Moving to Microsoft® ASP.NET 2.0

Dino Esposito

PUBLISHED BY
Microsoft Press
A Division of Microsoft Corporation
One Microsoft Way
Redmond, Washington 98052-6399

Printed and bound in the United States of America.

2 3 4 5 6 7 8 9   QWE   1 0 9 8 7 6

Distributed in Canada by H.B. Fenn and Company Ltd.

A CIP catalogue record for this book is available from the British Library.
Microsoft Press books are available through booksellers and distributors worldwide. For further information about international editions, contact your local Microsoft Corporation office or contact Microsoft Press International directly at fax (425) 936-7329. Visit our Web site at www.microsoft.com/mspress. Send comments to *mspinput@microsoft.com*.

Acquisitions Editor: Ben Ryan
Project Editors: Lynn Finnel
Technical Editor: Kenn Scribner
Copy Editor: Roger LeBlanc
Indexer: Lynn Armstrong

Body Part No. X12-14515

Table of Contents

What do you think of this book?
We want to hear from you!

Microsoft is interested in hearing your feedback about this publication so we can continually improve our books and learning resources for you. To participate in a brief online survey, please visit: *www.microsoft.com/learning/booksurvey/*

Introduction

Prior to the advent of Microsoft ASP.NET, three main technologies and platforms were available to de-velop Web applications: Active Server Pages (ASP), Java Server Pages (JSP), and the open source Web platform commonly referred to as LAMP (Linux plus Apache plus MySQL plus either Perl, Python, or PHP as the pro-gramming language).

Although each has language-specific and architecture-specific features, all these Web development platforms are designed to create interactive pages as part of a Web-based application. To some extent, they all enable developers to separate programming logic from the page layout through the use of components that the page itself is responsible to call and render. Aside from this common ultimate goal, significant differences exist among these platforms, most of which relate to the programming model and languages they promote and support. For example, JSP exploits the Java framework of classes, and, with JavaBeans, provides an extensibility model for reusing components.

Like ASP, JSP, and LAMP, ASP.NET also works on top of the HTTP protocol and takes advantage of HTTP commands and policies to set up two-way, browser-to-server communication and cooperation. What really differentiates ASP.NET from other Web development technologies, and what makes it especially revolu-tionary, is the abstract programming model it propounds-the Web Forms model. In addition, the whole ASP.NET platform comes as a native part of the Microsoft .NET Framework.

ASP.NET is the culmination of Web development technologies that have appeared over the past ten years-one building on another, and each filling the gaps left by its predecessor. As a result, ASP.NET is an advanced, feature-rich, and powerful platform for building distributed applications transported by the HTTP protocol.

Today, programming ASP.NET applications means becoming familiar with all techniques available and possible, no matter which version of the platform you're actually using. This book covers the state of the art in Web programming with Microsoft .NET technologies. You'll find it useful no matter which version of ASP.NET you use, and no matter what level of Web skills you may have or how you developed those skills. Each topic is covered in a top-down approach-from the broader perspective of the feature, down to the im-plementation and pro-gramming details of a particular ASP.NET version.

This book provides in-depth coverage of the ASP.NET fundamentals: the HTTP runtime, security, caching, state management, pages, controls, and data binding and data access.

Who Is This Book For?

To avoid beating around the bush, let me state clearly: this is not a book for novice developers. This is not the appropriate book if you have only a faint idea of what ASP.NET is or if you are looking for an introduction to ASP.NET technology. If you are a novice and looking for step-by-step instruction, start with *Microsoft ASP.NET 2.0 Step By Step*, by George Shepherd (Microsoft Press, 2005). Once you have grabbed hold of ASP.NET principles and features and want to apply them, this core reference is the book for you.

Here you won't find screen shots illustrating Visual Studio 2005 wizards or any mention of options to select or unselect to get a certain behavior from your code. Of course, this doesn't mean that I am against Visual Studio 2005 or that I don't recommend using Visual Studio 2005 to develop ASP.NET applications. Visual Studio 2005 is a great tool for writing ASP.NET 2.0 applications but, from an ASP.NET perspective, Visual Studio is merely a tool. This book, instead, is all about the ASP.NET technology.

If you already know Visual Studio 2005 and its wonderful set of tricks and time-saving features and feel ready to learn more about the underlying machinery, this is the right book for you.

I do recommend this book to developers who have read and digested *Microsoft ASP.NET 2.0 Step By Step* or have equivalent knowledge. This book is certainly a useful reference for your library; it's just not the book to begin with.

System Requirements

You'll need the following hardware and software to build and run the code samples for this book:

- Microsoft Windows XP with Service Pack 2, Microsoft Windows Server 2003 with Service Pack 1, or Microsoft Windows 2000 with Service Pack 4.
- Microsoft Visual Studio 2005 Standard Edition or Microsoft Visual Studio 2005 Professional Edition.
- Internet Information Services (IIS) is not strictly required, but it is helpful for testing sample applications in a realistic run-time environment.
- Microsoft SQL Server 2005 Express (included with Visual Studio 2005) or Microsoft SQL Server 2005.
- The Northwind database of Microsoft SQL Server 2000 is used in most examples in this book to demonstrate data-access techniques throughout the book.
- 766-MHz Pentium or compatible processor (1.5 GHz Pentium recommended).
- 256 MB RAM (512 MB or more recommended).
- Video (800 × 600 or higher resolution) monitor with at least 256 colors (1024 × 768 High Color 16-bit recommended).
- CD-ROM or DVD-ROM drive.
- Microsoft Mouse or compatible pointing device.

Code Samples

All of the code samples discussed in this book can be downloaded from the book's companion content page at the following address:

http://www.microsoft.com/mspress/companion/0-7356-2176-4/

Support for This Book

Every effort has been made to ensure the accuracy of this book and the companion content. As corrections or changes are collected, they will be added to a Microsoft Knowledge Base article. To view the list of known corrections for this book, visit the following article:

http://support.microsoft.com/kb/905045

Microsoft Press provides support for books and companion content at the following Web site:

http://www.microsoft.com/learning/support/books/

Questions and Comments

If you have comments, questions, or ideas regarding the book or the companion content, or questions that are not answered by visiting the preceding sites, please send them to Microsoft Press via e-mail to

mspinput@microsoft.com

or via postal mail to

Microsoft Press
Attn: *Programming Microsoft ASP.NET 2.0 Core Reference* Editor
One Microsoft Way
Redmond, WA 98052-6399

Please note that Microsoft software product support is not offered through the above addresses.

Chapter 1

The ASP.NET Programming Model

ASP.NET is a Web development platform that provides services, a programming model, and software infrastructure necessary to build enterprise-class applications. Although largely syntax compatible with its popular predecessor—Active Server Pages (ASP)—ASP.NET is a revolutionary new programming framework designed to enable the rapid development of Web applications. As part of the Microsoft .NET platform, ASP.NET provides a component-based, extensible, and easy-to-use way to build, deploy, and run Web applications that target any browser or mobile device.

ASP.NET is the culmination of Web development technologies that rapidly followed one another in the past ten years—one building on another, and each filling the gaps of its predecessor. As a result, ASP.NET is currently the most technologically advanced, feature-rich, and powerful platform for building distributed applications transported by the HTTP protocol.

While amazingly growing in popularity and successfully being employed in thousands of real-world projects, ASP.NET 1.1 is only the first step of a clearly longer road. The more one works with ASP.NET, the more he or she realizes that even more is needed. ASP.NET simplifies a number of tasks and is sort of a programming paradise, especially for developers coming from classic ASP, Internet Server Application Programming Interface (ISAPI) programming, or other Web platforms. ASP.NET 1.1 just whetted the appetite of the developer community. Thus, after the first months of working with and assessing ASP.NET, members of this community started asking and wishing for more—well, actually much more.

ASP.NET 2.0 is a major upgrade to the platform, even though it doesn't introduce any new or revolutionary programming paradigm. At first sight, there's no radically new approach to code design and implementation, and there's no new syntax model to become familiar with. Nonetheless, ASP.NET 2.0 is a milestone on the Microsoft Web development roadmap—for application architects as well as for developers. Many of the constituent classes have been reworked, and some underwent face-lift operations. Several new controls have been added for the sake of productivity, and a bunch of new and enhanced system modules now make the run-time pipeline more customizable, flexible, robust, and secure. As a result, new practices emerge as best practices, new programming techniques are available to architects and lead developers, and new system features provide native solutions to known issues with earlier versions. To maximize the benefits of using ASP.NET, you should first look at the overall model—the components, programmability, and infrastructure.

A close look at the overall model is exactly what this chapter provides. To start out, let's examine some basic concepts of the ASP.NET platform and its programming model.

What's ASP.NET, Anyway?

Prior to the advent of ASP.NET, three main technologies and platforms were available to develop Web applications: ASP, Java Server Pages (JSP), and the open source Web platform commonly referred to as LAMP (Linux plus Apache plus MySQL plus either Perl, Python, or PHP as the programming language).

> **Note**   For completeness, we should also mention a couple of platform-specific, lower-level technologies that ASP and JSP rely on. ASP is actually an ISAPI extension, whereas JSP is implemented as a special *servlet* application. ISAPI extensions on IIS-based platforms and servlets on Java-based systems, let you create server-side, Web-deployed applications using a more classic approach. You write a module that builds and renders the page rather than declaratively design the page using a mix of markup text and embedded code.

Although each has language-specific and architecture-specific features, all these Web development platforms are designed to create interactive pages as part of a Web-based application. To some extent, all enable developers to separate programming logic from the page layout through the use of components that the page itself is responsible to call and render. Aside from this common ultimate goal, significant differences exist among those platforms, most of which relate to the programming model and languages they promote and support. For example, JSP exploits the Java framework of classes and, with JavaBeans, provides an effective extensibility model for reusing components. In addition, JSP supports tag customization and lets developers associate code with a custom tag definition. Finally, because it's a key element of the Java 2 Enterprise Edition (J2EE) platform, JSP relies on the Java language, a first-class, compiled language as opposed to the scripting languages used by both ASP and LAMP platforms. So how does ASP.NET fit in exactly?

Like ASP and other Web development environments, ASP.NET also works on top of the HTTP protocol and takes advantage of HTTP commands and policies to set up two-way, browser-to-server communication and cooperation. What really differentiates ASP.NET from the plethora of other Web development technologies is the abstract programming model it propounds, the Web Forms model. In addition, the whole ASP.NET platform comes as a native part of the Microsoft .NET Framework. To be sure you grasp the importance of this last point, let me explain. ASP.NET applications are compiled pieces of code, are made of reusable and extensible components, can be authored with first-class languages (including C#, Microsoft Visual Basic .NET, Microsoft JScript .NET, and J#), and can access the entire hierarchy of classes in the .NET Framework.

In short, ASP.NET combines the best of all worlds. It is semantically compatible (and, to some extent, also language compatible) with ASP. It provides the same object-oriented features as JSP applications (tag customization, compiled languages, components, extensibility, and reusability). And as icing on the cake, ASP.NET delivers a wealth of goodies, tools, and powerful system features that can be effectively grouped within the blanket expression *tools for abstracting the HTTP programming model*. Lots of programmer-friendly classes let you develop pages using typical desktop methods. The Web Forms model promotes an overall event-driven approach, but it is deployed over the Web.

> **Note**   ASP.NET is supported on a variety of platforms, including Microsoft Windows 2000 with at least Service Pack 2, Windows XP Professional, and Windows Server 2003. To develop ASP.NET server applications, Internet Information Services (IIS) version 5.0 or later, is also required. Other software you need—for example, Microsoft Data Access Components (MDAC) 2.7—is automatically installed when you set up the .NET Framework. In terms of performance, robustness, and security, the ideal combination of system software for hosting ASP.NET applications appears to be Windows Server 2003 (preferably with Service Pack 1 applied) and IIS 6.0.

Programming in the Age of Web Forms

The rationale behind the ASP.NET Web Forms model is directly related to the search for a better strategy to deal with the growing demand for cheap but powerful Web interaction. As a matter of fact, the HTTP protocol represents the major strength and weakness of Web applications. The stateless nature of the HTTP protocol introduces vastly different programming concepts that are foreign to many desktop developers—first and foremost among these concepts is session state management. On the other hand, the inherent simplicity and scalability of HTTP is the key to its worldwide adoption and effectiveness—in short, we probably couldn't have the Internet as we know it without a protocol like HTTP. Yet, as demand for rich and powerful applications increases, programmers have to devise better ways of setting up easy and effective communication from the client to the server and vice versa.

Various techniques have been experimented with over time to smooth the communication across different pages and across multiple invocations of the same page. Most programmers are used to thinking in terms of a client-generated action that results in a server-side reaction. Such a basic and fundamental pattern cannot be accomplished, at least not literally, over the Web. A certain degree of abstraction and some system-provided services are needed to make smooth communication happen.

ASP, much more so than JSP, thinks declaratively and has quite a slim and scanty object model. Overall, programmers who become Web programmers are forced to adopt a different mindset and toss the familiar action/reaction paradigm out the door.

Event-Driven Programming over HTTP

ASP.NET Web Forms bring the event-driven model of interaction to the Web. Implementing an event model over the Web requires any data related to the client-side user's activity to be forwarded to the server for corresponding and *stateful* processing. The server processes the output of client actions and triggers reactions. The state of the application contains two types of information: the state of the client and the state of the session. The state of the client—mostly the contents of form input fields collectively referred to as the page state—is easily accessible through the server-side collections that store posted values. But what about the overall state of the session? The client expects that sending information to the server through one page is naturally related to any other page he or she might view later, such as when adding items to a shopping cart. Who remembers what a particular user has in the shopping cart? By itself, HTTP is incapable of keeping track of this information; that's where session state and a proper server-side infrastructure surrounding and integrating HTTP fit in.

I can't emphasize enough the importance of understanding the concepts involved with *state-less programming* when developing Web applications. As mentioned, HTTP is a stateless pro-tocol, which means two successive requests across the same session have no knowledge of each other. They are resolved by newly instantiated environments in which no session-specific information is maintained, except all the information the application itself might have stored in global objects. In ASP, reentrant forms are a common way to work around such a system limitation. A reentrant form is an HTML *<form>* element that posts to the same page that con-tains it. Reentrant forms alone do not fully solve the issue. However, by combining them with code blocks and hidden fields storing state information that is critical for the page, many developers elegantly overcame the obstacle.

What was once an ASP best-practice has been standardized and integrated in the ASP.NET runtime to become the key feature that endows ASP.NET applications with automatic state maintenance. The ASP.NET runtime carries the page state back and forth across page requests. When generating HTML code for a given page, ASP.NET encodes and stuffs the state of server-side objects into a few hidden, and transparently created, fields. When the page is requested, the same ASP.NET runtime engine checks for embedded state information—the hidden fields—and uses any decoded information to set up newly created instances of server-side objects. The net effect of such a mechanism is not unlike the Windows Forms model on the desktop and is summarized in Figure 1-1.

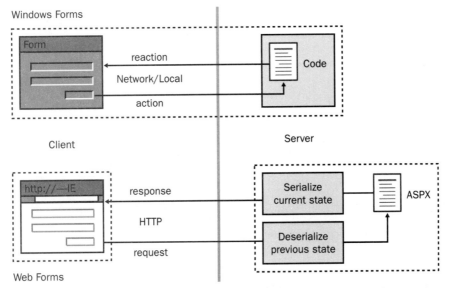

Figure 1-1   Comparing the Windows Forms and Web Forms models in the .NET Framework.

The Windows Forms model stems from the typical event-driven desktop programming style. No matter what connectivity exists between the client and server components, the server always works in reaction to the client's input. The server is aware of the overall application state and operates in a two-tier, connected manner. The Web Forms model needs some machinery to support the same event-driven programming model. In Figure 1-1, the needed *machinery* is represented by the state deserialization that occurs when the page is requested, and the state serialization performed when the HTML response is being generated.

In charge of this filtering work is the ASP.NET HTTP runtime—a piece of code that extends and specializes the overall capabilities of the hosting Web server. Reentrant forms and hidden fields are the low-level tools used to perform the trick. Such a model wouldn't be as effective without a back-end, rich object model spanning the whole content of the server page. Crucial to the building and effective working of the ASP.NET development platform is the component model.

The ASP.NET component model identifies and describes the building blocks of ASP.NET pages. It is implemented through an object model that provides a server-side counterpart to virtually any HTML page elements, such as HTML tags like <*form*> and <*input*>. In addition, the ASP.NET object model includes numerous components (called server controls or Web controls) that represent more complex elements of the user interface (UI). Some of these controls have no direct mapping with individual HTML elements but are implemented by combining multiple HTML tags. Typical examples of complex UI elements are the *Calendar* control and the *DataGrid* control.

In the end, an ASP.NET page is made of any number of server controls mixed with verbatim text, markup, and images. Sensitive data excerpted from the page and controls state is unobtrusively stored in hidden fields, and it forms the context of that page request. The association between an instance of the page and its state is unambiguous, not programmatically modifiable, and controlled by the ASP.NET HTTP runtime.

The ASP.NET component model is the first stop on the way to the full understanding of the ASP.NET platform. The component model escorts you through the whole development cycle, including the phase of page authoring and run-time system configuration, as shown in Figure 1-2.

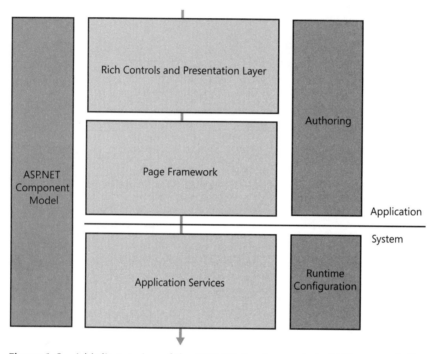

Figure 1-2   A bird's-eye view of the ASP.NET development stack. The arrow indicates the typical top-down application perspective, going down from the user interface to the system services.

Before we dive into the various elements shown in Figure 1-2, let's briefly review the basics of the HTTP protocol, which remains the foundation of Web interaction. After that, we'll move on to describe the structure of an ASP.NET page and how to write and deploy ASP.NET applications.

The HTTP Protocol

This section provides a quick overview of the way Web applications operate. If you already have a working knowledge of the Web underpinnings, feel free to jump ahead to the section "Structure of an ASP.NET Page."

The acronym *HTTP* has become so familiar to us developers that we sometimes don't remember exactly what it stands for. Actually, *HTTP* stands for Hypertext Transfer Protocol. HTTP is a text-based protocol that defines how Web browsers and Web servers communicate. The format of HTTP packets is fully described in RFC 2068 and is available for download from *http://www.w3.org/Protocols/rfc2068/rfc2068.txt*. HTTP packets travel over a Transmission Control Protocol (TCP) connection directed toward default port 80 at the target Internet Protocol (IP) address.

The HTTP Request

When you point the browser to a URL, it uses the available Domain Name System (DNS) to translate the server name you provided with the URL into an IP address. Next, the browser opens a socket and connects to port 80 at that address. The packet with the download request for *http://www.contoso.com/default.aspx* can take the following simple form:

```
GET /default.aspx HTTP/1.1
Host: www.contoso.com
```

The first line of text in a request is the *start line* of the request. It must contain the name of the HTTP command to execute (*GET* in this case), the URL of the resource, plus the version of the HTTP protocol you want to use.

An HTTP request can contain, and usually does contain, a number of headers. An HTTP header is a line of text that provides additional information about the request. In the HTTP request just shown, the line beginning with "Host:" is an HTTP header. Headers that can be found in an HTTP request include the following:

- **User-Agent.** Identifies the type of browser that originated the request
- **Connection.** Closes a connection or keeps a connection alive
- **If-Modified-Since.** Provides client-side cache validation

GET and POST are the most commonly used HTTP commands or verbs. The GET verb means retrieve whatever information is identified by the request URL. The POST verb is used to request that the origin server accept the content enclosed in the request and process it. Typically, the POST verb is used to provide a block of data (that is, the result of submitting a form) to a data-handling process.

The HTTP Response

The server's response includes a *status line* made from the message's protocol version and an exit code (indicating success or that an error has occurred). The status line is followed by a bunch of headers—typically the page content type and length—and the body content. A blank line separates the body content from the rest of the message, as shown in the following response:

```
HTTP/1.1 200 OK
Server: Microsoft-IIS/5.0
Content-Type: text/html
Content-Length: 51

<html><body><h1>ASP.NET is cool!</h1></body></html>
```

The preceding code illustrates the simple HTML output returned by the Web server. Requests and responses are strings formatted according to the HTTP schema, and they travel over a TCP connection. The code *200* means that all went OK with the request. The specified Web server processes the request and returns content of a certain length expressed in the given Multipurpose Internet Mail Extensions (MIME) type (*text/html*). HTTP codes that could be returned are listed in the HTTP specification, available at the aforementioned URL. In addition, it should be noted that the blank line between the last header and the content of the HTTP response is not just formatting—the pair carriage-return and line-feed are required and are a precise part of the standard.

What happens next mostly depends on the MIME type and the local browser's capabilities. As long as the MIME type is *text/html*, the browser displays the content as HTML. If the MIME type is, say, *text/xml*, some browsers will render the content as plain text, while others (for example, Microsoft Internet Explorer 6.0) will apply a built-in style sheet.

Building a Server-Side Abstraction Layer

Every conversation between browsers and Web servers consists of an exchange of packets similar to the ones we have just examined. If the requested URL is an HTML page, the Web server typically reads the contents of the *.html* file and flushes it into the body of the response packet. If the URL is an ASP.NET page, a special IIS module gets involved. The module is an IIS ISAPI plug-in.

An ISAPI extension is a dynamic-link library (DLL) registered on a per-file extension basis. An ISAPI extension registered to handle *.aspx* files gets involved whenever a request comes in for this type of resource. The ISAPI extension analyzes the request and configures the server-side environment that will actually process the source of the page. When the state for the request has been successfully retrieved and restored completely, the page is allowed to run and produce the HTML output.

Submitting Forms

The HTML *<form>* tag is the only element authorized to transmit client-side data to the server. When the user clicks on a button of type "submit," by design the browser stuffs the current content of all the controls that belong to the form into a string. The string is then passed to the server as part of the GET or POST command.

The following HTML snippet illustrates a simple form containing a text box and submit button. As you can see, the form is associated with the POST command and the default.aspx URL:

```
<form method="post" action="default.aspx">
    <input type="text" name="EmpCode" />
    <input type="submit" value="Send" />
</form>
```

The following request shows the POST command that hits the Web server when the user clicks the submit button:

```
POST /default.aspx HTTP/1.1
Host: www.contoso.com
Content-Type: application/x-www-form-urlencoded
Content-Length: 12

EmpCode=1001
```

While processing the page request, the ISAPI extension parses the body of the request and exposes any information found through a more programmer-friendly object model. For example, instead of remaining a simple name/value string, the *EmpCode* variable is moved within an application-wide collection—the *Request.Form* collection. This represents a first level of abstraction built over the raw HTTP programming model. Objects such as *Request*, *Response*, and *Server* form the HTTP context for the call and, as such, represent the minimum set of objects you find in most Web development platforms, including JSP and ASP. In ASP.NET, though, you find much more.

Structure of an ASP.NET Page

An ASP.NET page is a server-side text file saved with the *.aspx* extension. The internal structure of the page is extremely modular and comprises three distinct sections—page directives, code, and page layout:

- **Page directives**   Page directives set up the environment in which the page will run, specify how the HTTP runtime should process the page, and determine which assumptions about the page are safe to make. Directives also let you import namespaces to simplify coding, load assemblies not currently in the global assembly cache (GAC), and register new controls with custom tag names and namespace prefixes.

- **Code section**   The code section contains handlers for page and control events, plus optional helper routines. Any source code pertinent to the page can be inserted inline or attached to the page through a separate file. If inserted inline, the code goes into a tag with the misleading name of *<script>*. (The name *<script>* has been chosen for backward-compatibility reasons.) Server-side *<script>* tags are distinguished from client-side *<script>* tags by the use of the *runat=server* attribute. (More on this in a moment.) Any page code is always compiled before execution. In ASP.NET 2.0, it can also be precompiled and deployed in the form of a binary assembly.

- **Page layout**   The page layout represents the skeleton of the page. It includes server controls, literal text, and HTML tags. The user interface of the server controls can be fleshed out a bit using declared attributes and control properties.

For the page to work, you don't need to specify all sections. Although real-world pages include all the sections mentioned, perfectly valid and functional pages can include only the code section or page layout. In some special cases, you can even have an ASP.NET page made of a single directive.

In Chapter 2, and even more in Chapter 3, we'll delve deep into the features of a page and its building blocks.

A Sample ASP.NET Page

It is about time we see what an ASP.NET page looks like. To start, a simple text editor will suffice; so let's open Notepad and let the sleeping giant (Microsoft Visual Studio .NET) lie. The following code implements a simple ASP.NET page that lets you enter a string and then changes it to uppercase letters after you click a button. For the sake of simplicity, we use inline code. (As you'll learn later in the book, this is *not* what you'll be doing in real-world applications and in any page with some complexity.)

```
<!-- Directives -->
<% @Page Language="C#" %>

  <!-- Code Section -->
<script runat="server">
private void MakeUpper(object sender, EventArgs e)
{
    string buf = TheString.Value;
    TheResult.InnerText = buf.ToUpper();
}
</script>

  <!-- Layout -->
<html>
<head><title>Pro ASP.NET (Ch 01)</title></head>
<body>
<h1>Make It Upper</h1>
<form runat="server">
    <input runat="server" id="TheString" type="text" />
    <input runat="server" id="Button1" type="submit" value="Proceed..."
        OnServerClick="MakeUpper" />
    <hr>
    <h3>Results:</h3>
    <span runat="server" id="TheResult" />
</form>
</body>
</html>
```

Blank lines and comments in the preceding listing separate the three sections—directives, code, and page layout. Notice the unsparing use of the *runat* attribute—it's one of the most important pieces of the whole ASP.NET jigsaw puzzle. In the next section, we'll discuss *runat* in more detail. For now, it suffices to say that the *runat* attribute promotes an otherwise lifeless server-side tag to the rank of a component instance.

The page layout is made of literals and HTML tags, some of which contain the aforementioned *runat* attribute. Everything flagged this way, despite the appearances, is not really an HTML element. More precisely, it is the markup placeholder of a server-side component–an ASP.NET control–that is actually responsible for the final markup served to the browser. In an ASP.NET source, every tag marked with the *runat* attribute is not output as is, but undergoes a transformation process on the server at the end of which the real markup is generated. The ASP.NET runtime is in charge of mapping tags to control instances. Let's quickly review the code.

Quick Review of the Code

Thanks to the *runat* attribute the input text field becomes an instance of the *HtmlInputControl* class when the page is processed on the server. The *Value* property of the class determines the default text to assign to the input field. When the user clicks the submit button, the page automatically posts back to itself. The magic is performed by the *runat* attribute set for the *<form>* tag. Once on the server, the posted value of the input field is read and automatically assigned to the *Value* property of a newly created instance of the *HtmlInputControl*. Next, the code associated with the *OnServerClick* event runs. This code takes the current content of the text box– the posted string–and converts it to uppercase letters. Finally, the uppercase string is assigned it to the *InnerText* property of the server-side control bound to the HTML *<span>* tag. When the *MakeUpper* event handler completes, the page is ready for rendering. At this point, updated HTML code is sent to the browser.

To test the page, copy the *.aspx* file to your Web server's root directory. Normally, this is *c:\inetpub\wwwroot*. If you want, create an ad hoc virtual directory. Let's assume the page is named *hello.aspx*. Next, point the browser to the page. Figure 1-3 shows what you get.

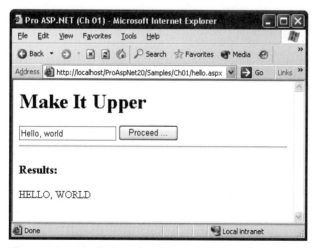

Figure 1-3   Our first (and rather simple) ASP.NET page in action.

It would be useful to take a look at the HTML source of the page when it is first displayed to the user—that is, before the user clicks to make the text uppercase.

```
<!-- Directives -->

<!-- Code Section -->

<!-- Layout -->
<html>
<head><title>Pro ASP.NET (Ch 01)</title></head>
<body>
<h1>Make It Upper</h1>
<form method="post" action="hello.aspx" id="Form1">
<div>
    <input type="hidden" name="__EVENTTARGET" value="" />
    <input type="hidden" name="__EVENTARGUMENT" value="" />
    <input type="hidden" name="__VIEWSTATE" value="/wEPDwUJNZM4N…==" />
</div>

<script type="text/javascript">
<!--
var theForm = document.forms['Form1'];
if (!theForm) {
    theForm = document.Form1;
}
function __doPostBack(eventTarget, eventArgument) {
    if (!theForm.onsubmit || (theForm.onsubmit() != false)) {
        theForm.__EVENTTARGET.value = eventTarget;
        theForm.__EVENTARGUMENT.value = eventArgument;
        theForm.submit();
    }
}
// -->
</script>

<input name="TheString" type="text" id="TheString" value="Hello, world" />
<input name="Button1" type="submit" id="Button1" value="Proceed ..." />
<hr>
<h3>Results: </h3><span id="TheResult"></span>
</form>
</body>
</html>
```

Within the *<form>* tag, a hard-coded *action* attribute has been added to force posting to the same page. This is by design and is one of the most characteristic aspects of ASP.NET. The various hidden fields you see are essential to the implementation of the postback mechanism and are generated automatically. The same can be said for the embedded script code. The *<input>* tags are nearly identical to their counterpart in the *.aspx* source—only the *runat* attribute disappeared.

Now that we've dirtied our hands with some ASP.NET code, let's step back and review the layers that actually make ASP.NET pages work in the context of an application.

The ASP.NET Component Model

ASP.NET is the key enabling technology for all Web-related functionality provided by the .NET Framework. The .NET Framework is made entirely of an object-oriented hierarchy of classes that span all programming topics for Windows operating systems. Generally speaking, a Web application is made of pages the user requests from a server and that the server processes and returns as markup code—mostly HTML. How the requested resource is processed, and therefore how the markup is generated, is server-specific. In particular, when the resource happens to have an *.aspx* extension, IIS delegates any further processing to the ASP.NET runtime system.

The ASP.NET runtime transforms the source code of the requested *.aspx* page into the living instance of a .NET Framework class that inherits from a base class named *Page*. At the end of the day, a running ASP.NET page is an object, and so it is for some of its components—the server-side controls.

A large number of new ASP.NET features are just a direct or an indirect propagation of the .NET infrastructure. ASP.NET benefits from cross-language integration and exception handling, garbage collection and code access security, deployment and configuration, and an incredibly rich class library. All these features aren't the products of a self-contained engine, they are available to you because ASP.NET applications are a special breed of a .NET application.

A Model for Component Interaction

Any element in an ASP.NET page that is marked with the *runat* attribute can be given a unique ID, allowing you to access that element from your server-side code. Accessing items by ID is a natural approach on the client (such as the use of Dynamic HTML pages), but it represents a brand new scheme for server applications. Two factors make this revolutionary approach possible:

- The component-based architecture of the .NET platform, and the fact that ASP.NET is a constituent part of that platform
- The ASP.NET built-in mechanism for the application's state management

The component-based design of .NET makes component interaction easy and effective in all environments including ASP.NET applications. ASP.NET components access page features and interact by calling one another's methods and setting properties.

The fact that all elements in the page are true components, and not simply parsable text, provides a flexible and powerful extensibility model. Creating new controls is as easy as deriving a new class; building a page inheritance hierarchy is as easy as specifying a parent class different from the base *Page* class.

> **Warning**   Visual Studio .NET 2005 returns a design-time error if you don't explicitly assign each ASP.NET control a unique ID. However, the page will work just fine at run time.

The *runat* Attribute

The *runat* attribute is what determines whether a piece of markup text is to be emitted verbatim at render time or transformed into a stateful instance of a particular .NET class. In the latter case, the class would make itself responsible for emitting the related markup. In an ASP.NET page, all markup elements that have the *runat* attribute set to *server* are considered server-side controls. The control class exposes methods and properties that let you configure the state of the component. The control is responsible for emitting HTML code when the page is rendered to the browser. Let's consider the following simple code that renders an anchor element in the client page:

```
Response.Write("<A id=myAnchor href=www.asp.net>Click me</A>")
```

The anchor element is created programmatically and is not defined in the page layout. In classic ASP, code blocks and the *Response.Write* method are the only ways you have to create or configure controls dynamically. In some development environments, such as Microsoft Visual InterDev, *design-time controls* provided an object-based way to output dynamically generated HTML. Design-time controls, though, were just what the name indicates—that is, controls you can use at design-time to generate markup and script code. In ASP.NET, you have a new breed of controls that we could call *run-time controls* to mark the contrast with design-time controls.

Working with Server-Side Controls

Within an ASP page, there's no way for you to code against the *myAnchor* element. It's just frozen, lifeless text, only good for sending to the browser. Once on a client, the *myAnchor* element gets back to life and can accept script instructions. Suppose now that you need to set the *href* attribute of the anchor based on run-time conditions. In classic ASP, you could first obtain the value for the *href* attribute and then call *Response.Write*:

```
strHref = "www.asp.net"
strHtml = "<A id=myAnchor "
strHtml = strHtml + "href=" + strHref
strHtml = strHtml + ">Click me</A>"
Response.Write(strHtml)
```

This code will work unchanged in an ASP.NET page but is certainly not the best you can do. By declaring the *<A>* tag with the *runat* attribute, you can give life to the anchor element on the server too:

```
<A runat="server" id="myAnchor">Click me</A>
```

When the page is loaded, the ASP.NET runtime parses the source code and creates instances of all controls marked with the *runat* attribute. Throughout the page, the *myAnchor* ID identifies an instance of the server-side control mapped to the *<A>* tag. The following code can be used to set the *href* attribute programmatically when the page loads:

```
<script runat="server" language="C#">
void Page_Load(object sender, EventArgs e)
{
    myAnchor.HRef = "http://www.asp.net";
}
</script>
```

The markup elements whose name matches an HTML element are mapped to the corresponding HTML server control. Note that not all feasible HTML tags have corresponding ASP.NET controls; for those that don't, a generic control is used. The list of tags and their associated controls is hard-coded in the ASP.NET runtime. Elements that belong to the *<asp>* namespace are mapped to Web server controls. Other markup elements are mapped to the assembly and class name declared by using an *@Register* directive.

Pagewide Tags

The *runat* attribute can be used also with pagewide tags such as *<head>* and *<body>*. These tags are represented through an instance of the *HtmlGenericControl* class. *HtmlGenericControl* is the .NET class used to represent an HTML server-side tag not directly represented by a .NET Framework class. The list of such tags also includes *<span>*, *<font>*, and *<iframe>*.

In the following page, the background color is set programmatically when the page loads:

```
<%@ Page Language="C#" %>
<script runat="server">
private void Page_Load(object sender, EventArgs e)
{
    TheBody.Style[HtmlTextWriterStyle.BackgroundColor] = "lightblue";
}
</script>
<html>
<body id="TheBody" runat="server">
   <h3>The background color of this page has been set programmatically.
       Open View|Source menu to see the source code.</h3>
</body>
</html>
The resulting HTML code is as follows:
<html>
<head><title>Pro ASP.NET (Ch 01)</title></head>
<body id="TheBody" style="background-color:lightblue;">
<form method="post" action="Body.aspx" id="Form1">
  <div>
    <input type="hidden" name="__VIEWSTATE" value="/wEPD… RVC+" />
  </div>
```

```
<h3>The background color of this page has been set programmatically.
    Open View|Source menu to see the source code.</h3>
</form>
</body>
</html>
```

Likewise, you can set any of the attributes of the *<body>* tag, thus deciding programmatically, say, which style sheet or background image to use. You use the *HtmlGenericControl*'s *Attributes* collection to create attributes on the tag. You use the *InnerText* property to set the inner text of a tag.

```
TheBody.Attributes["Background"] = "/proaspnet20/images/body.gif";
```

We'll discuss the programming interface of the *HtmlGenericControl* class in more detail in Chapter 4.

> **Note** In ASP.NET 2.0, the contents of the *<head>* tag can be accessed programmatically as long as it is flagged with the *runat* attribute. The *Page* class exposes a bunch of ad hoc methods and properties that we'll explore in Chapter 3.

Unknown Tags

In case of unknown tags, namely tags that are neither predefined in the current schema nor user-defined, the ASP.NET runtime can behave in two different ways. If the tag doesn't contain namespace information, ASP.NET treats it like a generic HTML control. The empty namespace, in fact, evaluates to the HTML namespace, thereby leading the ASP.NET runtime to believe the tag is really an HTML element. No exception is raised, and markup text is generated on the server. For example, let's consider the following ASP.NET page:

```
<%@ Page Language="C#" %>
<script runat="server">
void Page_Load(object sender, EventArgs e)
{
    dinoe.Attributes["FavoriteFood"] = "T-bone steak";
}
</script>
<html>
<head><title>Pro ASP.NET (Ch 01)</title></head>
<body>
<form runat="server">
  <Person id="dinoe" runat="server" />
  Click the <b>View|Source</b> menu item...
</form>
</body>
</html>
```

The *<Person>* tag is still processed as if it was a regular HTML tag, and the *FavoriteFood* attribute is added. Figure 1-4 shows what the HTML code for this page actually is. In the preceding sample, the type of the *dinoe* object is *HtmlGenericControl*.

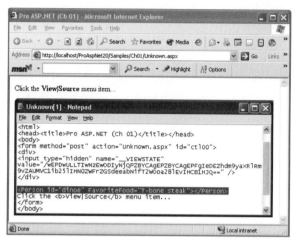

Figure 1-4   ASP.NET also processes namespace-less custom tags, mapping them to the *HtmlGenericControl* class.

If the tag does contain namespace information, it is acceptable as long as the namespace is *<asp>* or a namespace explicitly associated with the tag name using an *@Register* directive. If the namespace is unknown, a compile error occurs.

ASP.NET Server Controls

There are basically two families of ASP.NET server controls. They are HTML server controls and Web server controls. *System.Web.UI.HtmlControls* is the namespace of HTML server controls. *System.Web.UI.WebControls* groups all the Web server controls.

HTML Server Controls

HTML server controls are classes that represent a standard HTML tag supported by most browsers. The set of properties of an HTML server control matches a commonly used set of attributes of the corresponding tag. The control feature properties such as *InnerText*, *InnerHtml*, *Style*, and *Value* plus collections such as *Attributes*. Instances of HTML server controls are automatically created by the ASP.NET runtime each time the corresponding HTML tag marked with runat="server" is found in the page source.

As mentioned, the available set of HTML server controls doesn't cover all possible HTML tags of any given version of the HTML schema. Only most commonly used tags found their way to the *System.Web.UI.HtmlControls* namespace. Tags such as *<iframe>*, *<frameset>*, *<body>*, and *<hn>* have been left out as well as less frequently used tags such as *<fieldset>*, *<marquee>*, and *<pre>*.

The lack of a specialized server control, however, doesn't limit your programming power when it comes to using and configuring those tags on the server. You only have to use a more generic programming interface—the *HtmlGenericControl* class, which we looked at briefly in this section.

Web Server Controls

Web server controls are controls with more features than HTML server controls. Web server controls include not only input controls such as buttons and text boxes, but also special-purpose controls such as a calendar, an ad rotator, a drop-down list, a tree view, and a data grid. Web server controls also include components that closely resemble some HTML server controls. Web server controls, though, are more abstract than the corresponding HTML server controls in that their object model doesn't necessarily reflect the HTML syntax. For example, let's compare the HTML server text control and the Web server *TextBox* control. The HTML server text control has the following markup:

```
<input runat="server" id="FirstName" type="text" value="Dino" />
```

The Web server *TextBox* control has the following markup:

```
<asp:textbox runat="server" id="FirstName" text="Dino" />
```

Both controls generate the same HTML markup code. However, the programming interface of the HTML server text control matches closely that of the HTML *<input>* tag, while methods and properties of the Web server *TextBox* control are named in a more abstract way. For example, to set the content of an HTML server text control you must use the *Value* property because *Value* is the corresponding HTML attribute name. If you work with the Web server *TextBox* control, you must resort to *Text*. With very few exceptions (that I'll discuss in Chapter 3), using HTML server controls or Web server controls to represent HTML elements is only a matter of preference and ease of development and maintenance.

The ASP.NET Development Stack

At the highest level of abstraction, the development of an ASP.NET application passes through two phases—pages authoring and run-time configuration. You build the pages that form the application, implement its user's requirements, and then fine-tune the surrounding run-time environment to make it serve pages effectively and securely. As Figure 1-2 shows, the ASP.NET component model is the bedrock of all ASP.NET applications and their building blocks. With Figure 1-2 in mind, let's examine the various logical layers to see what they contain and why they contain it.

The Presentation Layer

An ASP.NET page is made of controls, free text, and markup. When the source code is transformed into a living instance of a page class, the ASP.NET runtime makes no further distinction between verbatim text, markup, and server controls—everything is a control, including literal text and carriage-return characters. At run time, any ASP.NET page is a mere graph of controls.

Rich Controls

The programming richness of ASP.NET springs from the wide library of server controls that covers the basic tasks of HTML interaction—for example, collecting text through input tags—as well as more advanced functionalities such as grid-based data display. The native set of controls is large enough to let you fulfill virtually any set of requirements. In addition, the latest version of ASP.NET adds a few new rich controls to take developer's productivity close to its upper limit.

In ASP.NET 2.0, you find controls to create Web wizards, collapsible views of hierarchical data, advanced data reports, commonly used forms, declarative data binding, menus, site navigation. You even find a tiny API to create portal-like pages. Availability of rich controls means reduction of development time and coding errors, more best practices implemented, and more advanced functionalities delivered to end users. We'll specifically cover controls in Chapter 4, Chapter 6, and later on in Chapter 10.

Custom Controls

ASP.NET core controls provide you with a complete set of tools to build Web functionalities. The standard set of controls can be extended and enhanced by adding custom controls. The underlying ASP.NET component model greatly simplifies the task by applying the common principles and rules of object-oriented programming.

You can build new controls by enhancing an existing control or aggregating two or more controls together to form a new one. ASP.NET 1.x comes with a small set of base classes to build brand new controls on. This set of classes has been extended in ASP.NET 2.0, in particular to simplify the development of new data-bound controls.

Adaptive Rendering

Starting with version 2.0, ASP.NET ships a new control adapter architecture that allows any server control to create alternate renderings for a variety of browsers. Note, though, that the new ASP.NET 2.0 adapter model doesn't apply to *mobile controls*. Mobile controls are a special family of Web controls designed to build applications for mobile devices. ASP.NET 2.0 mobile controls still use the old adapter model, which was available since ASP.NET 1.1, for controls that inherit from *MobileControl* and are hosted on pages that inherit from *MobilePage*. In short, if you need to write a mobile application with ASP.NET 2.0, you should use the mobile controls, as you would have done with ASP.NET 1.1.

So what's the added value of the new adapter model? With this form of adaptive rendering, you can write control adapters to customize server controls for individual browsers. For example, you can write a control adapter to generate a different HTML markup for the *Calendar* control for a given desktop browser.

The Page Framework

Any ASP.NET page works as an instance of a class that descends from the *Page* class. The *Page* class is the ending point of a pipeline of modules that process any HTTP request. The various system components that work on the original request build step by step all the information needed to locate the page object to generate the markup. The page object model sports several features and capabilities that could be grouped in terms of events, scripting, personalization, styling, and prototyping.

Page Events

The life cycle of a page in the ASP.NET runtime is marked by a series of events. By wiring their code up to these events, developers can dynamically modify the page output and the state of constituent controls. In ASP.NET 1.x, a page fires events such as *Init*, *Load*, *PreRender*, and *Unload* that punctuate the key moments in the life of the page. ASP.NET 2.0 adds quite a few new events to allow you to follow the request processing more closely and precisely. In particular, you find new events to signal the beginning and end of the initialization and loading phase. The page life cycle will be thoroughly examined in Chapter 3.

Page Scripting

The page scripting object model lets developers manage script code and hidden fields to be injected in client pages. This object model generates JavaScript code used to glue together the HTML elements generated by server controls, thus providing features otherwise impossible to program on the server. For example, in this way you can set the input focus to a particular control when the page displays in the client browser.

ASP.NET pages can be architected to issue client calls to server methods without performing a full postback and subsequently refresh the whole displayed page. This sort of remote scripting engine is implemented through a callback mechanism that offers a clear advantage to developers. When you use script callbacks, the results of the execution of a server-side method are passed directly to a JavaScript function that can then update the user interface via Dynamic HTML. A roundtrip still occurs, but the page is not fully refreshed.

Script callbacks, though, are not the only good news. Cross-page posting is another feature that the community of ASP.NET developers loudly demanded. It allows the posting of content of a form to another page. Sounds like teaching old tricks to a new dog? Maybe. As mentioned earlier in this chapter, one of the most characteristic aspects of ASP.NET is that each page contains just one *<form>* tag, which continuously posts to itself. That's the way ASP.NET has been designed, and it results in several advantages.

In previous versions of ASP.NET, cross-page posting could be implemented the same way as in classic ASP—that is, posting through an HTML pure *<form>* not marked with the *runat* attribute. This method works fine, but it leaves you far from the object-oriented and strongly typed world of ASP.NET. Cross-page posting as implemented in ASP.NET 2.0 fills the gap.

Page Personalization

In ASP.NET 2.0, you can store and retrieve user-specific information and preferences without the burden of having to write the infrastructural code. The application defines its own model of personalized data, and the ASP.NET runtime does the rest by parsing and compiling that model into a class. Each member of the personalized class data corresponds to a piece of information specific to the current user. Loading and saving personalized data is completely transparent to end users and doesn't even require the page author to know much about the internal plumbing. The user personalized information is available to the page author through a page property. Each page can consume previously saved information and save new information for further requests.

Page Styling

Much like Microsoft Windows XP themes, ASP.NET themes assign a set of styles and visual attributes to elements of the site that can be customized. These elements include control properties, page style sheets, images, and templates on the page. A theme is the union of all visual styles for all customizable elements in the pages—a sort of super–CSS (cascading style sheet) file. A theme is identified by name and consists of CSS files, images, and control skins. A *control skin* is a text file that contains default control declarations in which visual properties are set for the control. With this feature enabled, if the developer adds, say, a *DataGrid* control to a page, the control is rendered with the default appearance defined in the theme.

Themes are a great new feature because they allow you to change the look and feel of pages in a single shot and, perhaps more importantly, give all pages a consistent appearance.

Page Prototyping

Almost all Web sites today contain pages with a similar layout. For some sites, the layout is as simple as a header and footer; others sites might contain sophisticated navigational menus and widgets that wrap content. In ASP.NET 1.x, the recommended approach for developers was to wrap these UI blocks in user controls and reference them in each content page. As you can imagine, this model works pretty well when the site contains only a few pages; unfortunately, it becomes unmanageable if the site contains hundreds of pages. An approach based on user controls presents several key issues for content-rich sites. For one thing, you have duplicate code in content pages to reference user controls. Next, application of new templates requires the developer to touch every page. Finally, HTML elements that span the content area are likely split between user controls.

In ASP.NET 2.0, page prototyping is greatly enhanced thanks to *master pages*. Developers working on Web sites where many pages share some layout and functionality can now author any shared functionality in one master file, instead of adding the layout information to each page or separating the layout among several user controls. Based on the shared master, developers can create any number of similar-looking *content pages* simply by referencing the master page through a new attribute. We'll cover master pages in Chapter 6.

The HTTP Runtime Environment

The process by which a Web request becomes plain HTML text for the browser is not much different in ASP.NET 2.0 than in ASP.NET 1.1. The request is picked up by IIS, given an identity token, and passed to the ASP.NET ISAPI extension (*aspnet_isapi.dll*)—the entry point for any ASP.NET-related processing. This is the general process, but a number of key details depend on the underlying version of IIS and the process model in use.

The process model is the sequence of operations needed to process a request. When the ASP.NET runtime runs on top of IIS 5.x, the process model is based on a separate worker process named *aspnet_wp.exe*. This Microsoft Win32 process receives control directly from IIS through the hosted ASP.NET ISAPI extension. The extension is passed any request for ASP.NET resources, and it hands them over to the worker process. The worker process loads the common language runtime (CLR) and starts the pipeline of managed objects that transform the original request from an HTTP payload into a full-featured page for the browser. The *aspnet_isapi* module and the worker process implement advanced features such as process recycling, page output caching, memory monitoring, and thread pooling. Each Web application runs in a distinct AppDomain within the worker process. By default, the worker process runs under a restricted, poorly privileged account named ASPNET.

> **Note** In the CLR, an application domain (AppDomain) provides isolation, unloading, and security boundaries for executing managed code. An AppDomain is a kind of lightweight, CLR-specific process where multiple assemblies are loaded and secured to execute code. Multiple AppDomains can run in a single CPU process. There is not a one-to-one correlation between AppDomains and threads. Several threads can belong to a single AppDomain, and while a given thread is not confined to a single application domain, at any given time, a thread executes in a single AppDomain.

When ASP.NET runs under IIS 6.0, the default process model is different and the *aspnet_wp.exe* process is not used. The worker process in use is the standard IIS 6.0 worker process (*w3wp.exe*). It looks up the URL of the request and loads a specific ISAPI extension. For example, it loads aspnet_isapi.dll for ASP.NET-related requests. Under the IIS 6.0 process model, the aspnet_isapi extension is responsible for loading the CLR and starting the HTTP pipeline.

Once in the ASP.NET HTTP pipeline, the request passes through various system and user-defined components that work on it until a valid page class is found and successfully instantiated. Developers can modify and adapt the run-time environment to some extent. This can happen in three ways: changing the list of installed HTTP modules, configuration files, state and personalization providers, and other application services.

System HTTP Modules

HTTP modules are the ASP.NET counterpart of ISAPI filters. An HTTP module is a .NET Framework class that implements a particular interface. All ASP.NET applications inherit a few system HTTP modules as defined in the machine.config file. Preinstalled modules provide features such as authentication, authorization, and session-related services. Generally speaking, an HTTP module can preprocess and postprocess a request, and it intercepts and handles system events as well as events raised by other modules.

The good news is that you can write and register your own HTTP modules and make them plug into the ASP.NET runtime pipeline, handle system events, and fire their own events. In addition, you can adapt on a per-application basis the list of default HTTP modules. You can add custom modules and remove those that you don't need.

Application Configuration

The behavior of ASP.NET applications is subject to a variety of parameters; some are system-level settings, some depend on the characteristics of the application. The common set of system parameters is defined in the *machine.config* file. This file contains default and machine-specific values for all supported settings. Machine settings are normally controlled by the system administrator, and applications should not be given writing access to the *machine.config* file. The *machine.config* file is located outside the Web space of the application and, as such, cannot be reached even if an attacker succeeds in injecting malicious code in the system.

Any application can override most of the default values stored in the machine.config file by creating one or more application-specific web.config files. At a minimum, an application creates a web.config file in its root folder. The web.config file is a subset of machine.config, written according to the same XML schema. The goal of *web.config* is to override some of the default settings. Beware, however, that not all settings that are defined in machine.config can be overridden in a child configuration file. In particular, the information about the ASP.NET process model can be defined only in a machinewide manner using the machine.config file.

If the application contains child directories, it can define a web.config file for each folder. The scope of each configuration file is determined in a hierarchical, top-down manner. The settings valid for a page are determined by the sum of the changes that the various web.config files found along the way applied to the original machine configuration. Any web.config file can extend, restrict, and override any type of settings defined at an upper level, including the machine level. If no configuration file exists in an application folder, the settings that are valid at the upper level are applied.

Application Services

Authentication, state management, and caching are all examples of essential services that the ASP.NET runtime environment supplies to running applications. With ASP.NET 2.0, other services have been added to the list—including administration, membership, role management, and personalization—as shown in Figure 1-5.

Most application services must persist and retrieve some data for internal purposes. While doing so, a service chooses a data model and a storage medium, and it gets to the data through a particular sequence of steps. Applications based on these services are constrained by the design to using those settings—which usually includes a fixed data schema, a predefined storage medium, a hard-coded behavior. What if you don't like or don't want these restrictions?

Run-time configuration, as achieved through *machine.config* and *web.config* files, adds some more flexibility to your code. However, run-time configuration does not provide a definitive solution that is flexible enough to allow full customization of the service that would make it extensible and smooth to implement. A more definitive solution is provided by ASP.NET 2.0, which formalizes and integrates into the overall framework of classes a design pattern that was originally developed and used in several ASP.NET Starter Kits. Known as the *provider model*, this pattern defines a common API for a variety of operations—each known as the *provider*. At the same time, the provider's interface contains several hooks for developers to take complete control over the internal behavior of the API, data schema used, and storage medium.

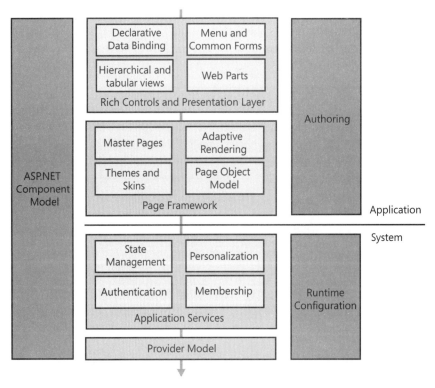

Figure 1-5   A more detailed view of the ASP.NET development stack. The arrow indicates the typical top-down application perspective, going down from the user interface to the system services.

> **Important** The provider model is one of the most important and critical aspects of ASP.NET. A good understanding of it is crucial to conduct effective design and implementation of cutting-edge applications. The provider model is formalized in ASP.NET 2.0, but it is simply the implementation of a design pattern. As such, it is completely decoupled at its core from any platform and framework. So once you understand the basic idea, you can start using it in any application, even outside the boundaries of ASP.NET.

The ASP.NET Provider Model

There's a well-known design pattern behind the ASP.NET provider model—the *strategy* pattern. Defined, the strategy pattern indicates an expected behavior (say, sorting) that can be implemented through a variety of interchangeable algorithms (say, Quicksort, Mergesort). Each application then selects the algorithm that best fits while keeping the public, observable behavior and programming API intact.

The most notable feature of the strategy pattern is that it provides a way for an object, or an entire subsystem, to expose its internals so that a client can unplug the default implementation of a given feature and plug his own in. This is exactly what happens in ASP.NET for a number of services, including membership, roles, state management, personalization, site navigation. The ASP.NET provider model is the ASP.NET implementation of the strategy pattern.

The Rationale Behind the Provider Model

The provider model is not an application feature that end users can see with their own eyes. In itself, it doesn't make an application show a richer content, run faster, or be more responsive. The provider model is an infrastructural feature that improves an application's architecture by enabling developers and architects to operate under the hood of some system components. At the same time, it enables developers to build new components that expose hooks for clients to plug in and customize behavior and settings. Implementing the strategy pattern doesn't transform an application into an open-source project, allowing anybody to modify anything. It simply means that you have a simple, elegant, and effective pattern to make certain parts of your application customizable by clients. At the same time, the ASP.NET implementation of the pattern—the provider model—makes you capable of customizing certain parts of the ASP.NET runtime environment through special classes named providers from which you can derive your own.

Exemplifying the Provider Model

To see an example of the provider model and its major benefits, let's look at Figure 1-6. The figure outlines the classic schema for authenticating a user. The blocks of the diagram follow closely the flow of operations in ASP.NET 1.1.

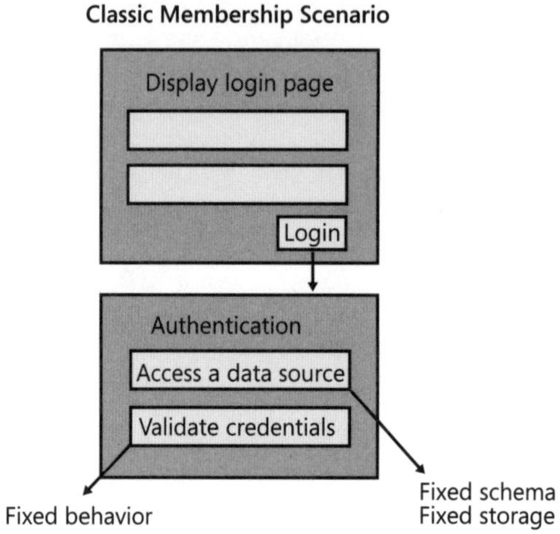

Classic Membership Scenario

Figure 1-6   Classic membership schema for ASP.NET 1.1 applications.

The user who attempts to connect to a protected page is shown a login page and invited to type credentials. Next, the name and password are passed on to a function, which is ultimately responsible for validating the user. ASP.NET 1.x can automatically check users against Windows accounts or a list of names in the web.config file. None of these approaches work well in a realistic Web application; in most cases, developers just end up writing a custom piece of code to validate credentials against a homemade data source. The schema and storage medium of the data source are fixed and determined by the developer. Likewise, the algorithm employed to validate credentials is constrained by the design.

Is there anything wrong with this solution? Not necessarily. It works just fine, puts you in control of everything, and can be adapted to work in other applications. The rub is that there's no well-defined pattern that emerges from this solution. Sure, you can port it from one application to the next, but overall the solution relates to the adapter pattern mostly like cut-and-paste relates to object-oriented inheritance.

Let's briefly consider another scenario—session state management. In ASP.NET 1.x, you can store the session state in a process separate from the running application—be it SQL Server or a Windows service (the ASP.NET state server). If you do so, though, you're constrained to using the data schema that ASP.NET hard-codes for you. Furthermore, imagine you're not a SQL Server customer. In this case, either you abandon the idea of storing session state to a database or you buy a set of licenses for SQL Server. Finally, there's nothing you can do about the internal behavior of the ASP.NET session module. If you don't like the way it, say, serializes data to the out-of-process storage, you can't change it. Take it or leave it—there's no intermediate choice.

Can you see the big picture? There are modules in ASP.NET that force you to take (or leave) a fixed schema of data, a fixed storage medium, and a fixed internal behavior. The most that you can do is (sometimes) avoid using those modules and write your own from scratch, as we outlined in the membership example. However, rolling your own replacement is not necessarily a smart move. You end up with a proprietary and application-specific system that is not automatically portable from one application to another. In addition, if you hire new people, you have to train those people before they get accustomed to using your API. Finally, you have to put forth a lot of effort to make such a proprietary API general enough to be reusable and extensible in a variety of contexts. (Otherwise, you get to reinvent the wheel time after time.)

In which way is the provider model a better solution? In the first place, it supplies a well-documented and common programming interface to perform common tasks. In addition, you gain the ability to completely control the internal business and data access logic of each API that falls under its umbrella.

In the end, in ASP.NET 1.1 you often have no other choice than writing your own API to roll certain functions the way you want. In ASP.NET 2.0, the provider model offers a much better alternative. So much better that it's practically a crime not to use it.

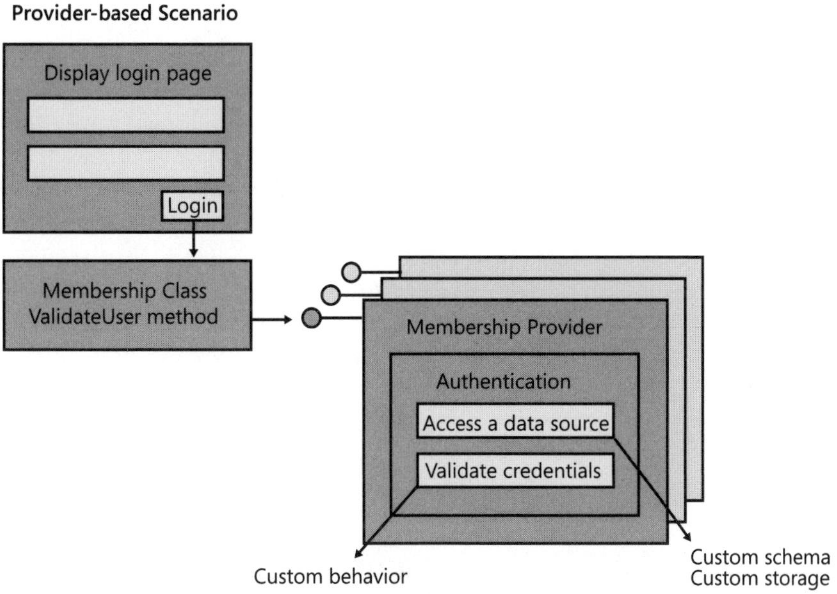

Figure 1-7   Membership revisited to use the provider model in ASP.NET 2.0.

Figure 1-7 revisits Figure 1-6 in light of the provider model. ASP.NET 2.0 makes available a bunch of static methods on a global class—*Membership*. (We'll cover the membership API in great detail in Chapter 15.) At the application level, you always invoke the same method to perform the same operation (for example, validating user credentials, creating new users, changing passwords.) Below this common API, though, you can plug in your own provider to do the job just the way you want. Writing a new provider is as easy as deriving a new class from a known base and overriding a few well-known methods. The selection of the current provider for a given task takes place in the configuration file.

Benefits of the Provider Model

In the ASP.NET implementation, the strategy pattern brings you two major benefits: extensive customization of the application's run-time environment, and code reusability. Several areas in ASP.NET are affected by the provider model. You can write providers to handle user membership and roles, persist session state, manage user profiles through personalization, and load site map information from a variety of sources. For example, by writing a provider you can change the schema of the data used to persist credentials, store this data in an Oracle or DB2 database, and store passwords hashed rather than as clear text. This level of customization of system components is unprecedented, and it opens up a new world of possibilities for application developers. At the same time, it gives you an excellent starting point for writing new providers and even extending the model to your own components.

If you look at ASP.NET 2.0 from the perspective of existing applications, the provider model gains even more technical relevance because it is the key to code reuse and subsequent preservation of investments in programming and development time. As we pointed out, a realistic membership system in ASP.NET 1.1 requires you to roll your own API as far as validation and user management are concerned. What should you do when the decision to upgrade to ASP.NET 2.0 is made? Should you drop all that code to embrace the new dazzling membership API of ASP.NET 2.0? Or would you be better sticking to the old-fashioned and proprietary API for membership?

The provider model delivers the answer (and a good answer, indeed) in its unique ability of switching the underlying algorithm while preserving the overall behavior. This ability alone wouldn't be sufficient, though. You also need to adapt your existing code to make it pluggable in the new runtime environment. Another popular pattern helps out here—the adapter pattern. The declared intent of the adapter pattern is convert a class A to an interface B that a client C understands. You wrap the existing code into a new provider class that can be seamlessly plugged into the existing ASP.NET 2.0 framework. You change the underlying implementation of the membership API, and you use your own schema and storage medium while keeping the top-level interface intact. And, more importantly, you get to fully reuse your code.

A Quick Look at the ASP.NET Implementation

The implementation of the ASP.NET provider model consists of three distinct elements—the provider class, configuration layer, and storage layer. The provider class is the component you plug into the existing framework to provide a desired functionality the way you want. The configuration layer supplies information used to identify and instantiate the actual provider. The storage layer is the physical medium where data is stored. Depending on the feature, it can be Active Directory, an Oracle or SQL Server table, an XML file, or whatever else.

The Provider Class

A provider class implements an interface known to its clients. In this way, the class provides clients with the functionality promised by that interface. Clients are not required to know anything about the implementation details of the interface. This code opacity allows for the magic of code driving other code it doesn't even know about. In the ASP.NET provider model, the only variation to the original definition of the strategy pattern is that base classes are used instead of interfaces.

In ASP.NET, a provider class can't just be any class that implements a given interface. Quite the reverse, actually. A provider class must inherit from a well-known base class. There is a base class for each supported type of provider. The base class defines the programming interface of the provider through a bunch of abstract methods.

All provider base classes derive from a common class named *ProviderBase*. This base class provides one overridable method—*Initialize*—through which the run-time environment passes any pertinent settings from configuration files. Figure 1-8 outlines the hierarchy of provider classes for membership.

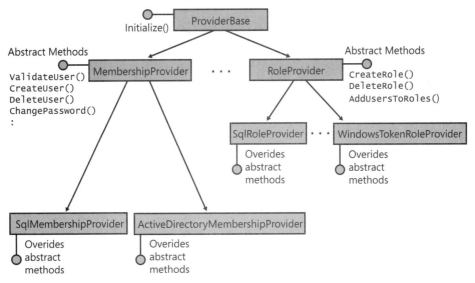

Figure 1-8   The hierarchy of provider classes.

Interfaces vs. Base Classes

Raise your hand if you are a developer who has never been involved in hours and hours of debate on the subject of interfaces versus base classes. It's a discussion that rarely comes to an end and always leave folks from different camps firmly holding to their respective positions. Should you use interfaces, or are base classes better? Which considerations is your answer based on? Consider the following fact, first.

Prebeta builds of ASP.NET 2.0 implemented the provider model literally with the definition of the strategy pattern—that is, through interfaces. In the Beta 1 timeframe, interfaces were replaced with base classes, and so it is with the released version. The ASP.NET team seemingly came to a conclusion on the issue, did it not?

An interface is a collection of logically related methods that contains only member definitions and no code. An interface type is a partial description of a type, which multiple classes can potentially support. In other words, a good interface is one that is implemented by a number of different types and encapsulates a useful, generalized piece of functionality that clients want to use. That's why many interfaces just end with the suffix "able", such as *IDisposable*, *IComparable*, and *IFormattable*. If an interface has only one useful implementing class, it is likely the offspring of a bad design choice. As a practical rule, new interfaces should be introduced sparingly and with due forethought.

A base class defines a common behavior and a common programming interface for a tree of child classes. Classes are more flexible than interfaces and support versioning. If you add a new method to version 2.0 of a class, any existing derived classes continue to function unchanged, as long as the new method is not abstract. This is untrue for interfaces.

In light of these considerations, the emerging rule is that one should use base classes instead of interfaces whenever possible (which doesn't read as, "always use base classes"). To me, base classes appear to be an excellent choice, as far as the provider model is concerned.

The Configuration Layer

Each supported provider type is assigned a section in the configuration file, which is where the default provider for the feature is set and all available providers are listed. If the provider sports public properties, default values for these properties can be specified through attributes. The contents of the section are passed as an argument to the *Initialize* method of the *ProviderBase* class—the only method that all providers have in common. Within this method, each provider uses the passed information to initialize its own state. Here's a snapshot of the configuration section for the membership provider.

```
<membership defaultProvider="AspNetSqlProvider">
    <providers>
        <add name="AspNetSqlProvider"
            type="System.Web.Security.SqlMembershipProvider, System.Web"
            connectionStringName="LocalSqlServer"
            enablePasswordRetrieval="false"
            enablePasswordReset="true"
            requiresQuestionAndAnswer="true"
            ⋮
            passwordFormat="Hashed" />
        ⋮
    </providers>
</membership>
```

The Storage Layer

All providers need to read and write information to a persistent storage medium. In many cases, two providers of the same type differ only for the storage they employ. Details of the storage medium are packed in the attributes of the provider in the *<providers>* section, as shown in the preceding code sample. For example, the preceding *AspNetSqlProvider* provider is the predefined membership provider that reads and writes to a SQL Server table. The connection string for the provider is specified through the *connectionStringName* attribute, which in turn refers to another centralized section of the configuration files that lists all available connection strings.

For the provider to work, any needed infrastructure (that is, database, tables, relationships) must exist. Setting up the working environment is a task typically accomplished at deployment time. ASP.NET makes it a breeze thanks to the Web site administration console, which is shown in Figure 1-9.

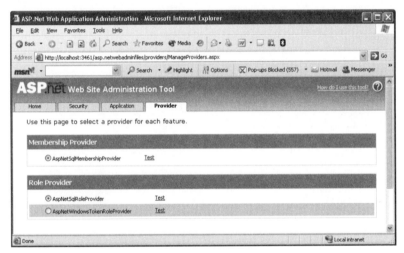

Figure 1-9   The ASP.NET Web site administration console you invoke from within Visual Studio .NET 2005.

Available Types of Providers

The provider model is used to achieve several tasks, the most important of which are as follows:

- The implementation of a read/write mechanism to persist the user profile

- The creation of a user-defined repository of user credentials that supports most common operations, such as checking a user for existence, adding and deleting users, and changing passwords

- The creation of a user-defined repository for user roles

- The definition of the site map

- The introduction of newer types of data storage for the session state

Table 1-1 shows the list of the provider classes available in ASP.NET.

Table 1-1   Available ASP.NET Provider Base Classes

Class	Description
MembershipProvider	Base class for membership providers used to manage user account information.
ProfileProvider	Base class for personalization providers used to persist and retrieve user's profile information.
RoleProvider	Base class for role providers used to manage user role information.
SessionStateStoreProviderBase	Base class for session state store providers. These providers are used to save and retrieve session state information from persistent storage media.
SiteMapProvider	Base class for managing site map information.

The classes listed in Table 1-1 define an abstract method for each aspect that's customizable in the feature they represent. For example, regarding membership management, the class *MembershipProvider* exposes methods such as *ValidateUser*, *CreateUser*, *DeleteUser*, *ChangePassword*, and so forth. Note that you'll never use *MembershipProvider* in your code just because it's an abstract class. Instead, you'll use a derived class such as *SqlMembershipProvider* or, perhaps, *ActiveDirectoryMembershipProvider*. The same holds true for other types of providers.

Finally, if you're going to write a custom membership provider that wraps your existing code, you'd create a class that inherits from *MembershipProvider* or similar classes if other provider-based features are involved.

> **Note**   The provider architecture is one of ASP.NET 2.0's most important new features and also one of the most delicate with regard to applications. To prevent developers from producing buggy providers, the ASP.NET team supplies a made-to-measure provider toolkit that details what you can and cannot do in a provider, plus lots of sample code to serve as a guide. Writing a custom provider can be tricky for at least a couple of reasons. First, ASP.NET providers must be thread-safe. Second, their initialization step can lead you straight into a deadly reentrancy. Be sure you download the ASP.NET provider toolkit from the ASP.NET Developer Center before you leap into a new provider project.

Conclusion

As part of the .NET Framework, ASP.NET allows you to take full advantage of features of the common-language runtime (CLR), such as type safety, inheritance, language interoperability, and versioning. As the newest platform for Web applications, ASP.NET builds on the successes of a variety of other platforms, including classic ASP, JSP, and LAMP. ASP.NET promotes a programming model that, although built on top of the stateless HTTP protocol, appears to be stateful and event-driven to programmers.

In this chapter, we first analyzed the component model that backs up ASP.NET Web pages and then went through the development stack from top (presentation layer and rich controls) to bottom (infrastructure and providers). The provider model—in the end, an implementation of the strategy pattern—is a key element in the new ASP.NET architecture and a pillar of support for new applications. Extensively applied, it allows you to customize several low-level aspects of the application's run-time environment and reuse large portions of existing code. Fully understood, it gives you a way to build new components that are flexible and extensible beyond imagination and, as such, seamless to plug in to a variety of projects and easier to customize for clients.

Just the Facts

- In ASP.NET, you take full advantage of all CLR features, such as type safety, inheritance, code access security, language interoperability.

- At execution time, ASP.NET pages are represented by an instance of a class that descends from the *Page* class.

- The *Page* class is the ending point of a pipeline of modules that process any HTTP request.

- Only elements in an ASP.NET page marked with the *runat* attribute can be programmatically accessed when the page is executed on the server.

- Page elements devoid of the *runat* attribute are not processed on the server and emitted verbatim.

- The *runat* attribute applies to virtually any possible tags you can use in an ASP.NET page, including custom and unknown tags.

- The process model is the sequence of operations needed to process a request. The process model is determined by IIS and determines which worker process takes care of running ASP.NET applications and under which account.

- ASP.NET applications run under a weak account.

- The behavior of ASP.NET applications can be configured through a bunch of configuration files.

- The ASP.NET provider model is an infrastructural feature that improves an application's architecture by enabling developers and architects to operate under the hood of some system components.

- The ASP.NET provider model brings you two major benefits: extensive customization of the application's run-time environment and code reusability.

Chapter 6
Rich Page Composition

A large number of Web sites these days contain similar-looking, rich pages that share the same graphics, appearance, user interface (UI) widgets, and perhaps some navigational menus or search forms. These pages are rich in content and functionality, are visually appealing, and, more important, have an overall look and feel that abides by the golden rule of Web usability: be consistent. What's the recommended approach for building such pages and Web sites?

One possibility is wrapping these UI elements in user controls and referencing them in each page. Although such a model is extremely powerful and produces modular code, when you have hundreds of pages to work with, it soon becomes unmanageable. Both classic ASP and ASP.NET 1.x provide some workarounds for this type of issue, but neither tackles such a scenario openly and provides a definitive, optimal solution. ASP.NET 2.0 faces up to the task through a new technology—*master pages*—and basically benefits from the ASP.NET Framework's ability to merge a "supertemplate" with user-defined content replacements.

With themes, you can easily give the whole site a consistent (and, you hope, appealing) user interface and easily export that look from one application to the next. Much like Microsoft Windows XP themes, ASP.NET themes assign a set of styles and visual attributes to the customizable elements of the site. Themes are a superset of cascading style sheets (CSS) and are supported only in ASP.NET 2.0.

A recurring task in Web development is collecting user input by using forms. When the input to collect is large and pretty much articulated (in other words, easy to categorize), multiple forms are typically used to accomplish the task. The whole procedure is divided into various steps, each of which takes care of collecting and validating a particular subset of the expected data. This multistep procedure is often called a *wizard*. ASP.NET 2.0 introduces a new view control that makes building wizards a snap.

Overall, building rich pages is a much more approachable task in ASP.NET today than it was with previous versions. With master pages, you build pages based on an existing template of code and markup; with themes, you use skins to control pages and achieve visual consistency as well as profile capabilities. Finally, with wizards, you add rich functionality to pages.

Working with Master Pages

As a matter of fact, ASP.NET and Microsoft Visual Studio .NET greatly simplified the process of authoring Web pages and Web sites and made it affordable to a wide range of people with different skills. However, after a few months of real-world experience, many developers recognized that something was missing in the ASP.NET approach to page authoring. While building simple sites is easy, architecting real-world sites with hundreds of complex and rich pages still requires additional work and, more important, key decisions to be made without guidance.

Almost all Web sites use a similar graphical layout for all their pages. This doesn't happen by chance—it grows out of accepted guidelines for design and usability. A consistent layout is characteristic of all cutting-edge Web sites, no matter how complex. For some Web sites, the layout consists of the header, body, and footer; for others, it is a more sophisticated aggregation of navigational menus, buttons, and panels that contain and render the actual content. Needless to say, manual duplication of code and HTML elements is simply out of the question. Making code automatically reusable clearly represents a better approach, but how do you implement it *in practice*?

Authoring Rich Pages in ASP.NET 1.x

In ASP.NET 1.x, the best approach to authoring pages with a common layout is to employ *user controls*. User controls are aggregates of ASP.NET server controls, literal text, and code. (We'll cover user controls in my other recent book, *Programming Microsoft ASP.NET 2.0 Applications: Advanced Topics* [Microsoft Press, 2005], which is published as a companion volume to this book.) The ASP.NET runtime exposes user controls to the outside world as programmable components. The idea is that you employ user controls to tailor your own user interface components and share them among the pages of the Web site. For example, all the pages that need a navigational menu can reference and configure the user control that provides that feature.

What's Good About User Controls

User controls are like embeddable pages. Turning an existing ASP.NET page into a user control requires only a few minor changes. User controls can be easily linked to any page that needs their services. Furthermore, changes to a user control's implementation do not affect the referencing page and only require you (or the runtime) to recompile the user control into an assembly.

> **Note**   In ASP.NET, user controls make the use of classic ASP include files obsolete. A typical
> ASP include file contains either static or dynamic content for the portion of the page it repre-
> sents. There's no object orientation in this approach, making thoughtful design and easy main-
> tainability very difficult, if not impossible, for very large Web sites. In addition, include file tags
> opened in one file are frequently closed in another file. This situation makes WYSIWYG
> designer support virtually impossible.

What's Bad About User Controls

If you change the *internal* implementation of the user control, no referencing page will be
affected. However, if you alter any aspect of the control's *public* interface (such as the class
name, properties, methods, or events), all the pages that reference the control must be
updated. This means you must manually retouch all the pages in the application that use the
control. Then you must recompile these pages and deploy the assemblies. In addition, the
next time a user views each page, the ASP.NET runtime will take a while to respond because
the dynamic assembly for the page must be re-created.

Architecturally speaking, the solution based on user controls works just fine. In practice,
though, it is not a very manageable model for large-scale applications—its effectiveness
decreases as the complexity of the application (the number of pages involved) increases. If
your site contains hundreds of pages, handling common elements through user controls can
quickly become inefficient and unmanageable.

Visual Inheritance

ASP.NET pages are built as instances of special classes—code-behind or code file classes.
Because pages are ultimately classes, what happens if you stuff part of the common UI in some
base class and inherit new pages from there? This approach resembles the visual inheritance
feature that Windows Forms developers have been familiar with for a long time.

Pure visual inheritance *a là* Windows Forms is impractical in ASP.NET. This is because
ASP.NET pages are made of code *and* markup. The markup determines the position of the
controls, while code adds logic and functionality. Building predefined graphic templates in
the base class doesn't pose issues, but how would you import those standard UI blocks
in derived pages, and, more important, how would you merge those with controls local to
the derived page?

In Windows Forms, controls have an absolute position that the designer reproduces, making
it easy for developers to insert new controls anywhere. Web Forms, though, typically use relative positioning, which leads to either of the next two design choices. Option one is to supply
predefined and named UI blocks in base classes and have derived classes load them in matching

placeholders. Option two involves using master pages as defined in ASP.NET 2.0. To implement the former technique do the following:

1. Derive your page from a base class that knows how to create special UI blocks such as toolbars, headers, and footers. Each of these UI blocks has a unique name.

2. Add *<asp:placeholder>* controls to the derived page whose ID matches any of the predefined names. The base class contains the code to explore the control's tree and expand placeholders with predefined UI blocks.

This approach exploits inheritance but provides no WYSIWYG facilities and forces you to create UI blocks in code-only mode with no markup. This option is demonstrated in the companion code, but it should be considered only for ASP.NET 1.x applications. The second option mentioned—using master pages—is described in the following section.

Writing a Master Page

In ASP.NET 2.0, a master page is a distinct file referenced at both the application level and the page level that contains the static layout of the page. Regions that each derived page can customize are referenced in the master page with a special placeholder control. A *derived* page is simply a collection of blocks the runtime will use to fill the holes in the master. True visual inheritance *à la* Windows Forms is not a goal of ASP.NET 2.0 master pages. The contents of a master page are merged into the content page, and they dynamically produce a new page class that is served to the user upon request. The merge process takes place at compile time and only once. In no way do the contents of the master serve as a base class for the content page.

What's a Master Page, Anyway?

A master page is similar to an ordinary ASP.NET page except for the top *@Master* directive and the presence of one or more *ContentPlaceHolder* server controls. A *ContentPlaceHolder* control defines a region in the master page that can be customized in a derived page. A master page without content placeholders is technically correct and will be processed correctly by the ASP.NET runtime. However, a placeholderless master fails in its primary goal—to be the supertemplate of multiple pages that look alike. A master page devoid of placeholders works like an ordinary Web page but with the extra burden required to process master pages. Here is a simple master page:

```
<%@ Master Language="C#" CodeFile="Simple.master.cs" Inherits="Simple" %>
<html>
<head runat="server">
    <title>Hello, master pages</title>
</head>
<body>
    <form id="form1" runat="server">
        <asp:Panel ID="HeaderPanel" runat="server"
            BackImageUrl="Images/SkyBkgnd.png" Width="100%">
```

```
            <asp:Label ID="TitleBox" runat="server"
                Text="Programming ASP.NET 2.0" />
        </asp:Panel>
        <asp:contentplaceholder id="PageBody" runat="server">
         <!-- derived pages will define content for this placeholder -->
        </asp:contentplaceholder>
        <asp:Panel ID="FooterPanel" runat="server"
            BackImageUrl="Images/SeaBkgnd.png">
            <asp:Label ID="SubTitleBox" runat="server"
                Text="Dino Esposito" />
        </asp:Panel>
    </form>
</body>
</html>
```

As you can see, the master page looks like a standard ASP.NET page. Aside from the identifying *@Master* directive, the only key differences are *ContentPlaceHolder* controls. A page bound to this master automatically inherits all the contents of the master (the header and footer, in this case) and can attach custom markup and server controls to each defined placeholder. The content placeholder element is fully identified by its *ID* property and normally doesn't require other attributes.

The *@Master* Directive

The *@Master* directive distinguishes master pages from content pages and allows the ASP.NET runtime to properly handle each. A master page file is compiled to a class that derives from the *MasterPage* class. The *MasterPage* class, in turn, inherits *UserControl*. So, at the end of the day, a master page is treated as a special kind of ASP.NET user control.

The *@Master* supports quite a few attributes. For the most part, though, they are the same attributes that we reviewed in Chapter 3 for the *@Page* directive. Table 6-1 details the attributes that have a special meaning to master pages.

Table 6-1   Attributes of the *@Master* Directive

Attribute	Description
ClassName	Specifies the name for the class that will be created to render the master page. This value can be any valid class name but should not include a namespace. By default, the class name for simple.master is *ASP.simple_master*.
CodeFile	Indicates the URL to the file that contains any source code associated with the master page.
Inherits	Specifies a code-behind class for the master page to inherit. This can be any class derived from *MasterPage*.
MasterPageFile	Specifies the name of the master page file that this master refers to. A master can refer to another master through the same mechanisms a page uses to attach to a master. If this attribute is set, you will have nested masters.

The master page is associated with a code file that looks like the following:

```
public partial class Simple : System.Web.UI.MasterPage {
    protected void Page_Load(object sender, EventArgs e) {
        ...
    }
    §
}
```

The *@Master* directive doesn't override attributes set at the *@Page* directive level. For example, you can have the master set the language to Visual Basic .NET and one of the content pages can use C#. The language set at the master page level never influences the choice of the language at the content page level. You can use other ASP.NET directives in a master page—for example, *@Import*. However, the scope of these directives is limited to the master file and does not extend to child pages generated from the master.

> **Note** You can create master pages programmatically. You build your own class and make it inherit *MasterPage*. Then you create *.master* files in which the *Inherits* attribute points to the fully qualified name of your class. Rapid application development (RAD) designers such as the one embedded in Microsoft Visual Studio .NET 2005 use this approach to create master pages.

The *ContentPlaceHolder* Container Control

The *ContentPlaceHolder* control acts as a container placed in a master page. It marks places in the master where related pages can insert custom content. A content placeholder is uniquely identified by an ID. Here's an example:

```
<asp:contentplaceholder runat="server" ID="PageBody" />
```

A content page is an ASP.NET page that contains only *<asp:Content>* server tags. This element corresponds to an instance of the *Content* class that provides the actual content for a particular placeholder in the master. The link between placeholders and content is established through the ID of the placeholder. The content of a particular instance of the *Content* server control is written to the placeholder whose ID matches the value of the *ContentPlaceHolderID* property, as shown here:

```
<asp:Content runat="server" contentplaceholderID="PageBody">
    ...
</asp:Content>
```

In a master page, you define as many content placeholders as there are customizable regions in the page. A content page doesn't have to fill all the placeholders defined in the bound master. However, a content page can't do more than just fill placeholders defined in the master.

> **Note** A placeholder can't be bound to more than one content region in a single content page. If you have multiple *<asp:Content>* server tags in a content page, each must point to a distinct placeholder in the master.

Specifying Default Content

A content placeholder can be assigned default content that will show up if the content page fails to provide a replacement. Each *ContentPlaceHolder* control in the master page can contain default content. If a content page does not reference a given placeholder in the master, the default content will be used. The following code snippet shows how to define default content:

```
<asp:contentplaceholder runat="server" ID="PageBody">
    <!-- Use the following markup if no custom
        content is provided by the content page -->
    ...
</asp:contentplaceholder>
```

The default content is completely ignored if the content page populates the placeholder. The default content is never merged with the custom markup provided by the content page.

> **Note** A *ContentPlaceHolder* control can be used only in a master page. Content placeholders are not valid on regular ASP.NET pages. If such a control is found in an ordinary Web page, a parser error occurs.

Writing a Content Page

The master page defines the skeleton of the resulting page. If you need to share layout or any UI block among all the pages, placing it in a master page will greatly simplify management of the pages in the application. You create the master and then think of your pages in terms of a delta from the master. The master defines the common parts of a certain group of pages and leaves placeholders for customizable regions. Each *content page*, in turn, defines what the content of each region has to be for a particular ASP.NET page. Figure 6-1 shows how to create a content page in Visual Studio .NET 2005.

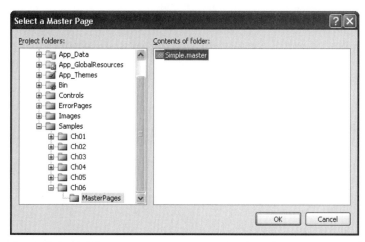

Figure 6-1   Adding a content page to a Visual Studio .NET 2005 project.

The *Content* Control

The key part of a content page is the *Content* control—a mere container for other controls. The *Content* control is used only in conjunction with a corresponding *ContentPlaceHolder* and is not a standalone control. The master file that we considered earlier defines a single placeholder named *PageBody*. This placeholder represents the body of the page and is placed right below an HTML table that provides the page's header. Figure 6-2 shows a sample content page based on the aforementioned master page.

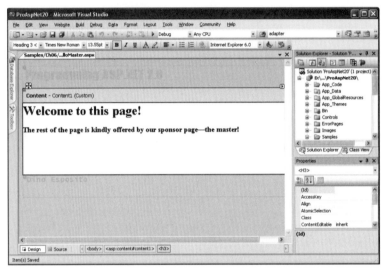

Figure 6-2   A preview of the content page. Notice the layout of the master page grayed out in the background.

Let's take a look at the source code of the content page:

```
<%@ Page Language="C#" MasterPageFile="Simple.master"
        CodeFile="HelloMaster.aspx.cs" Inherits="HelloMaster" %>

<asp:Content ID="Content1" ContentPlaceHolderID="PageBody" Runat="Server">
    <h1>Welcome to this page!</h1>
    <h3>The rest of the page is kindly offered by our sponsor
        page-the master!</h3>
</asp:Content>
```

The content page is the resource that users invoke through the browser. When the user points her or his browser to this page, the output in Figure 6-3 is shown.

The replaceable part of the master is filled with the corresponding content section defined in the derived pages. A content page—that is, a page bound to a master—is a special breed of page in that it can *only* contain *<asp:Content>* controls. A content page is not permitted to host server controls outside of an *<asp:Content>* tag.

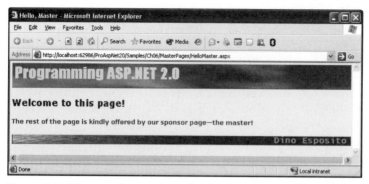

Figure 6-3   The sample page in action.

Let's explore the attachment of pages to masters in a bit more detail.

Attaching Pages to a Master

In the previous example, the content page is bound to the master by using the *MasterPageFile* attribute in the *@Page* directive. The attribute points to a string representing the path to the master page. Page-level binding is just one possibility—although it is the most common one.

You can also set the binding between the master and the content at the application or folder level. Application-level binding means that you link all the pages of an application to the same master. You configure this behavior by setting the *Master* attribute in the *<pages>* element of the principal *web.config* file:

```
<configuration>
    <system.web>
        <pages master="MyApp.master" />
    </system.web>
</configuration>
```

If the same setting is expressed in a child *web.config* file—a *web.config* file stored in a site subdirectory—all ASP.NET pages in the folder are bound to a specified master page.

Note that if you define binding at the application or folder level, all the Web pages in the application (or the folder) must have *Content* controls mapped to one or more placeholders in the master page. In other words, application-level binding prevents you from having (or later adding) a page to the site that is not configured as a content page. Any classic ASP.NET page in the application (or folder) that contains server controls will throw an exception.

Device-Specific Masters

Like all ASP.NET pages and controls, master pages can detect the capabilities of the underlying browser and adapt their output to the specific device in use. ASP.NET 2.0 makes choosing a device-specific master easier than ever. If you want to control how certain pages of your site appear on a particular browser, you can build them from a common master and design the master to address the specific features of the browser. In other words, you can create multiple versions of the same master, each targeting a different type of browser.

How do you associate a particular version of the master and a particular browser? In the content page, you define multiple bindings using the same *MasterPageFile* attribute, but you prefix it with the identifier of the device. For example, suppose you want to provide ad hoc support for Microsoft Internet Explorer and Netscape browsers and use a generic master for any other browsers that users employ to visit the site. You use the following syntax:

```
<%@ Page masterpagefile="Base.master"
    ie:masterpagefile="ieBase.master"
    netscape6to9:masterpagefile="nsBase.master" %>
```

The ieBase.master file will be used for Internet Explorer; the nsBase.master, on the other hand, will be used if the browser belongs to the Netscape family, versions 6.x to 9.0. In any other case, a device-independent master (Base.master) will be used. When the page runs, the ASP.NET runtime automatically determines which browser or device the user is using and selects the corresponding master page, as shown in Figure 6-4.

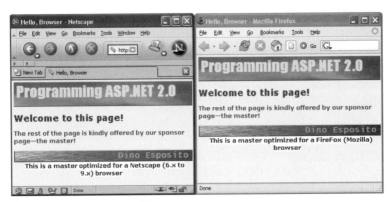

Figure 6-4   Browser-specific master pages.

The prefixes you can use to indicate a particular type of browser are those defined in the ASP.NET configuration files for browsers. Table 6-2 lists the most commonly used Brower IDs.

Table 6-2   ID of Most Common Browsers

Browser ID	Browser Name
IE	Any version of Internet Explorer
Netscape3	Netscape Navigator 3.x
Netscape4	Netscape Communicator 4.x
Netscape6to9	Any version of Netscape higher than 6.0
Mozilla	Firefox
Opera	Opera
Up	Openwave-powered devices

It goes without saying that you can distinguish not only between up-level and down-level browsers but also between browsers and other devices, such as cellular phones and personal digital assistants (PDAs). If you use device-specific masters, you must also indicate a device-independent master.

> **Warning**   Browser information is stored differently in ASP.NET 1.x and ASP.NET 2.0. In ASP.NET 1.x, you find it in the *<browserCaps>* section of the *machine.config* file. In ASP.NET 2.0, it is stored in text files with a *.browser* extension located in the *Browsers* folder under the ASP.NET installation path on the Web server: WINDOWS%\Microsoft.NET\Framework\ [**version**]\Config\Browsers.

Setting the Title of a Page

As a collection of *<asp:Content>* tags, a content page is not allowed to include any markup that can specify the title of the page. Using the *<title>* tag is possible in the master page, but the master page—by design—works as the base for a variety of pages, each requiring its own title. The trick to setting the title is in using the *Title* property of the *@Page* directive in the content page:

```
<@Page MasterPageFile="simple.master" Title="Hello, master" %>
```

Note, though, that the setting of the title of the page is possible only if the *<title>* or the *<head>* tag in the master is flagged as *runat=server*.

Processing Master and Content Pages

The use of master pages slightly changes how pages are processed and compiled. For one thing, a page based on a master has a double dependency—on the *.aspx* source file (the content page) and on the *.master* file (the master page). If either of these pages changes, the dynamic page assembly will be re-created. Although the URL that users need is the URL of the content page, the page served to the browser results from the master page fleshed out with any replacement provided by the content page.

Compiling Master Pages

When the user requests an *.aspx* resource mapped to a content page—that is, a page that references a master—the ASP.NET runtime begins its job by tracking the dependency between the source *.aspx* file and its master. This information is persisted in a local file created in the ASP.NET temporary files folder. Next, the runtime parses the master page source code and creates a Visual Basic .NET or C# class, depending on the language set in the master page. The class inherits *MasterPage*, or the master's code file, and is then compiled to an assembly.

If multiple .*master* files are found in the same directory, they are all processed at the same time. Thus a dynamic assembly is generated for any master files found, even if only one of them is used by the ASP.NET page whose request triggered the compilation process. Therefore, don't leave unused master files in your Web space—they will be compiled anyway. Also note that the compilation tax is paid only the first time a content page is accessed within the application. When a user accesses another page that requires the second master, the response is faster because the previously compiled master is cached.

Serving the Page to Users

As mentioned, any ASP.NET page bound to a master page must have a certain structure—no server controls or literal text are allowed outside the <*asp:Content*> tag. As a result, the layout of the page looks like a plain collection of content elements, each bound to a particular placeholder in the master. The connection is established through the ID property. The <*asp:Content*> element works like a control container, much like the *Panel* control of ASP.NET or the HTML <*div*> tag. All the markup text is compiled to a template and associated with the corresponding placeholder property on the master class.

The master page is a special kind of user control with some templated regions. It's not coincidental, in fact, that the *MasterPage* class inherits from the *UserControl* class. Once instantiated as a user control, the master page is completed with templates generated from the markup defined in the content page. Next, the resulting control is added to the control tree of the current page. No other controls are present in the final page except those brought in by the master. Figure 6-5 shows the skeleton of the final page served to the user.

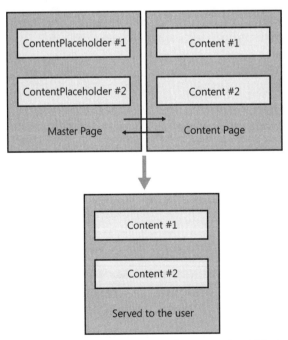

Figure 6-5   The structure of the final page in which the master page and the content page are merged.

Nested Master Pages

So far we've seen a pretty simple relationship between a master and a collection of content pages. However, the topology of the relationship can be made as complex and sophisticated as needed. A master can, in fact, be associated with another master and form a hierarchical, nested structure. When nested masters are used, any child master is seen and implemented as a plain content page in which extra *ContentPlaceHolder* controls are defined for an extra level of content pages. Put another way, a child master is a kind of content page that contains a combination of *<asp:Content>* and *<asp:ContentPlaceHolder>* elements. Like any other content page, a child master points to a master page and provides content blocks for its parent's place-holders. At the same time, it makes available new placeholders for its child pages.

> **Note**   There's no architectural limitation in the number of nesting levels you can implement in your Web sites. Performance-wise, the depth of the nesting has a negligible impact on the overall functionality and scalability of the solution. The final page served to the user is always compiled on demand and never modified as long as dependent files are not touched.

Let's expand on the previous example to add an intermediate master page. The root master page—named *parent.master*—defines the header, the footer, and a replaceable region. Except for the class names, the source code is identical to the example we considered earlier. Let's have a closer look at the intermediate master—named *content.master*:

```
<%@ Master Language="C#" MasterPageFile="Parent.master"
    CodeFile="Content.master.cs" Inherits="ContentMaster" %>

<asp:Content Runat="Server" ContentPlaceHolderID="ContentOfThePage" >
    <table width="100%"><tr>
        <td>
            <h1>Welcome to this page!</h1>
            <h3>The rest of the page is kindly offered by our
                sponsor page—the master!</h3>
        </td>
        <td align="center">
            <h2>Select Your Favorite Chapter</h2>
            <asp:ContentPlaceHolder runat="server" ID="ChapterMenu" />
        </td>
    </tr></table>
</asp:Content>
```

As you can see, the master contains both a collection of *<asp:Content>* and *<asp:ContentPlaceHolder>* tags. The top directive is that of a master but contains the *MasterPageFile* attribute, which typically characterizes a content page.

The *content.master* resource is not directly viewable because it contains a virtual region. If you're familiar with object-oriented programming (OOP) terminology, I'd say that an intermediate master class is much like an intermediate virtual class that overrides some methods on the parent but leaves other abstract methods to be implemented by another derived class. Just as abstract classes can't be instantiated, nested master pages can't be viewed through a browser. In any case, the *content.master* resource is undoubtedly a master class, and its code file contains a class that inherits from *MasterPage*.

> **Warning**   Because Visual Studio .NET 2005 doesn't support visual editing of nested master pages, you have to create an intermediate master page as a content page, change the top directive to @*Master*, remove the *Title* attribute and, last but not least, change the base class of the code file to *MasterPage*.

The following code illustrates a content page that builds on two masters:

```
<%@ Page Language="C#" MasterPageFile="Content.master"
        CodeFile="ViewBook.aspx.cs" Inherits="ViewBook"
        Title="Book Viewer" %>

<asp:Content ContentPlaceHolderID="ChapterMenu" Runat="Server">
    <asp:DropDownList runat="server">
        ...
    </asp:DropDownList><br />
    <asp:Button runat="server" Text="Read ..." />
</asp:Content>
```

Figure 6-6 shows the final results.

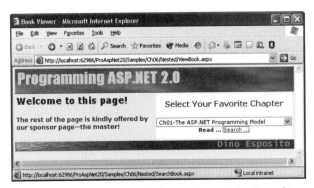

Figure 6-6   The page results from the combination of two master pages.

Admittedly, there's nothing in the figure that clearly indicates the existence of two masters; for your information, the innermost master controls the leftmost area where the drop-down list is laid out. This means that writing another page that offers an alternative technique to find a chapter is particularly easy. Have a look at the code and Figure 6-7:

```
<%@ Page Language="C#" MasterPageFile="Content.master"
    CodeFile="SearchBook.aspx.cs" Inherits="SearchBook" %>

<asp:Content ContentPlaceHolderID="ChapterMenu" Runat="Server">
    <asp:TextBox runat="server" Text="[Enter keywords]" />
    <asp:LinkButton runat="server" Text="Search ..." />
</asp:Content>
```

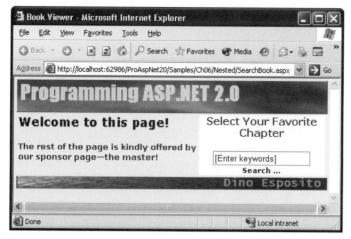

Figure 6-7   A slightly different page requires slightly different code!

A sapient use of master and content pages leads straight to an obvious conclusion: slightly different pages require slightly different code.

Programming the Master Page

You can use code in content pages to reference properties, methods, and controls in the master page, with some restrictions. The rule for properties and methods is that you can reference them if they are declared as public members of the master page. This includes public page-scope variables, public properties, and public methods.

Exposing Master Properties

To give an identity to a control in the master, you simply set the *runat* attribute and give the control an ID. Can you then access the control from within a content page? Not directly. The only way to access the master page object model is through the *Master* property. Note, though, that the *Master* property of the *Page* class references the master page object for the content page. This means that only public properties and methods defined on the master page class are accessible.

The following code enhances the previous master page to make it expose the text of the header as a public property:

```
public partial class SimpleWithProp : System.Web.UI.MasterPage
{
    protected void Page_Load(object sender, EventArgs e)
    {
    }

    public string TitleBoxText
    {
```

```
        get { return TitleBox.Text; }
        set { TitleBox.Text = value; }
    }
}
```

The header text of Figure 6-3 (shown earlier) is represented by a *Label* control named *TitleBox*. The control's protection level makes it inaccessible from the outside world, but the public property *TitleBoxText* defined in the preceding code represents a public wrapper around the *Label*'s Text property. In the end, the master page has an extra public property through which programmers can set the text of the header.

Invoking Properties on the Master

The *Master* property is the only point of contact between the content page and its master. The bad news is that the *Master* property is defined to be of type *MasterPage*; as such, it doesn't know anything about any property or method definition specific to the master you're really working with. In other words, the following code wouldn't compile because no *TitleBoxText* property is defined on the *MasterPage* class:

```
public partial class HelloMaster : System.Web.UI.Page
{
    protected void Page_Load(object sender, EventArgs e)
    {
        Master.TitleBoxText = "Programming ASP.NET-version 2.0";
    }
}
```

What's the real type behind the *Master* property?

The *Master* property represents the master page object as compiled by the ASP.NET run-time engine. This class follows the same naming convention as regular pages—*ASP.XXX_master*, where *XXX* is the name of the master file. Developers can override the default class name by setting the *ClassName* attribute on the @*Master* directive. The attribute lets you assign a user-defined name to the master page class:

```
<%@ Master Inherits="SimpleWithProp" … Classname="MyMaster" %>
```

In light of this, to be able to call custom properties or methods, you must first cast the object returned by the *Master* property to the actual type:

```
((ASP.MyMaster)Master).TitleBoxText = "Programming ASP.NET-version 2.0";
```

Interestingly enough, Visual Studio .NET 2005 provides some facilities to let you identify the right dynamically generated type already at design time. (See Figure 6-8.)

The *ASP* namespace is the system namespace that all system dynamically defined types belong to. In Visual Studio .NET 2005, that namespace is properly recognized and handled by Microsoft IntelliSense. That was not the case with the previous version of Visual Studio .NET.

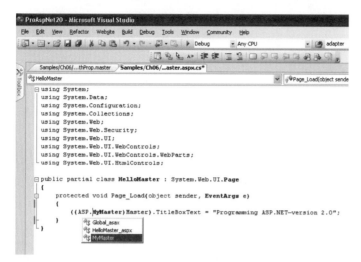

Figure 6-8   Visual Studio .NET 2005 pops up names of classes that will be created only during the page execution.

The @*MasterType* Directive

By adding the @*MasterType* directive in the content page, you can avoid all the casting just shown. The @*MasterType* informs the compiler about the real type of the *Master* property. The *Master* property is declared of the right type in the dynamically created page class, and this allows you to write strong-typed code, as follows:

```
<%@ Page Language="C#" MasterPageFile="SimpleWithProp.master"
    CodeFile="HelloMasterType.aspx.cs" Inherits="HelloMasterType" %>
<%@ MasterType VirtualPath="SimpleWithProp.master" %>
```

In the code file, you can have the following statements:

```
protected void Page_Load(object sender, EventArgs e)
{
    Master.TitleBoxText = "Programming ASP.NET-version 2.0";
}
```

The @*MasterType* directive supports two mutually exclusive attributes—*VirtualPath* and *Type-Name*. Both serve to identify the master class to use. The former does it by URL; the latter does it by type name.

Changing the Master Page Dynamically

To associate an ASP.NET content page with a master page—keeping in mind that in no case can you associate a classic ASP.NET page with a master—you use the *MasterPageFile* attribute of the @*Page* directive. *MasterPageFile*, though, is also a read/write property on the *Page* class that points to the name of the master page file. Can you dynamically select the master page via code and based on run-time conditions?

Using a dynamically changing master page is definitely possible in ASP.NET 2.0 and is suitable, for example, for applications that can present themselves to users through different skins. However, programmatically selecting the master page is not a task that you can accomplish at any time. To be precise, you can set the *MasterPageFile* property only during the *PreInit* page event—that is, before the runtime begins working on the request:

```
protected void Page_PreInit(object sender, EventArgs e)
{
    MasterPageFile = "simple2.master";
}
```

If you try to set the *MasterPageFile* property in *Init* or *Load* event handlers, an exception is raised.

> **Note**   The *Master* property represents the current instance of the master page object, is a read-only property, and can't be set programmatically. The *Master* property is set by the runtime after loading the content of the file referenced by the *MasterPageFile* property.

Working with Themes

For years, CSS styles have helped site developers to easily and efficiently design pages with a common and consistent look and feel. Although page developers can select the CSS file programmatically on the server, at its core CSS remains an inherent client-side technology, devised and implemented to apply skins to HTML elements. When you build ASP.NET pages, though, you mostly work with server controls.

CSS styles can be used to style server controls, but they're not the right tool for the job. The main issue here is that ASP.NET controls can have properties that are not the direct emanation of a CSS style property. The appearance of an ASP.NET control can be affected by an array of resources—images, strings, templates, markup, combinations of various CSS styles. To properly apply skins to ASP.NET server controls, CSS files are necessary but not sufficient. Enter ASP.NET themes.

ASP.NET themes are closely related to Windows XP themes. Setting a theme is as simple as setting a property, and all the settings the theme contains are applied in a single shot. Themes can be applied to individual controls and also to a page or an entire Web site.

> **Warning**   Themes are a specific feature of ASP.NET 2.0. There's no built-in support for themes in ASP.NET 1.x. I discussed how to build a theme infrastructure for ASP.NET 1.x in the June 2004 issue of *MSDN Magazine*. The article is online at *http://msdn.microsoft.com/ msdnmag/issues/04/06/CuttingEdge*.

Understanding ASP.NET Themes

In ASP.NET 1.x, when you author a page you don't just focus on the tasks a certain set of controls must be able to accomplish. You also consider their appearance. Most of the time, you end up setting visual attributes such as colors, font, borders, and images. The more sophisticated the control, the more time you spend making it look nice rather than just functional.

In ASP.NET 1.x, the *DataGrid* control—one of the most popular and customizable controls—provides a gallery of predefined styles from which you choose the most appealing. This gallery of predefined styles is the *DataGrid*'s auto-format feature. *DataGrid*'s built-in styles are implemented through a set of predefined settings that Visual Studio .NET 2003 applies to the control at design time. The auto-format feature saves testing and typing and lets you choose the style visually. Added as a time-saving feature, auto-format addresses the issue only partially, as it has two main drawbacks. First, a lot of visual attributes are still persisted to the *.aspx* source file, making rich pages hard to read and maintain. Second, the list of available formats is closed and can't be further extended or personalized.

Wouldn't it be great if you could compose your pages just by picking controls off the toolbox and connecting them, without even bothering about their final look? Wouldn't it be nice if you could then simply create an additional file in the project to define visual attributes for each type of control? In this way, the *.aspx* source file would be free of verbose visual attributes, and you could change the style of controls at will while performing few or no modifications to the original page. ASP.NET themes provide exactly this capability.

What's a Theme, Anyway?

A *theme* is a set of skins and associated files such as style sheets and images—a sort of super CSS file. Once enabled, the theme determines the appearance of all controls under its jurisdiction. Consider the following simple markup:

```
<asp:Calendar ID="Calendar1" runat="server" />
```

Without themes, the calendar will look spare and spartan. With a theme added, the same markup renders a more colorful and appealing calendar. As you can see, a neat separation exists between the page contents and formatting rules. Look at Figure 6-9. Which do you think is the unthemed calendar?

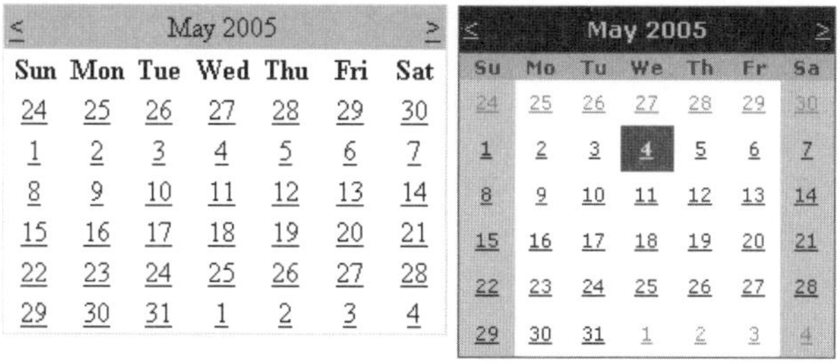

Figure 6-9   The same controls, with and without themes.

To fully understand ASP.NET themes, you must be familiar with a few terms, which are detailed in Table 6-3.

Table 6-3   ASP.NET Themes Terminology

Term	Definition
Skin	A named set of properties and templates that can be applied to one or more controls on a page. A skin is always associated with a specific control type.
Style sheet	A CSS or server-side style sheet file that can be used by pages on a site.
StyleSheet Theme	A theme used to abstract control properties from controls. The application of this theme means that the control can still override the theme.
Customization Theme	A theme used to abstract control properties from controls, but the theme overrides the control and any style sheet theme.

Imagine you are creating a new Web site and would like it to be visually appealing from the start. Instead of having to learn all the available style properties of each employed control, you just use ASP.NET themes. Using a built-in theme in a page is as easy as setting a property, as we'll see in a moment. With this change, pages automatically inherit a new and, one hopes, attractive appearance. For example, if you add a *Calendar* control to a page, it automatically renders with the default appearance defined in the theme.

Selecting a theme for one or more pages doesn't necessarily bind you to the settings of that theme. Through the Visual Studio .NET designer, you can review the pages and manually adjust some styles in a control if you want to.

> **Note**   The following convention holds true in this book and, in general, in related literature. Unless otherwise suggested by the context, the word *theme* indicates a customization theme. A style sheet theme is usually referred to as a *style sheet theme*.

Structure of a Theme

Themes are expressed as the union of various files and folders living under a common root directory. Themes can be global or local. Global themes are visible to all Web applications installed on a server machine. Local themes are visible only to the application that defines them. Global themes are contained in child directories located under the following path. The name of the directory is the name of the theme:

```
%WINDOWS%\Microsoft.NET\Framework\[version]\ASP.NETClientFiles\Themes
```

Local themes are specialized folders that live under the *App_Themes* folder at the root of the application. Figure 6-10 shows a sample theme (named ProAspNet20) in a Web application.

Figure 6-10   A view of this book's companion code's official theme in Visual Studio .NET 2005.

As you can see, the theme in the figure consists of a *.css* file and a *.skin* file. Generally, themes can contain a mix of the following resources:

■ **CSS files.**   Also known as *style sheets*, CSS files contain style definitions to be applied to elements in an HTML document. Written according to a tailor-made syntax, CSS styles define how elements are displayed and where they are positioned on your page. Web browsers that support only HTML 3.2 and earlier will not apply CSS styles. The World Wide Web Consortium (W3C) maintains and constantly evolves CSS standards. Visit *http://www.w3.org* for details on current CSS specifications. CSS files are located in the root of the theme folder.

■ **Skin files.**   A skin file contains the theme-specific markup for a given set of controls. A skin file is made by a sequence of control definitions that include predefined values for most visual properties and supported templates. Each skin is control-specific and has a unique name. You can define multiple skins for a given control. A skinned control has the original markup written in the *.aspx* source file modified by the content of the skin. The way the modification occurs depends on whether a customization or a style sheet theme is used. Skin files are located in the root of the theme folder.

■ **Image files.**   Feature-rich ASP.NET controls might require images. For example, a pageable *DataGrid* control might want to use bitmaps for first or last pages that are graphically compliant to the skin. Images that are part of a skin are typically located in an *Images* directory under the theme folder. (You can change the name of the folder as long as the name is correctly reflected by the skin's attributes.)

■ **Templates.**   A control skin is not limited to graphical properties but extends to define the layout of the control—for templated controls that support this capability. By stuffing template definitions in a theme, you can alter the internal structure of a control while leaving the programming interface and behavior intact. Templates are defined as part of the control skin and persisted to skin files.

The content types just listed are not exhaustive, but they do cover the most commonly used data you might want to store in a theme. You can have additional subdirectories filled with any sort of data that makes sense to skinned controls. For example, imagine you have a custom control that displays its own user interface through the services of an external ASP.NET user control (*.ascx*). Skinning this control entails, among other things, indicating the URL to the user control. The user control becomes an effective part of the theme and must be stored under the theme folder. Where exactly? That depends on you, but opting for a *Controls* subdirectory doesn't seem to be a bad idea. We'll return to this point later when building a sample theme.

Customization Themes vs. Style Sheet Themes

There are two forms of themes—customization themes and style sheet themes. Customization themes are used for post-customization of a site. The theme overrides any property definition on the control found in the *.aspx* source. By changing the page's theme, you entirely modify the appearance of the page without touching the source files. If you opt for customization theming, you just need minimal markup for each control in the ASP.NET page.

Style sheet themes are similar to CSS style sheets, except that they operate on control properties rather than on HTML element styles. Style sheet themes are applied immediately after the control is initialized and before the attributes in the *.aspx* file are applied. In other words, with a style sheet theme developers define default values for each control that are in fact overridden by settings in the *.aspx* source.

> **Important**   Customization themes and style sheet themes use the same source files. They differ only in how the ASP.NET runtime applies them to a page. The same theme can be applied as a customization theme or a style sheet theme at different times.

The difference between customization and style sheet themes is purely a matter of which takes priority over which. Let's review the resultant form of a control when a customization theme and style sheet theme are applied. Imagine you have the following markup:

```
<asp:Calendar ID="Calendar1" runat="server" backcolor="yellow" />
```

If the page that contains this markup is bound to a customization theme, the calendar shows up as defined in the theme. In particular, the background of the calendar will be of the color defined by the theme.

If the page is bound to a style sheet theme, instead, the background color of the calendar is yellow. The other properties are set in accordance with the theme.

Theming Pages and Controls

You can apply themes at various levels—application, folder, and individual pages. In addition, within the same theme you can select different skins for the same type of control.

Setting a theme at the application level affects all the pages and controls in the application. It's a feature you configure in the application's *web.config* file:

```
<system.web>
    <pages theme="ProAspNet20" />
</system.web>
```

The *theme* attribute sets a customization theme, while the *styleSheetTheme* attribute sets a style sheet theme. Note that the case is important in the *web.config*'s schema. Likewise, a theme can be applied to all the pages found in a given folder and below that folder. To do so, you create a new *web.config* file in an application's directory and add the section just shown to it. All the pages in that directory and below it will be themed accordingly. Finally, you can select the theme at the page level and have styles and skins applied only to that page and all its controls.

Enabling Themes on a Page

To associate a theme with a page, you set the *Theme* or *StyleSheetTheme* attribute on the *@Page* directive, and you're all set:

```
<% @Page Language="C#" Theme="ProAspNet20" %>
<% @Page Language="C#" StyleSheetTheme="ProAspNet20" %>
```

Also in this case, *Theme* sets a customization theme, whereas *StyleSheetTheme* indicates a style sheet theme.

Bear in mind that the name of the selected theme must match the name of a subdirectory under the *App_Themes* path or the name of a global theme. If a theme with a given name exists both locally to the application and globally to the site, the local theme takes precedence. Figure 6-11 shows IntelliSense support for themes in Visual Studio .NET 2005.

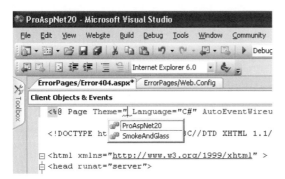

Figure 6-11 IntelliSense support for themes in Visual Studio .NET 2005.

While we're speaking of precedence, it is important to note that themes have a hierarchical nature: directory-level themes takes precedence over application-level themes, and page-level themes override any other themes defined around the application. This hierarchy is independent of which attributes are used—*Theme* or *StyleSheetTheme*—to enable theming.

> **Note**   Setting both *Theme* and *StyleSheetTheme* attributes is not prohibited, though it is not a recommended practice. There's a behavioral gap between the two forms of themes that should make clear which one you need in any situation. However, if you set both attributes, consider that both themes will be applied—first the style sheet theme and then the customization theme. The final results depend on the CSS cascading mechanism and ultimately are determined by the CSS settings of each theme.

Applying Skins

A skin file looks like a regular ASP.NET page as it is populated by control declaration and import directives. Each control declaration defines the default appearance of a particular control. Consider the following excerpt from a skin file:

```
<!-- This is a possible skin for a Button control -->
<asp:Button runat="server"
    BorderColor="darkgray"
    Font-Bold="true"
    BorderWidth="1px"
    BorderStyle="outset"
    ForeColor="DarkSlateGray"
    BackColor="gainsboro" />
```

The net effect of the skin is that every *Button* control in a themed page will be rendered as defined by the preceding markup. If the theme is applied as a style sheet, the settings just shown will be overridable by the developer; if the theme is a customization theme, those settings determine the final look and feel of the control. Properties that the theme leave blank are set according to the control's defaults or the *.aspx* source.

> **Important**   Whatever theme you apply—customization or style sheet—control properties can always be modified through code in page events such as *Init* and *Load*.

A theme can contain multiple skins for a given control, each identified with a unique name— the *SkinID* attribute. When the *SkinID* attribute is set, the skin is said to be a named *skin*. A theme can contain any number of named skins per control, but just one unnamed (default) skin. You select the skin for a control in an ASP.NET themed page by setting the control's *SkinID* property. The value of the control's *SkinID* property should match an existing skin in the current theme. If the page theme doesn't include a skin that matches the *SkinID* property, the default skin for that control type is used. The following code shows two named skins for a button within the same theme:

```
<!-- Place these two definitions in the same .skin file -->
<asp:button skinid="skinClassic" BackColor="gray" />
<asp:button skinid="skinTrendy" BackColor="lightcyan" />
```

When you enable theming on a page, by default all controls in that page will be themed except controls, and individual control properties, that explicitly disable theming.

> **Note**   The automatic application of themes to all controls in a page makes it easy to customize a page that has no knowledge of skins, including existing pages written for ASP.NET 1.x.

Taking Control of Theming

The ASP.NET 2.0 theming infrastructure provides the *EnableTheming* Boolean property to disable skins for a control and all its children. You can configure a page or control to ignore themes by setting the *EnableTheming* property to *false*. The default value of the property is *true*. *EnableTheming* is defined on the *Control* class and inherited by all server controls and pages. If you want to disable theme support for all controls in a page, you can set the *EnableTheming* attribute on the *@Page* directive.

> **Important**   Note that the *EnableTheming* property can be set only in the *Page_PreInit* event for static controls—that is, controls defined in the *.aspx* source. For dynamic controls—controls created programmatically—you must have set the property before adding the control to the page's control tree. A control is added to the page's control tree when you add to the *Controls* collection of the parent control—typically, the form or another control in the form.

When is disabling themes useful? Themes are great at ensuring that all page controls have a consistent look and feel, but at the same time themes override the visual attributes of any control for which a skin is defined. You can control the overriding mechanism a bit by switching style sheet and customization themes. However, when you want a control or page to maintain its predefined look, you just disable themes for that page or control.

Note that disabling themes affects *only* skins, not CSS styles. When a theme includes one or more CSS style-sheet files, they are linked to the *<head>* tag of the resulting HTML document and, after that, are handled entirely by the browser. As you can easily guess, there's not much a Web browser can know about ASP.NET themes!

Theming Controls

Themes style server controls to the degree that each control allows. By default, all control properties are themeable. Theming can be disabled on a particular property by applying the *Themeable* attribute on the property declaration, as follows:

```
[Themeable(false)]
public virtual bool CausesValidation
{
    get { … }
    set { … }
}
```

You can't change the *Themeable* attribute for built-in server controls. You have that option for custom controls instead. Moreover, for custom controls you should use the *Themeable* attribute to prevent theming of behavioral properties such as the *CausesValidation* property just shown. Themes should be used only on visual properties that uniquely affect the appearance of the control:

```
[Themeable(false)]
public MyControl : Control
{
    ...
}
```

Finally, the *Themeable* attribute can be applied to the class declaration of a custom control to stop it from ever bothering about themes.

Putting Themes to Work

Finding a bunch of themes that suit your needs, free or for a small fee, shouldn't be a problem. However, this is a bad reason for not learning how to build your own themes. As mentioned, themes consist of several supporting files, including CSS style sheets and control skins to decorate HTML elements and server controls, respectively, and any other supporting images or files that make up the final expected result.

I firmly believe that building nice-looking, consistent, usable themes is not a programmer's job. It is a task that designers and graphics people can easily accomplish ten times better and faster. However, themes are more than CSS files, and what's more, they are in the area of control properties—exactly the realm of the developer. In short, developers should provide guidance to theme designers much more than we did in the past with CSS authors.

As a first step, let's review the key differences between CSS files and themes.

CSS vs. Themes

Themes are similar to CSS style sheets in that both apply a set of common attributes to any page where they are declared. Themes differ from CSS style sheets in a few key ways, however.

First and foremost, themes work on control properties, whereas CSS style sheets operate on styles of HTML elements. Because of this, with themes you can include auxiliary files and specify standard images for a *TreeView* or *Menu* control, the paging template of a *DataGrid*, or the layout of a *Login* control. In addition, themes can optionally force overriding of local property values (customization themes) and not cascade as CSS style sheets do.

Because themes incorporate CSS style-sheet definitions and apply them along with other property settings, there's no reason for preferring CSS style sheets over themes in ASP.NET 2.0 applications.

Creating a Theme

To create a new theme in a Visual Studio .NET 2005 solution, you start by creating a new folder under *App_Themes*. The simplest way to do this is by right-clicking the *App_Themes* node and selecting a theme folder. Next, you add theme files to the folder, and, when you're done, you can even move the entire directory to the root path of global themes on the Web server.

Typical auxiliary files that form a theme are listed in Figure 6-12. They are CSS style-sheet files, skin files, XML or text files, and extensible style-sheet files (XSLT). Empty files of the specified type are created in the theme folder and edited through more or less specialized text editors in Visual Studio .NET 2005.

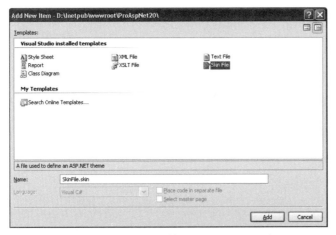

Figure 6-12   Adding auxiliary files to an ASP.NET theme.

A skin file is a collection of a control's markup chunks, optionally named through the *SkinID* attribute. You can create a skin file by cutting and pasting the markup of controls you visually configured in a sample page. If some properties of the skinned controls require resources, you can point them to a path inside the theme folder. Here's an example:

```
<asp:BulletedList runat="server"
    Font-Names="Verdana"
```

```
BulletImageURL="Images/smokeandglass_bullet2.gif"
BulletStyle="CustomImage"
BackColor="transparent"
ForeColor="#585880" />
```

This skin of the *BulletedList* control points to a theme-specific URL for the bullet image. The directory *Images* is intended to be relative to the theme folder. Needless to say, the name *Images* is totally arbitrary. Should the skin require other external files, you could group them in other theme subdirectories.

A skin file can define the appearance of built-in server controls as well as custom controls. To skin a custom control, though, you must first reference it in the file, as follows:

```
<%@ Register TagPrefix="expo"
             Namespace="Expoware.ProAspNet20.Controls"
             Assembly="ProAspNet20.Controls" %>
```

Next, you add the desired default markup for any control defined in the specified assembly and namespace.

Loading Themes Dynamically

You can apply themes dynamically, but this requires a bit of care. The ASP.NET runtime loads theme information immediately after the *PreInit* event fires. When the *PreInit* event fires, the name of any theme referenced in the *@Page* directive is already known and will be used unless it is overridden during the event. If you want to enable your users to change themes on the fly, you create a *Page_PreInit* event handler. The following code shows the code file of a sample page that changes themes dynamically:

```
public partial class TestThemes : System.Web.UI.Page
{
    protected void Page_Load(object sender, EventArgs e)
    {
        if (!IsPostBack) {
            ThemeList.DataSource = GetAvailableThemes();
            ThemeList.DataBind();
        }
    }

    void Page_PreInit(object sender, EventArgs e)
    {
        string theme = "";
        if (Page.Request.Form.Count > 0)
            theme = Page.Request["ThemeList"].ToString();
        if (theme == "None")
            theme = "";
        this.Theme = theme;
    }

    protected StringCollection GetAvailableThemes()
```

```
    {
        string path = Request.PhysicalApplicationPath + @"App_Themes";
        DirectoryInfo dir = new DirectoryInfo(path);
        StringCollection themes = new StringCollection();
        foreach (DirectoryInfo di in dir.GetDirectories())
            themes.Add(di.Name);

        return themes;
    }
}
```

Figure 6-13 shows the page in action. The drop-down list control enumerates the installed application themes and lets you choose the one to apply. The selected theme is then applied in the *PreInit* event and immediately reflected. In the *PreInit* event, no view state has been restored yet; *Request.Form* is the only safe way to access a posted value like the selected theme.

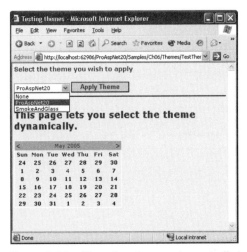

Figure 6-13 Changing themes dynamically in a sample page.

Working with Wizards

Master pages and themes give you the power of building similar-looking, rich pages that share graphics, control layout, and even some functionality. A special type of rich page is the page that implements a wizard. More common in Windows desktop applications than in Web scenarios, wizards are typically used to break up large forms to collect user input. A wizard is a sequence of related steps, each associated with an input form and a user interface. Users move through the wizard sequentially, but they are normally given a chance to skip a step or jump back to modify some of the entered values. A wizard is conceptually pretty simple, but implementing it over HTTP connections can be tricky. Everybody involved with serious Web development can only heartily welcome the introduction of the *Wizard* control in ASP.NET 2.0.

An Overview of the *Wizard* Control

The *Wizard* control supports both linear and nonlinear navigation. It allows you to move backward to change values and to skip steps that are unnecessary due to previous settings or because users don't want to fill those fields. Like many other ASP.NET 2.0 controls, the *Wizard* supports themes, styles, and templates.

The *Wizard* is a composite control and automatically generates some constituent controls such as navigation buttons and panels. As you'll see in a moment, the programming interface of the control has multiple templates that provide for in-depth customization of the overall user interface. The control also guarantees that state is maintained no matter where you move—backward, forward, or to a particular page. All the steps of a wizard must be declared within the boundaries of the same *Wizard* control. In other words, the wizard must be self-contained and not provide page-to-page navigation.

Structure of a Wizard

As shown in Figure 6-14, a wizard has four parts: header, view, navigation bar, and sidebar.

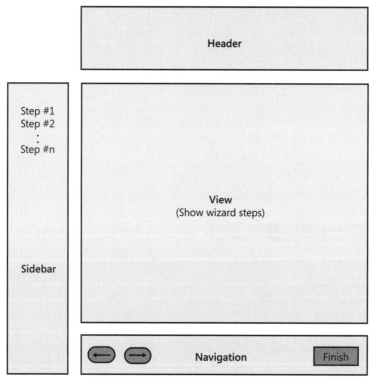

Figure 6-14   The four parts of a *Wizard* control.

The header consists of text you can set through the *HeaderText* property. You can change the default appearance of the header text by using its style property; you can also change the structure of the header by using the corresponding header template property. If *HeaderText* is empty and no custom template is specified, no header is shown for the wizard.

The view displays the contents of the currently active step. The wizard requires you to define each step in an *<asp:wizardstep>* element. An *<asp:wizardstep>* element corresponds to a *WizardStep* control. Different types of wizard steps are supported; all wizard step classes inherit from a common base class named *WizardStepBase*.

All wizard steps must be grouped in a single *<wizardsteps>* tag, as shown in the following code:

```
<asp:wizard runat="server" DisplaySideBar="true">
  <wizardsteps>
    <asp:wizardstep runat="server" steptype="auto" id="step1">
      First step
    </asp:wizardstep>
    <asp:wizardstep runat="server" steptype="auto" id="step2">
      Second step
    </asp:wizardstep>
    <asp:wizardstep runat="server" steptype="auto" id="finish">
      Final step
    </asp:wizardstep>
  </wizardsteps>
</asp:wizard>
```

The navigation bar consists of auto-generated buttons that provide any needed functionality— typically, going to the next or previous step or finishing. You can modify the look and feel of the navigation bar by using styles and templates.

The optional sidebar is used to display content in the left side of the control. It provides an overall view of the steps needed to accomplish the wizard's task. By default, it displays a description of each step, with the current step displayed in boldface type. You can customize styles and templates. Figure 6-15 shows the default user interface. Each step is labeled using the ID of the corresponding *<asp:wizardstep>* tag.

Figure 6-15   A wizard with the default sidebar on the left side.

Wizard Styles and Templates

You can style all the various parts and buttons of a *Wizard* control by using the properties listed in Table 6-4.

Table 6-4 The *Wizard* Control's Style Properties

Style	Description
CancelButtonStyle	Sets the style properties for the wizard's Cancel button
FinishCompleteButtonStyle	Sets the style properties for the wizard's Finish button
FinishPreviousButtonStyle	Sets the style properties for the wizard's Previous button when at the *Finish* step
HeaderStyle	Sets the style properties for the wizard's header
NavigationButtonStyle	Sets the style properties for navigation buttons
NavigationStyle	Sets the style properties for the navigation area
SideBarButtonStyle	Sets the style properties for the buttons on the sidebar
SideBarStyle	Sets the style properties for the wizard's sidebar
StartStepNextButtonStyle	Sets the style properties for the wizard's Next button when at the *Start* step
StepNextButtonStyle	Sets the style properties for the wizard's Next button
StepPreviousButtonStyle	Sets the style properties for the wizard's Previous button
StepStyle	Sets the style properties for the area where steps are displayed

The contents of the header, sidebar, and navigation bar can be further customized with templates. Table 6-5 lists the available templates.

Table 6-5 The *Wizard* Control's Template Properties

Style	Description
FinishNavigationTemplate	Specifies the navigation bar shown before the last page of the wizard. By default, the navigation bar contains the Previous and Finish buttons.
HeaderTemplate	Specifies the title bar of the wizard.
SideBarTemplate	Used to display content in the left side of the wizard control.
StartNavigationTemplate	Specifies the navigation bar for the first view in the wizard. By default, it contains only the Next button.
StepNavigationTemplate	Specifies the navigation bar for steps other than first, finish, or complete. By default, it contains Previous and Next buttons.

In addition to using styles and templates, you can control the programming interface of the *Wizard* control through a few properties.

The Wizard's Programming Interface

Table 6-6 lists the properties of the *Wizard* control, excluding style and template properties and properties defined on base classes.

Table 6-6   Main Properties of the *Wizard* Control

Property	Description
ActiveStep	Returns the current wizard step object. The object is an instance of the *WizardStep* class.
ActiveStepIndex	Gets and sets the 0-based index of the current wizard step.
DisplayCancelButton	Toggles the visibility of the *Cancel* button. The default value is *false*.
DisplaySideBar	Toggles the visibility of the sidebar. The default value is *false*.
HeaderText	Gets and sets the title of the wizard.
SkipLinkText	The ToolTip string that the control associates with an invisible image, as a hint to screen readers. The default value is *Skip Navigation Links* and is localized based on the server's current locale.
WizardSteps	Returns a collection containing all the *WizardStep* objects defined in the control.

A wizard in action is fully represented by its collection of step views and buttons. In particular, you'll recognize the following buttons: *StartNext*, *StepNext*, *StepPrevious*, *FinishComplete*, *FinishPrevious*, and *Cancel*. Each button is characterized by properties to get and set the button's image URL, caption, type, and destination URL after click. The name of a property is the name of the button followed by a suffix. The available suffixes are listed in Table 6-7.

Table 6-7   Suffixes of Button Properties

Suffix	Description
ButtonImageUrl	Gets and sets the URL of the image used to render the button
ButtonText	Gets and sets the text for the button
ButtonType	Gets and sets the type of the button: push button, image, or link button
DestinationPageUrl	Gets and sets the URL to jump to once the button is clicked

Note that names in Table 6-7 do not correspond to real property names. You have the four properties in this table for each distinct type of wizard button. The real name is composed by the name of the button followed by any of the suffixes—for example, *CancelButtonText*, *Finish-CompleteDestinationPageUrl*, and so on.

The *Wizard* control also supplies a few interesting methods—for example, *GetHistory*, which is defined as follows:

```
public ICollection GetHistory()
```

GetHistory returns a collection of *WizardStepBase* objects. The order of the items is determined by the order in which the wizard's pages were accessed by the user. The first object returned—the one with an index of 0—is the currently selected wizard step. The second object represents the view before the current one, and so on.

The second method, *MoveTo*, is used to move to a particular wizard step. The method's prototype is described here:

```
public void MoveTo(WizardStepBase step)
```

The method requires you to pass a *WizardStepBase* object, which can be problematic. However, the method is a simple wrapper around the setter of the *ActiveStepIndex* property. If you want to jump to a particular step and not hold an instance of the corresponding *WizardStep* object, setting *ActiveStepIndex* is just as effective.

Table 6-8 lists the key events in the life of a *Wizard* control in an ASP.NET 2.0 page.

Table 6-8   Events of the *Wizard* Control

Event	Description
ActiveViewChanged	Raised when the active step changes
CancelButtonClick	Raised when the Cancel button is clicked
FinishButtonClick	Raised when the Finish Complete button is clicked
NextButtonClick	Raised when any Next button is clicked
PreviousButtonClick	Raised when any Previous button is clicked
SideBarButtonClick	Raised when a button on the sidebar is clicked

As you can see, there's a common click event for all Next and Previous buttons you can find on your way. A Next button can be found on the Start page as well as on all step pages. Likewise, a Previous button can be located on the Finish page. Whenever a Next button is clicked, the page receives a *NextButtonClick* event; whenever a Previous button is clicked, the control raises a *PreviousButtonClick* event.

Adding Steps to a Wizard

A *WizardStep* object represents one of the child views that the wizard can display. The *WizardStep* class ultimately derives from *View* and adds just a few public properties to it. A *View* object represents a control that acts as a container for a group of controls. A view is hosted within a *MultiView* control. (See Chapter 4.) To create its output, the wizard makes internal use of a *MultiView* control. However, the wizard is not derived from the *MultiView* class.

You define the views of a wizard through distinct instances of the *WizardStep* class, all grouped under the *<WizardSteps>* tag. The *<WizardSteps>* tag corresponds to the *WizardSteps* collection property exposed by the *Wizard* control:

```
<WizardSteps>
    <asp:WizardStep>
        ...
    </asp:WizardStep>
    <asp:WizardStep>
        ...
    </asp:WizardStep>
</WizardSteps>
```

Each wizard step is characterized by a title and a type. The *Title* property provides a brief description of the view. This information is not used unless the sidebar is enabled. If the sidebar is enabled, the title of each step is used to create a list of steps. If the sidebar is enabled but no title is provided for the various steps, the ID of the *WizardStep* objects is used to populate the sidebar, as shown earlier in Figure 6-15.

While defining a step, you can also set the *AllowReturn* property, which indicates whether the user is allowed to return to the current step from a subsequent step. The default value of the property is *true*.

Types of Wizard Steps

The *StepType* property indicates how a particular step should be handled and rendered within a wizard. Acceptable values for the step type come from the *WizardStepType* enumeration, as listed in Table 6-9.

Table 6-9   Wizard Step Types

Property	Description
Auto	The default setting, which forces the wizard to determine how each contained step should be treated.
Complete	The last page that the wizard displays, usually after the wizard has been completed. The navigation bar and the sidebar aren't displayed.
Finish	The last page used for collecting user data. It lacks the Next button, and it shows the Previous and Finish buttons.
Start	The first screen displayed, with no Previous button.
Step	All other intermediate pages, in which the Previous and Next buttons are displayed.

When the wizard is in automatic mode—the default type *Auto*—it determines the type of each step based on the order in which the steps appear in the source code. For example, the first step is considered of type *Start* and the last step is marked as *Finish*. No *Complete* step is assumed. If you correctly assign types to steps, the order in which you declare them in the *.aspx* source is not relevant.

Creating an Input Step

The following code shows a sample wizard step used to collect the provider name and the connection string to connect to a database and search for some data. For better graphical results, the content of the step is encapsulated in a fixed-height *<div>* tag. If all the steps are configured in this way, users navigating through the wizard won't experience sudden changes in the overall page size and layout.

```
<asp:wizardstep ID="Wizardstep1" runat="server" title="Connect">
    <div style="height:200px;width:400px;margin:10;">
        <table>
            <tr><td>Provider</td><td>
                <asp:textbox runat="server" id="ProviderName" width="250px"
                            text="System.Data.SqlClient" />
            </td></tr>
            <tr><td>Connection String</td><td>
```

```
                    <asp:textbox runat="server" id="ConnString" width="250px"
                            text="SERVER=(local);DATABASE=northwind;UID=…;" />
                </td></tr>
                <tr><td height="100px"></td></tr>
            </table>
        </div>
    </asp:wizardstep>
```

Figure 6-16 shows a preview of the step. As you can guess, the step is recognized as a *Start* step. As a result, the wizard is added only to the Next button.

Figure 6-16   A sample *Start* wizard step.

A wizard is usually created for collecting input data, so validation becomes a critical issue. You can validate the input data in two nonexclusive ways—using validators and using transition event handlers.

The first option involves placing validator controls in the wizard step. This guarantees that invalid input—empty fields or incompatible data types—is caught quickly and, optionally, already on the client:

```
<asp:requiredfieldvalidator ID="RequiredField1" runat="server"
    text="*"
    errormessage="Must indicate a connection string"
    setfocusonerror="true"
    controltovalidate="ConnString" />
```

If you need to access server-side resources to validate the input data, you're better off using transition event handlers. A transition event is an event the wizard raises when it is about to switch to another view. For example, the *NextButtonClick* event is raised when the user clicks the Next button to jump to the subsequent step. You can intercept this event, do any required validation, and cancel the transition if necessary. We'll return to this topic in a moment.

Defining the Sidebar

The sidebar is a left-side panel that lists buttons to quickly and randomly reach any step of the wizard. It's a sort of quick-launch menu for the various steps that form the wizard. You control the sidebar's visibility through the Boolean *DisplaySideBar* attribute and define its contents through the *SideBarTemplate* property.

Regardless of the template, the internal layout of the sidebar is not left entirely to your imagination. In particular, the *<SideBarTemplate>* tag must contain a *DataList* control with a well-known ID–*SideBarList*. In addition, the *<ItemTemplate>* block must contain a button object with the name of *SideBarButton*. The button object must be any object that implements the *IButtonControl* interface.

> **Note**   For better graphical results, you might want to use explicit heights and widths for all steps and the sidebar as well. Likewise, the push buttons in the navigation bar might look better if they are made the same size. You do this by setting the *Width* and *Height* properties on the *NavigationButtonStyle* object.

Navigating Through the Wizard

When a button is clicked to move to another step, an event is fired to the hosting page. It's up to you to decide when and how to perform any critical validation, such as deciding whether conditions exist to move to the next step.

In most cases, you'll want to perform server-side validation only when the user clicks the Finish button to complete the wizard. You can be sure that whatever route the user has taken within the wizard, clicking the Finish button will complete it. Any code you bind to the *FinishButtonClick* event is executed only once, and only when strictly necessary.

By contrast, any code bound to the Previous or Next button executes when the user moves back or forward. The page posts back on both events.

Filtering Page Navigation with Events

You should perform server-side validation if what the user can do next depends on the data he or she entered in the previous step. This means that in most cases you just need to write a *NextButtonClick* event handler:

```
<asp:wizard runat="server" id="QueryWizard"
    OnNextButtonClick="OnNext">
    ...
</asp:wizard>
```

If the user moves back to a previously visited page, you can usually ignore any data entered in the current step and avoid validation. Because the user is moving back, you can safely assume he or she is not going to use any fresh data. When a back movement is requested, you can assume that any preconditions needed to visit that previous page are verified. This happens by design if your users take a sequential route.

If the wizard's sidebar is enabled, users can jump from page to page in any order. If the logic you're implementing through the wizard requires that preconditions be met before a certain step is reached, you should write a *SideBarButtonClick* event handler and ensure that the requirements have been met.

A wizard click event requires a *WizardNavigationEventHandler* delegate:

```
public delegate void WizardNavigationEventHandler(
    object sender,
    WizardNavigationEventArgs e);
```

The *WizardNavigationEventArgs* structure contains two useful properties that inform you about the 0-based indexes of the page being left and the page being displayed. The *CurrentStepIndex* property returns the index of the last page visited; the *NextStepIndex* returns the index of the next page. Note that both properties are read-only.

The following code shows a sample handler for the Next button. The handler prepares a summary message to show when the user is going to the Finish page.

```
void OnNext(object sender, WizardNavigationEventArgs e)
{
    // Collect the input data if going to the last page
    // -1 because of 0-based indexing, add -1 if you have a Complete page
    if (e.NextStepIndex == QueryWizard.WizardSteps.Count - 2)
        PrepareFinalStep();
}
void PrepareFinalStep()
{
    string cmdText = DetermineCommandText();

    // Show a Ready-to-go message
    StringBuilder sb = new StringBuilder("");
    sb.AppendFormat("You're about to run: <br><br>{0}<hr>", cmdText);
    sb.Append("<b><br>Ready to go?</b>");
    ReadyMsg.Text = sb.ToString();
}

string DetermineCommandText()
{
    // Generate and return command text here
}
```

Each page displayed by the wizard is a kind of panel (actually, a view) defined within a parent control—the wizard. This means that all child controls used in all steps must have a unique ID. It also means that you can access any of these controls just by name. For example, if one of the pages contains a text box named, say, ProviderName, you can access it from any event handler by using the *ProviderName* identifier.

The preceding code snippet is an excerpt from a sample wizard that collects input and runs a database query. The first step picks up connection information, whereas the second step lets users define table, fields, and optionally a *WHERE* clause. The composed command is shown in the Finish page, where the wizard asks for final approval. (See Figure 6-17.)

The full source code of the wizard is in the companion code for this book.

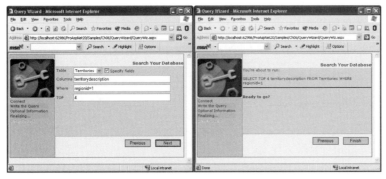

Figure 6-17   Two successive pages of the sample wizard: query details and the *Finish* step.

Canceling Events

The *WizardNavigationEventArgs* structure also contains a read/write Boolean property named *Cancel*. If you set this property to *true*, you just cancel the ongoing transition to the destination page. The following code shows how to prevent the display of the next step if the user is on the Start page and types in **sa** as the user ID:

```
void OnNext(object sender, WizardNavigationEventArgs e)
{
    if (e.CurrentStepIndex == 0 &&
        ConnString.Text.IndexOf("UID=sa") > -1)
    {
        e.Cancel = true;
        return;
    }
}
```

You can cancel events from within any transition event handler and not just from the *NextButtonClick* event handler. This trick is useful to block navigation if the server-side validation of the input data has failed. In this case, though, you're responsible for showing some feedback to the user.

> **Note**   You can't cancel navigation from within the *ActiveViewChanged* event. This event follows any transition events, such as the *NextButtonClick* or *PreviousButtonClick* event, and occurs when the transition has completed. Unlike transition events, the *ActiveViewChanged* event requires a simpler, parameterless handler—*EventHandler*.

Finalizing the Wizard

All wizards have some code to execute to finalize the task. If you use the ASP.NET 2.0 *Wizard* control, you place this code in the *FinishButtonClick* event handler. Figure 6-18 shows the final step of a wizard that completed successfully.

```
void OnFinish(object sender, WizardNavigationEventArgs e)
{
    string finalMsg = "The operation completed successfully.";
    try {
        // Complete the wizard (compose and run the query)
        string cmd = DetermineCommandText();
        DataTable table = ExecuteCommand(ConnString.Text, cmd);
        grid.DataSource = table;
        grid.DataBind();

        // OK color
        FinalMsg.ForeColor = Color.Blue;
    }
    catch (Exception ex) {
        FinalMsg.ForeColor = Color.Red;
        finalMsg = String.Format("The operation cannot be completed
                                    due to:<br>{0}", ex.Message);
    }
    finally {
        FinalMsg.Text = finalMsg;
    }
}

string DetermineCommandText()
{
    // Generate and return command text here
}

DataTable ExecuteCommand()
{
    // Execute database query here
}
```

If the wizard contains a *Complete* step, that page should be displayed after the Finish button is clicked and the final task has completed. If something goes wrong with the update, you should either cancel the transition to prevent the Complete page from even appearing or adapt the user interface of the completion page to display an appropriate error message. Which option you choose depends on the expected behavior of the implemented operation. If the wizard's operation can fail or succeed, you let the wizard complete and display an error message in case something went wrong. If the wizard's operation must complete successfully unless the user quits, you should not make the transition to the Complete page; instead, provide users with feedback on what went wrong and give them a chance to try again.

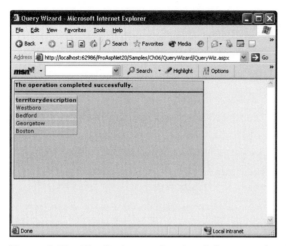

Figure 6-18   The final step of a wizard that completed successfully.

Conclusion

Since version 1.0, ASP.NET has been characterized by a well-balanced mix of low-level and feature-rich tools. Using low-level tools such as events, HTTP modules, and HTTP handlers, you can plug into the ASP.NET pipeline to influence the processing of requests at every stage. At the same time, ASP.NET offers a wealth of feature-rich components for those who don't need control over every little step.

The quantity and quality of application services has grown significantly in ASP.NET 2.0, which was designed with the goal of making things happen with the least amount of code. The introduction of rich composition tools for building pages like the ones we examined in this chapter is just a confirmation of the trend. In this chapter, we explored master pages to create content pages based on a predefined template made of graphics and, optionally, code. Master pages are not pure object-oriented visual inheritance *a là* Windows Forms; instead, they benefit from aggregation and let derived pages personalize well-known regions of the master. With full support from the Visual Studio .NET 2005 environment, master pages are a time-saving feature that brings concrete added value to ASP.NET 2.0 solutions.

Likewise, themes let developers code pages and controls that allow users to apply skins at will. ASP.NET themes work like Windows XP themes, and overall they're a superset of CSS that covers control properties in addition to HTML element styles. Themes work well in conjunction with the user profile API we discussed in Chapter 5. Using both, developers can let end users choose the theme and persist its name back to the personalization storage layer.

Finally, wizards are made-to-measure controls to quickly and efficiently write multistep input forms that divide complex operations into simple steps.

With this chapter, we completed the first part of the book, dedicated to building ASP.NET pages. With the next chapter, we approach the world of data access and explore ways to add data to a Web site.

Just the Facts

- A master page is a distinct file referenced at the application or page level that contains the static layout of the page.
- A master page contains regions that each *derived* page can customize.
- A *derived* page, known as a content page, is a collection of markup blocks that the runtime will use to fill the regions in the master page.
- Content pages can't contain information other than contents for the master's placeholders.
- Regions in the master page can have default content that can be used if the content page doesn't provide any.
- You can define various masters for a page and have the system automatically pick up a particular one based on the browser's user agent string.
- Master pages can be nested and expose a strong-typed object model.
- Themes are a collection of settings spread over various files that the ASP.NET runtime uses to give the whole site (or page) a consistent user interface.
- Themes become a kind of attribute, and they can be exported from one application to the next and applied to pages on the fly.
- Themes differ from CSS files because they let you style ASP.NET control properties and not just HTML elements.
- A theme contains skin files, CSS files, and images, plus any other auxiliary file you might find useful.
- A skin file is a collection of ASP.NET control declarations. The system ensures that after instantiation each control of that type in the page will have exactly the same set of attributes.
- The wizard control manages multiple views inside a single control and provides an auto-generated user interface for you to move back and forth between views as you do in a desktop wizard.

Chapter 7
ADO.NET Data Providers

ADO.NET is a data-access subsystem in the Microsoft .NET Framework. It was heavily inspired by ActiveX Data Objects (ADO), which has emerged over the past few years as a very successful object model for writing data-aware applications. The key design criteria for ADO.NET are simplicity and performance. Those criteria typically work against each other, but with ADO.NET you get the power and performance of a low-level interface combined with the simplicity of a modern object model. Unlike ADO, though, ADO.NET has been purposely designed to observe general, rather than database-oriented, guidelines.

Several syntactical differences exist between the object models of ADO and ADO.NET. In spite of this, the functionalities of ADO and ADO.NET look much the same. This is because Microsoft put a lot of effort in aligning some programming aspects of the ADO.NET object model with ADO. In this way, seasoned data developers new to .NET don't need to become familiar with too many new concepts and can work with a relatively short learning curve. With ADO.NET, you probably won't be able to reuse much of your existing code. You'll certainly be able, though, to reuse all your skills. At the same time, novice developers face a relatively simple and easy-to-understand model, with a consistent design and a powerful set of features.

The ADO.NET framework is made of two distinct but closely related sets of classes–data providers and data containers. We tackle providers in this chapter and save containers for the next chapter.

.NET Data Access Infrastructure

ADO.NET is the latest in a long line of database-access technologies that began with the Open Database Connectivity (ODBC) API several years ago. Written as a C-style library, ODBC was designed to provide a uniform API to issue SQL calls to various database servers. In the ODBC model, database-specific drivers hide any difference and discrepancy between the SQL language used at the application level and the internal query engine. Next, COM landed in the database territory and started a colonization process that culminated with OLE DB.

OLE DB has evolved from ODBC and, in fact, the open database connectivity principle emerges somewhat intact in it. OLE DB is a COM-based API aimed at building a common layer of code for applications to access any data source that can be exposed as a tabular rowset of data. The OLE DB architecture is composed of two elements—a consumer and a provider. The consumer is incorporated in the client and is responsible for setting up COM-based communication with the data provider. The OLE DB data provider, in turn, receives calls from the consumer and executes commands on the data source. Whatever the data format and storage medium are, an OLE DB provider returns data formatted in a tabular layout—that is, with rows and columns. OLE DB uses COM to make client applications and data sources to communicate.

Because it isn't especially easy to use and is primarily designed for coding from within C++ applications, OLE DB never captured the hearts of programmers, even though it could guarantee a remarkable mix of performance and flexibility. Next came ADO—roughly, a COM automation version of OLE DB—just to make the OLE DB technology accessible from Microsoft Visual Basic and classic Active Server Pages (ASP) applications. When used, ADO acts as the real OLE DB consumer embedded in the host applications. ADO was invented in the age of connected, two-tier applications, and the object model design reflects that. ADO makes a point of programming redundancy: it usually provides more than just one way of accomplishing key tasks, and it contains a lot of housekeeping code. For all these reasons, although it's incredibly easy to use, an ADO-based application doesn't perform as efficiently as a pure OLE DB application.

> **Note**   Using ADO in .NET applications is still possible, but for performance and consistency reasons its use should be limited to a few very special cases. For example, ADO is the only way you have to work with server cursors. In addition, ADO provides a schema management API to .NET Framework 1.x applications. On the other hand, ADO recordsets can't be directly bound to ASP.NET or Microsoft Windows Forms data-bound controls. We'll cover ASP.NET data binding in Chapter 9 and Chapter 10. The key improvements in ADO.NET are the rather powerful disconnected model exposed through the *DataSet* object, the strong integration with XML, and the seamless integration with the rest of the .NET Framework. Additionally, the performance of ADO.NET is very good, and the integration with Microsoft Visual Studio .NET is unprecedented. If you're writing a new application in the .NET Framework, deciding whether to use ADO.NET is a no-brainer.

.NET Managed Data Providers

A key architectural element in the ADO.NET infrastructure is the *managed provider*, which can be considered the .NET counterpart of the OLE DB provider. A managed data provider enables you to connect to a data source and retrieve and modify data. Compared to the OLE DB provider, a .NET managed provider has a simplified data-access architecture made of a smaller set of interfaces and based on .NET Framework data types.

Building Blocks of a .NET Data Provider

The classes in the managed provider interact with the specific data source and return data to the application using the data types defined in the .NET Framework. The logical components implemented in a managed provider are those graphically featured in Figure 7-1.

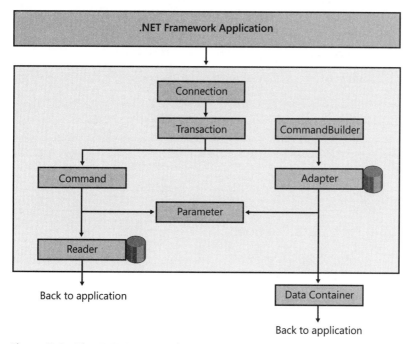

Figure 7-1 The .NET Framework classes that form a typical managed provider and their interconnections.

The functionalities supplied by a .NET data provider fall into a couple of categories:

- Support for disconnected data—that is, the capability of populating ADO.NET container classes with fresh data

- Support for connected data access, which includes the capability of setting up a connection and executing a command

Table 7-1 details the principal components of a .NET data provider.

Table 7-1   Principal Components of a .NET Data Provider

Component	Description
Connection	Creates a connection with the specified data source, including Microsoft SQL Server, Oracle, and any data source for which you can indicate either an OLE DB provider or an ODBC driver
Transaction	Represents a transaction to be made in the source database server
Command	Represents a command that hits the underlying database server
Parameter	Represents a parameter you can pass to the command object
DataAdapter	Represents a database command that executes on the specified database server and returns a disconnected set of records
CommandBuilder	Represents a helper object that automatically generates commands and parameters for a DataAdapter
DataReader	Represents a read-only, forward-only cursor created on the underlying database server

Each managed provider that wraps a real-world database server implements all the objects in Table 7-1 in a way that is specific to the data source.

> **Caution**   You won't find any class named *Connection* in the .NET Framework. You'll find instead several connection-like classes, one for each supported .NET managed provider—for example, *SqlConnection* and *OracleConnection*. The same holds true for the other objects listed in Table 7-1.

Interfaces of a .NET Data Provider

The components listed in Table 7-1 are implemented based on methods and properties defined by the interfaces you see in Table 7-2.

Table 7-2   Interfaces of .NET Data Providers

Interface	Description
IDbConnection	Represents a unique session with a data source
IDbTransaction	Represents a local, nondistributed transaction
IDbCommand	Represents a command that executes when connected to a data source
IDataParameter	Allows implementation of a parameter to a command
IDataReader	Reads a forward-only, read-only stream of data created after the execution of a command
IDataAdapter	Populates a DataSet object, and resolves changes in the DataSet object back to the data source
IDbDataAdapter	Supplies methods to execute typical operations on relational databases (such as insert, update, select, and delete)

Note that all these interfaces except *IDataAdapter* are officially considered to be optional. However, any realistic data provider that manages a database server would implement them all.

> **Note**   Individual managed providers are in no way limited to implementing all and only the interfaces listed in Table 7-2. Based on the capabilities of the underlying data source and its own level of abstraction, each managed provider can expose more components. A good example of this is the data provider for Microsoft SQL Server that you get in the .NET Framework 2.0. It adds several additional classes to handle special operations such as bulk copy, data dependency, and connection string building.

Managed Providers vs. OLE DB Providers

OLE DB providers and managed data providers are radically different types of components that share a common goal—to provide a unique and uniform programming interface for data access. The differences between OLE DB providers and .NET data providers can be summarized in the following points:

- **Component technology.**   OLE DB providers are in-process COM servers that expose a suite of COM interfaces to consumer modules. The dialog between consumers and providers takes place through COM and involves a number of interfaces. A .NET data provider is a suite of managed classes whose overall design looks into one *particular* data source rather than blinking at an abstract and universal data source, as is the case with OLE DB.

- **Internal implementation.**   Both types of providers end up making calls into the data-source programming API. In doing so, though, they provide a dense layer of code that separates the data source from the calling application. Learning from the OLE DB experience, Microsoft designed .NET data providers to be more agile and simple. Fewer interfaces are involved, and the conversation between the caller and the callee is more direct and as informal as possible.

- **Application integration.**   Another aspect of .NET that makes the conversation between caller and callee more informal is the fact that managed providers return data using the same data structures that the application would use to store it. In OLE DB, the data-retrieval process is more flexible, but it's also more complex because the provider packs data in flat memory buffers and leaves the consumer responsible for mapping that data into usable data structures.

Calling into an OLE DB provider from within a .NET application is more expensive because of the data conversion necessary to make the transition from the managed environment of the common language runtime (CLR) to the COM world. Calling a COM object from within a .NET application is possible through the COM interop layer, but doing so comes at a cost. In general, to access a data source from within a .NET application, you should always use a managed provider instead of OLE DB providers or ODBC drivers. You should be doing this primarily because of the transition costs, but also because managed providers are normally more modern tools based on an optimized architecture.

Some data sources, though, might not have a .NET data provider available. In these cases, resorting to old-fashioned OLE DB providers or ODBC drivers is a pure necessity. For this reason, the .NET Framework encapsulates in managed wrapper classes the logic needed to call into a COM-style OLE DB provider or a C-style ODBC driver.

Data Sources You Access Through ADO.NET

The .NET data provider is the managed component of choice for database vendors to expose their data in the most effective way. Ideally, each database vendor should provide a .NET-compatible API that is seamlessly callable from within managed applications. Unfortunately, this is not always the case. However, at least for the major database management systems (DBMS), a managed data provider can be obtained from either Microsoft or third-party vendors.

As of version 2.0, the .NET Framework supports the data providers listed in Table 7-3.

Table 7-3   Managed Data Providers in the .NET Framework

Data Source	Namespace	Description
SQL Server	*System.Data.SqlClient*	Targets various versions of SQL Server, including SQL Server 7.0, SQL Server 2000, and the newest SQL Server 2005
OLE DB providers	*System.Data.OleDb*	Targets OLE DB providers, including SQLOLEDB, MSDAORA, and the Jet engine
ODBC drivers	*System.Data.Odbc*	Targets several ODBC drivers, including those for SQL Server, Oracle, and the Jet engine
Oracle	*System.Data.OracleClient*	Targets Oracle 9i, and supports all of its data types

The OLE DB and ODBC managed providers listed in Table 7-3 are not specific to a physical database server, but rather they serve as a bridge that gives instant access to a large number of existing OLE DB providers and ODBC drivers. When you call into OLE DB providers, your .NET applications jumps out of the managed environment and issues COM calls through the COM interop layer.

Accessing SQL Server

As mentioned, Microsoft supplies a managed provider for SQL Server 7.0 and newer versions. Using the classes contained in this provider is by far the most effective way of accessing SQL Server. Figure 7-2 shows how SQL Server is accessed by .NET and COM clients.

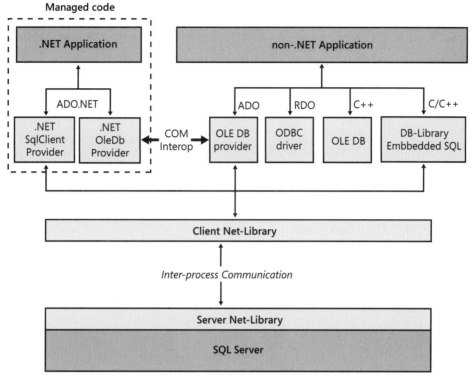

Figure 7-2 Accessing SQL Server by using the managed provider for OLE DB adds overhead because the objects called must pass through the COM interop layer.

A .NET application should always access a SQL Server database using the native data provider. Although it's possible to do so, you should have a good reason to opt for an alternative approach such as using the OLE DB provider for SQL Server (named SQLOLEDB). A possible good reason is the need to use ADO rather than ADO.NET as the data-access library. The SQL Server native provider not only avoids paying the performance tax of going down to COM, but it also implements some small optimizations when preparing the command for SQL Server.

Accessing Oracle Databases

The .NET Framework 1.1 and 2.0 include a managed provider for Oracle databases. The classes are located in the *System.Data.OracleClient* namespace in the *System.Data.OracleClient* assembly. Instead of using the managed provider, you can resort to the COM-based OLE DB provider (named MSDAORA) or the ODBC driver. Note, though, that the Microsoft OLE DB provider for Oracle does not support Oracle 9i and its specific data types. In contrast, Oracle 9i data types are fully supported by the .NET managed provider. So by using the .NET component to connect to Oracle, you not only get a performance boost but also increased programming power.

> **Note**   The .NET data provider for Oracle requires Oracle client software (version 8.1.7 or later) to be installed on the system before you can use it to connect to an Oracle data source.

Microsoft is not the only company to develop a .NET data provider for Oracle databases. Data Direct, Core Lab, and Oracle itself also shipped one. Each provider has its own set of features; for example, the Oracle provider (named ODP.NET) has many optimizations for retrieving and manipulating Oracle native types, such as any flavor of large objects (LOBs) and REF cursors. ODP.NET can participate in transactional applications, with the Oracle database acting as the resource manager and the Microsoft Distributed Transaction Coordinator (DTC) coordinating transactions.

Using OLE DB Providers

The .NET data provider for OLE DB providers is a data-access bridge that allows .NET applications to call into data sources for which a COM OLE DB provider exists. While this approach is architecturally less effective than using native providers, it is the only way to access those data sources when no managed providers are available.

The classes in the *System.Data.OleDb* namespace, though, don't support all types of OLE DB providers and have been optimized to work with only a few of them, as listed in Table 7-4.

Table 7-4   OLE DB Providers Tested

Name	Description
Microsoft.Jet.OLEDB.4.0	The OLE DB provider for the Jet engine implemented in Microsoft Office Access
MSDAORA	The Microsoft OLE DB provider for Oracle 7 that partially supports some features in Oracle 8
SQLOLEDB	The OLE DB provider for SQL Server 6.5 and newer

Table 7-4 does not include all the OLE DB providers that really work through the OLE DB .NET data provider. However, only the components in Table 7-4 are guaranteed to work well in .NET. In particular, the classes in the *System.Data.OleDb* namespace don't support OLE DB providers that implement any of the OLE DB 2.5 interfaces for semistructured and hierarchical rowsets. This includes the OLE DB providers for Exchange (EXOLEDB) and for Internet Publishing (MSDAIPP).

In general, what really prevents existing OLE DB providers from working properly within the .NET data provider for OLE DB is the set of interfaces they actually implement. Some OLE DB providers—for example, those written using the Active Template Library (ATL) or with Visual Basic and the OLE DB Simple Provider Toolkit—are likely to miss one or more COM interfaces that the .NET wrapper requires.

Using ODBC Drivers

The .NET data provider for ODBC lets you access ODBC drivers from managed, ADO.NET-driven applications. Although the ODBC .NET data provider is intended to work with all compliant ODBC drivers, it is guaranteed to work well only with the drivers for SQL Server, Oracle, and Jet. Although ODBC might appear to now be an obsolete technology, it is still used in several production environments, and for some vendors it is still the only way to connect to their products.

You can't access an ODBC driver through an OLE DB provider. There's no technical reason behind this limitation—it's just a matter of common sense. In fact, calling the MSDASQL OLE DB provider from within a .NET application would drive your client through a double data-access bridge—one going from .NET to the OLE DB provider, and one going one level down to the actual ODBC driver.

The Provider Factory Model

Unlike ADO and OLE DB, ADO.NET takes into careful account the particularity of each DBMS and provides a programming model tailor-made for each one. All .NET data providers share a limited set of common features, but each has unique capabilities. The communication between the user code and the DBMS takes place more directly using ADO.NET. This model works better and faster and is probably clearer to most programmers.

But until version 2.0 of the .NET Framework, ADO.NET has one key snag. Developers must know in advance the data source they're going to access. Generic programming—that is, programming in which the same code targets different data sources at different times—is hard (but not impossible) to do. You can create a generic command object and a generic data reader, but not a generic data adapter and certainly not a generic connection. However, through the *IDbConnection* interface, you can work with a connection object without knowing the underlying data source. But you can never create a connection object in a weakly typed manner—that is, without the help of the *new* operator.

Instantiating Providers Programmatically

ADO.NET 2.0 enhances the provider architecture and introduces the factory class. Each .NET data provider encompasses a factory class derived from the base class *DbProviderFactory*. A factory class represents a common entry point for a variety of services specific to the provider. Table 7-5 lists the main methods of a factory class.

Table 7-5   Principal Methods of a Factory Class

Method	Description
CreateCommand	Returns a provider-specific command object
CreateCommandBuilder	Returns a provider-specific command builder object
CreateConnection	Returns a provider-specific connection object
CreateDataAdapter	Returns a provider-specific data adapter object
CreateParameter	Returns a provider-specific parameter object

How do you get the factory of a particular provider? By using a new class, *DbProviderFactories*, that has a few static methods. The following code demonstrates how to obtain a factory object for the SQL Server provider:

```
DbProviderFactory fact;
fact = DbProviderFactories.GetFactory("System.Data.SqlClient");
```

The *GetFactory* method takes a string that represents the invariant name of the provider. This name is hard-coded for each provider in the configuration file where it is registered. By convention, the provider name equals its unique namespace.

GetFactory enumerates all the registered providers and gets assembly and class name information for the matching invariant name. The factory class is not instantiated directly. Instead, the method uses reflection to retrieve the value of the static *Instance* property of the factory class. The property returns the instance of the factory class to use. Once you hold a factory object, you can call any of the methods listed earlier in Table 7-5.

The following pseudocode gives an idea of the internal implementation of the *CreateConnection* method for the *SqlClientFactory* class—the factory class for the SQL Server .NET data provider:

```
public DbConnection CreateConnection()
{
    return new SqlConnection();
}
```

Enumerating Installed Data Providers

In the .NET Framework 2.0, you can use all .NET data providers registered in the configuration file. The following excerpt is from the *machine.config* file:

```
<system.data>
  <DbProviderFactories>
    <add name="SqlClient Data Provider"
        invariant="System.Data.SqlClient"
        description=".Net Framework Data Provider for SqlServer"
        type="System.Data.SqlClient.SqlClientFactory, System.Data "/>
    <add name="OracleClient Data Provider"
        invariant="System.Data.OracleClient"
        description=".Net Framework Data Provider for Oracle"
        type="System.Data.OracleClient.OracleFactory,
            System.Data.OracleClient" />
    ...
  </DbProviderFactories>
</system.data>
```

Each provider is characterized by an invariant name, a description, and a type that contains assembly and class information. The *GetFactoryClasses* method on the *DbProviderFactories* class returns this information packed in an easy-to-use *DataTable* object. The following sample page demonstrates how to get a quick list of the installed providers:

```
<%@ page language="C#" %>
<%@ import namespace="System.Data" %>
<%@ import namespace="System.Data.Common" %>

<script runat="server">
    void Page_Load (object sender, EventArgs e) {
        DataTable providers = DbProviderFactories.GetFactoryClasses();
        provList.DataSource = providers;
        provList.DataBind();
    }
</script>

<html>
<head runat="server"><title>List Factory Objects</title></head>
<body>
    <form runat="server">
        <asp:datagrid runat="server" id="provList" />
    </form>
</body>
</html>
```

The final page is shown in Figure 7-3.

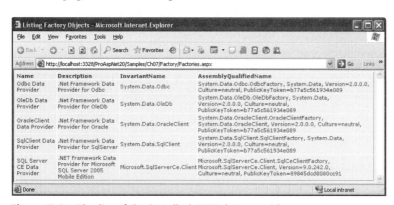

Figure 7-3   The list of the installed .NET data providers.

Database-Agnostic Pages

Let's write out some sample code to demonstrate how to craft database-agnostic pages. The sample page will contain three text boxes to collect the name of the provider, connection string, and command text:

```
protected void RunButton_Click(object sender, EventArgs e)
{
    string provider = ProviderNameBox.Text;
    string connString = ConnectionStringBox.Text;
    string commandText = CommandTextBox.Text;
```

```
    // Get the provider
    DbProviderFactory fact = DbProviderFactories.GetFactory(provider);

    // Create the connection
    DbConnection conn = fact.CreateConnection();
    conn.ConnectionString = connString;

    // Create the data adapter
    DbDataAdapter adapter = fact.CreateDataAdapter();
    adapter.SelectCommand = conn.CreateCommand();
    adapter.SelectCommand.CommandText = commandText;

    // Run the query
    DataTable table = new DataTable();
    adapter.Fill(table);

    // Shows the results
    Results.DataSource = table;
    Results.DataBind();
}
```

By changing the provider name and properly adapting the connection string and command, the same core code can now be used to work on other database servers.

> **Caution**   Nothing presented here is invented; no magic and no tricks apply. This said, though, don't be fooled by the apparent simplicity of this approach. Be aware that in real-world applications data access is normally insulated in the boundaries of the Data Access Layer (DAL) and that practice suggests you have one DAL per supported data source. This is because the complexity of real problems needs to be addressed by getting the most out of each data server. In the end, you need optimized data access code to exploit all the features of the DBMS rather than generic code that you write once and which queries everywhere and everything.

Connecting to Data Sources

The ADO.NET programming model is based on a relatively standard and database-independent sequence of steps. You first create a connection, then prepare and execute a command, and finally process the data retrieved. As far as basic operations and data types are involved, this model works for most providers. Some exceptions are binary large object (BLOB) fields management for Oracle databases and perhaps bulk copy and XML data management for SQL Server databases.

In the rest of the chapter, we'll mostly discuss how ADO.NET data classes work with SQL Server 7.0 and newer versions. However, we'll promptly point out any aspect that is significantly different from other .NET data providers. To start out, let's see how connections take place.

> **More Info** For in-depth coverage of ADO.NET 2.0, see *Programming Microsoft ADO.NET 2.0 Applications: Advanced Topics* by Glenn Johnson (Microsoft Press, 2005) and *Programming ADO.NET 2.0 Core Reference* by David Sceppa (Microsoft Press, 2005).

The *SqlConnection* Class

The first step in working with an ADO.NET-based application is setting up the connection with the data source. The class that represents a physical connection to SQL Server is *SqlConnection*, and it is located in the *System.Data.SqlClient* namespace. The class is sealed (that is, not inheritable) and cloneable, and it implements the *IDbConnection* interface. In ADO.NET 2.0, the interface is implemented through the intermediate base class *DbConnection*, which also provides additional features shared by all providers. (In fact, adding new members to the interface would have broken existing code.)

The *SqlConnection* class features two constructors, one of which is the default parameterless constructor. The second class constructor, on the other hand, takes a string containing the connection string:

```
public SqlConnection();
public SqlConnection(string);
```

The following code snippet shows the typical way to set up and open a SQL Server connection:

```
string connString = "SERVER=…;DATABASE=…;UID=...;PWD=...";
SqlConnection conn = new SqlConnection(connString);
conn.Open();
...
conn.Close();
```

Properties of the *SqlConnection* Class

Table 7-6 details the public properties defined on the *SqlConnection* class.

Table 7-6 Properties of the *SqlConnection* Class

Property	*IDbConnection* Interface	Description
ConnectionString	Yes	Gets or sets the string used to open the database.
ConnectionTimeout	Yes	Gets the number of seconds to wait while trying to establish a connection.
Database	Yes	Gets the name of the database to be used.
DataSource		Gets the name of the instance of SQL Server to connect to. It corresponds to the *Server* connection string attribute.

Table 7-6 Properties of the *SqlConnection* Class

Property	IDbConnection Interface	Description
PacketSize		Gets the size in bytes of network packets used to communicate with SQL Server. Set to 8192, it can be any value in the range from 512 through 32767.
ServerVersion		Gets a string containing the version of the current instance of SQL Server. The version string is in the form of *major.minor.release*.
State	Yes	Gets the current state of the connection: open or closed. Closed is the default.
StatisticsEnabled		Enables the retrieval of statistical information over the current connection. *Not available in ADO.NET 1.x.*
WorkStationId		Gets the network name of the client, which normally corresponds to the *WorkStation ID* connection string attribute.

An important characteristic to note about the properties of the connection classes is that they are all read-only except *ConnectionString*. In other words, you can configure the connection only through the tokens of the connection string, but you can read attributes back through handy properties. This characteristic of connection class properties in ADO.NET is significantly different than what you find in ADO, where many of the connection properties—for example, *ConnectionTimeout* and *Database*—were read/write.

Methods of the *SqlConnection* Class

Table 7-7 shows the methods available in the *SqlConnection* class.

Table 7-7 Methods of the *SqlConnection* Class

Method	IDbConnection Interface	Description
BeginTransaction	Yes	Begins a database transaction. Allows you to specify a name and an isolation level.
ChangeDatabase	Yes	Changes the current database on the connection. Requires a valid database name.
Close	Yes	Closes the connection to the database. Use this method to close an open connection.
CreateCommand	Yes	Creates and returns a *SqlCommand* object associated with the connection.

Table 7-7 **Methods of the *SqlConnection* Class**

Method	IDbConnection Interface	Description
Dispose		Calls *Close*.
EnlistDistributedTransaction		If auto-enlistment is disabled, enlists the connection in the specified distributed Enterprise Services DTC transaction. *Not supported in version 1.0 of the .NET Framework.*
EnlistTransaction	No, but defined on *DbConnection* in ADO.NET 2.0	Enlists the connection on the specified local or distributed transaction. *Not available in ADO.NET 1.x.*
GetSchema	No, but defined on *DbConnection* in ADO.NET 2.0	Retrieve schema information for the specified scope (that is, tables, databases). *Not available in ADO.NET 1.x.*
ResetStatistics		Resets the statistics service. *Not available in ADO.NET 1.x.*
RetrieveStatistics		Gets a hash table filled with the information about the connection, such as data transferred, user details, transactions. *Not available in ADO.NET 1.x.*
Open	Yes	Opens a database connection.

Note that if the connection goes out of scope, it is not automatically closed. Later on, but not especially soon, the garbage collector picks up the object instance, but the connection won't be closed because the garbage collector can't recognize the peculiarity of the object and handle it properly. Therefore, you must explicitly close the connection by calling *Close* or *Dispose* before the object goes out of scope.

> **Note**   Like many other disposable objects, connection classes implement the *IDisposable* interface, thus providing a programming interface for developers to dispose of the object. The dispose pattern entails the sole *Dispose* method; *Close* is not officially part of the pattern, but most classes implement it as well.

Changing Passwords

In ADO.NET 2.0, the *SqlConnection* class provides a static method named *ChangePassword* to let developers change the SQL Server password for the user indicated in the supplied connection string:

```
public static void ChangePassword(
    string connectionString, string newPassword)
```

An exception will be thrown if the connection string requires integrated security (that is, *Integrated Security=True* or an equivalent setting). The method opens a new connection to the server, requests the password change, and closes the connection once it has completed. The connection used to change the password is not taken out of the connection pool. The new password must comply with any password security policy set on the server, including minimum length and requirements for specific characters.

Note that *ChangePassword* works only on SQL Server 2005.

Accessing Schema Information

In ADO.NET 2.0, all managed providers are expected to implement a *GetSchema* method for retrieving schema information. The standard providers offer the following overloads of the method:

```
public override DataTable GetSchema();
public override DataTable GetSchema(string collection);
public override DataTable GetSchema(string collection, string[] filterVal)
```

The schema information you can retrieve is specific to the back-end system. For the full list of valid values, call *GetSchema* with no parameters. The following code shows how to retrieve all available collections and bind the results to a drop-down list:

```
// Get schema collections
SqlConnection conn = new SqlConnection(connString);
conn.Open();
DataTable table = conn.GetSchema();
conn.Close();

// Display their names
CollectionNames.DataSource = table;
CollectionNames.DataTextField = "collectionname";
CollectionNames.DataBind();
```

Figure 7-4 shows the available schema collections for a SQL Server 2000 machine. (For SQL Server 2005, it adds only a *UserDefinedTypes* collection.) Call *GetSchema* on, say, the *Databases* collection and you will get the list of all databases for the instance of SQL Server you are connected to. Likewise, if you call it on *Tables*, you will see the tables in the connected database.

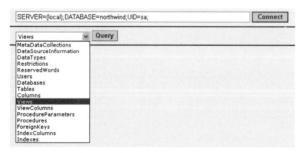

Figure 7-4 The list of available schema collections for SQL Server 2000.

> **Note** The preceding code snippet introduces the *DataTable* class as well as data binding. We will cover the *DataTable* class—one of the most important ADO.NET container classes—in the next chapter. Data binding, on the other hand, will be the subject of Chapter 9.

The list of schema collections is expressed as a *DataTable* object with three columns—*CollectionName* is the column with names. The following code shows how to retrieve schema information regarding the collection name currently selected in the drop-down list—the *Views*:

```
string coll = CollectionNames.SelectedValue;
string connString = ConnStringBox.Text;
SqlConnection conn = new SqlConnection(connString);
conn.Open();
DataTable table = conn.GetSchema(coll);
conn.Close();
GridView1.DataSource = table;
GridView1.DataBind();
```

As Figure 7-5 demonstrates, the data is then bound to a grid for display.

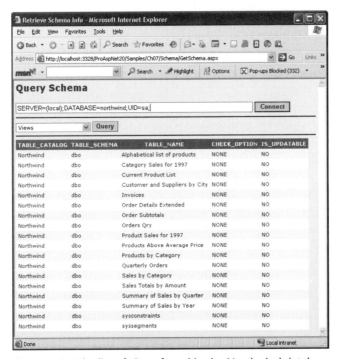

Figure 7-5   The list of views found in the Northwind database.

In ADO.NET 2.0, all connection objects support *GetSchema* methods, as they are part of the new intermediate *DbConnection* class. In ADO.NET 1.x, you have different approaches depending on the target source. If you work with OLE DB, you get schema information through the OLE DB native provider calling the *GetOleDbSchemaTable* method. The following code shows how to get table information:

```
OleDbConnection conn = new OleDbConnection(connString);
conn.Open();
DataTable schema = cConn.GetOleDbSchemaTable(
    OleDbSchemaGuid.Tables,
    new object[] {null, null, null, "TABLE"});
conn.Close();
```

GetOleDbSchemaTable takes an *OleDbSchemaGuid* argument that identifies the schema information to return. In addition, it takes an array of values to restrict the returned columns. *GetOleDbSchemaTable* returns a *DataTable* populated with the schema information. Alternately, you can get information on available databases, tables, views, constraints, and so on through any functionality provided by the specific data source, such as stored procedures and views.

```
SqlConnection conn = new SqlConnection(connString);
SqlDataAdapter adapter = new SqlDataAdapter(
    "SELECT * FROM INFORMATION_SCHEMA.TABLES " +
            "WHERE TABLE_TYPE = 'BASE TABLE' " +
            "ORDER BY TABLE_TYPE", conn);
DataTable schema = new DataTable();
adapter.Fill(schema);
```

In ADO.NET 2.0, the *GetSchema* method unifies the approach for retrieving schema information. The *SqlDataAdapter* class that appears in the preceding code snippet is a special type of command that we'll explore in depth in the next chapter. One of its key characteristics is that it returns disconnected data packed in a *DataTable* or *DataSet*.

Connection Strings

To connect to a data source, you need a connection string. Typically made of semicolon-separated pairs of names and values, a connection string specifies settings for the database runtime. Typical information contained in a connection string includes the name of the database, location of the server, and user credentials. Other, more operational information, such as connection timeout and connection pooling settings, can be specified, too.

In many enterprise applications, the usage of connection strings is related to a couple of issues: how to store and protect them, and how to build and manage them. The .NET Framework 2.0 provides excellent solutions to both issues, as we'll see in a moment.

Needless to say, connection strings are database-specific, although huge differences don't exist between, say, a connection string for SQL Server and Oracle databases. In this chapter, we mainly focus on SQL Server but point out significant differences.

Configuring Connection Properties

The *ConnectionString* property of the connection class can be set only when the connection is closed. Many connection string values have corresponding read-only properties in the connection class. These properties are updated when the connection string is set. The contents of the connection string are checked and parsed immediately after the *ConnectionString* property is set. Attribute names in a connection string are not case-sensitive, and if a given name appears multiple times, the value of the last occurrence is used. Table 7-8 lists the keywords that are supported.

Table 7-8   Connection String Keywords for SQL Server

Keyword	Description
Application Name	Name of the client application as it appears in the SQL Profiler. Defaults to *.Net SqlClient Data Provider*.
Async	When *true*, enables asynchronous operation support. *Not supported in ADO.NET 1.x.*
AttachDBFileName or *Initial File Name*	The full path name of the file (.mdf) to use as an attachable database file.
Connection Timeout	The number of seconds to wait for the connection to take place. Default is 15 seconds.
Current Language	The SQL Server language name.
Database or *Initial Catalog*	The name of the database to connect to.
Encrypt	Indicates whether Secure Sockets Layer (SSL) encryption should be used for all data sent between the client and server. Needs a certificate installed on the server. Default is *false*.
Failover Partner	The name of the partner server to access in case of errors. Connection failover allows an application to connect to an alternate, or backup, database server if the primary database server is unavailable. *Not supported in ADO.NET 1.x.*
Integrated Security or *Trusted_Connection*	Indicates whether current Windows account credentials are used for authentication. When set to *false*, explicit user ID and password need to be provided. The special value *sspi* equals *true*. Default is *false*.
MultipleActiveResultSets	When *true*, an application can maintain multiple active result sets. Set to *true* by default, this feature requires SQL Server 2005. *Not supported in ADO.NET 1.x.*
Network Library or *Net*	Indicates the network library used to establish a connection to SQL Server. Default is *dbmssocn*, which is based on TCP/IP.
Packet Size	Bytes that indicate the size of the packet being exchanged. Default is 8192.
Password or *pwd*	Password for the account logging on.

Table 7-8   **Connection String Keywords for SQL Server**

Keyword	Description
Persist Security Info	Indicates whether the managed provider should include password information in the string returned as the connection string. Default is *false*.
Server or *Data Source*	Name or network address of the instance of SQL Server to connect to.
User ID or *uid*	User name for the account logging on.
Workstation ID	Name of the machine connecting to SQL Server.

The network DLL specified by the *Network Library* keyword must be installed on the system to which you connect. If you use a local server, the default library is *dbmslpcn*, which uses shared memory. For a list of options, consult the MSDN documentation.

Any attempt to connect to an instance of SQL Server should not exceed a given time. The *Connection Timeout* keyword controls just this. Note that a connection timeout of 0 causes the connection attempt to wait indefinitely; it does not indicate no wait time.

You normally shouldn't change the default packet size, which has been determined based on average operations and workload. However, if you're going to perform bulk operations in which large objects are involved, increasing the packet size can be of help because it decreases the number of reads and writes.

Some of the attributes you see listed in Table 7-8 are specific to ADO.NET 2.0 and address features that have been introduced lately. They are asynchronous commands and multiple active result sets (MARS). MARS, in particular, removes a long-time constraint of the SQL Server programming model—that is, the constraint of having at most one pending request on a given session at a time. Before ADO.NET 2.0 and SQL Server 2005, several approaches have been tried to work around this limitation, the most common of which is using server-side cursors through ADO. We'll return to MARS later, in the section dedicated to SQL Server 2005.

Connection String Builders

How do you build the connection string to be used in an application? In many cases, you just consider it constant and read it out of a secured source. In other cases, though, you might need to construct it based on user input—for example, when retrieving user ID and password information from a dialog box. In ADO.NET 1.x, you can build the string only by blindly concatenating any name/value pairs. There are two major drawbacks with this technique. One is that the use of wrong keywords is caught only when the application undergoes testing. More serious than the lack of compile-time check, though, is that a blind-pair concatenation leaves room for undesired data injections to attach users to a different database or to change in some way the final goal of the connection. Any measures to fend off injections and check the syntax should be manually coded, resulting in a specialized builder class—just like the brand new connection string builder classes you find in ADO.NET 2.0.

All default data providers support connection string builders in a guise that perfectly applies to the underlying provider. The following code snippet (and its result, shown in Figure 7-6) builds and displays a connection string for SQL Server:

```
SqlConnectionStringBuilder builder = new SqlConnectionStringBuilder();
builder.DataSource = serverName;
builder.UserID = userid;
builder.Password = pswd;
NewConnString.Text = builder.ConnectionString;
```

Figure 7-6 Building connection strings programmatically and securely.

By using connection string builders, you gain a lot in terms of security because you dramatically reduce injection. Imagine that a malicious user types in the password **Foo;Trusted_Connection=true**. If you blindly concatenate strings, you might get the following:

```
Password=Foo;Trusted_Connection=true
```

Because the last pair wins, the connection will be opened based on the credentials of the logged-on user. If you use the builder class, you get the following appropriately quoted string:

```
Password="Foo;Trusted_Connection=true"
```

In addition, the builder class exposes the 20-plus supported keywords through easier-to-remember properties recognized by Microsoft IntelliSense.

Storing and Retrieving Connection Strings

Savvy developers avoid hard-coding connection strings in the compiled code. Configuration files (such as the *web.config* file) purposely support the *<appSettings>* named section, which is used to store custom data through name/value pairs. All these values populate the *AppSettings* collection and can be easily retrieved programmatically, as shown here:

```
string connString = ConfigurationSettings.AppSettings["NorthwindConn"];
```

This approach is far from perfect for two reasons. First, connection strings are not just data—they're a special kind of data not to be mixed up with general-purpose application settings. Second, connection strings are a critical parameter for the application and typically contain sensitive data. Therefore, at a minimum they need transparent encryption. Let's tackle storage first.

In the .NET Framework 2.0, configuration files define a new section specifically designed to contain connection strings. The section is named <*connectionStrings*> and is laid out as follows:

```
<connectionStrings>
    <add name="NWind"
        connectionString="SERVER=…;DATABASE=…;UID=…;PWD=…;"
        providerName="System.Data.SqlClient"  />
</connectionStrings>
```

You can manipulate the contents of the section by using <*add*>, <*remove*>, and <*clear*> nodes. You use an <*add*> node to add a new connection string to the current list, <*remove*> to remove a previously defined connection, and <*clear*> to reset all connections and create a new collection. By placing a *web.config* file in each of the application's directories, you can customize the collection of connection strings that are visible to the pages in the directory. Configuration files located in child directories can remove, clear, and extend the list of connection strings defined at the upper level. Note that each stored connection is identified with a name. This name references the actual connection parameters throughout the application. Connection names are also used within the configuration file to link a connection string to other sections, such as the <*providers*> section of <*membership*> and <*profile*> nodes.

All the connection strings defined in the *web.config* file are loaded into the new *ConfigurationManager.ConnectionStrings* collection. To physically open a connection based on a string stored in the *web.config* file, use following code:

```
string connStr;
connStr = ConfigurationManager.ConnectionStrings["NWind"].ConnectionString;
SqlConnection conn = new SqlConnection(connStr);
```

The full support from the configuration API opens up an interesting possibility for consuming connection strings—declarative binding. As we'll see in Chapter 9, ASP.NET 2.0 supports quite a few data source objects. A data source object is a server control that manages all aspects of data source interaction, including connection setup and command execution. You bind data source objects to data-bound controls and instruct the data source to retrieve data from a specific source. The great news is that you can now indicate the connection string declaratively, as follows:

```
<asp:SqlDataSource id="MySource" runat="server"
  ProviderName="System.Data.SqlClient"
  ConnectionString='<%#
    ConfigurationSettings.ConnectionStrings["NWind"].ConnectionString %>'
  SelectCommand="SELECT * FROM employees">
```

There's a lot more to be known about this feature, though, and we'll delve deeply into that later in the book. For now, it suffices to say that connection strings are much more than strings in the .NET Framework 2.0.

Protecting Connection Strings

ASP.NET 2.0 introduces a system for protecting sensitive data stored in the configuration system. It uses industry-standard XML encryption to encrypt specific sections of configuration files that might contain sensitive data. XML encryption (which you can learn more about at *http://www.w3.org/TR/xmlenc-core*) is a way to encrypt data and represent the result in XML. Prior to version 2.0, only a few specific ASP.NET sections that contain sensitive data support protection of this data using a machine-specific encryption in a registry key. This approach requires developers to come up with a utility to protect their own secrets—typically connection strings, credentials, and encryption keys.

In the .NET Framework 2.0, encryption of configuration sections is optional, and you can enable it for any configuration sections you want by referencing the name of the section in the <*protectedData*> section of the *web.config* file, as shown here:

```
<protectedData>
    <protectedDataSections>
        <add name="connectionStrings"
            provider="RSAProtectedConfigurationProvider" />
    </protectedDataSections>
</protectedData>
```

You can specify the type of encryption you want by selecting the appropriate provider from the list of available encryption providers. The .NET Framework 2.0 comes with two predefined providers:

- **DPAPIProtectedConfigurationProvider.** Uses the Windows Data Protection API (DPAPI) to encrypt and decrypt data

- **RSAProtectedConfigurationProvider.** Default provider; uses the RSA encryption algorithm to encrypt and decrypt data

Being able to protect data stored in the *web.config* file is not a feature specific to connection strings. It applies, instead, to all sections, with very few exceptions. This said, let's see how to encrypt connection strings stored in the *web.config* file.

You can use the newest version of a popular system tool—*aspnet_regiis.exe*—or write your own tool by using the ASP.NET 2.0 configuration API. If you use *aspnet_regiis*, examine the following code, which is a sample used to encrypt connection strings for the ProAspNet20 application:

```
aspnet_regiis.exe -pe connectionStrings -app /ProAspNet20
```

Note that the section names are case-sensitive. Note also that connection strings are stored in a protected area that is completely transparent to applications, which continue working as before. If you open the *web.config* file after encryption, you see something like the following:

```
<configuration>
  <protectedData>
    <protectedDataSections>
      <add name="connectionStrings"
           provider="RSAProtectedConfigurationProvider" />
    </protectedDataSections>
  </protectedData>
  <connectionStrings>
    <EncryptedData …>
      . . .
      <CipherData>
        <CipherValue>cQyofWFQ… =</CipherValue>
      </CipherData>
    </EncryptedData>
  </connectionStrings>
</configuration>
```

To restore the *web.config* file to its original clear state, you use the *–pd* switch in lieu of the *–pe* in the aforementioned command line.

Caution   Any page that uses protected sections works like a champ as long as you run it inside the local Web server embedded in Visual Studio .NET 2005. You might get an RSA provider configuration error if you access the same page from within a canonical (and much more realistic) IIS virtual folder. What's up with that?

The RSA-based provider—the default protection provider—needs a key container to work. A default key container is created upon installation and is named *NetFrameWorkConfiguration-Key*. The *aspnet_regiis.exe* utility provides a lot of command-line switches for you to add, remove, and edit key containers. The essential point is that you have a key container created before you dump the RSA-protected configuration provider. The container must not only exist, it also needs to be associated with the user account attempting to call it. The system account (running the local Web server) is listed with the container; the ASP.NET account on your Web server might not be. Assuming you run ASP.NET under the NETWORK SERVICE account (the default on Windows Server 2003 machines), you need the following code to add access to the container for the user:

```
aspnet_regiis.exe -pa "NetFrameworkConfigurationKey"
               "NT AUTHORITY\NETWORK SERVICE"
```

It is important that you specify a complete account name, as in the preceding code. Note that granting access to the key container is necessary only if you use the RSA provider.

Both the RSA and DPAPI providers are great options for encrypting sensitive data. The DPAPI provider dramatically simplifies the process of key management–keys are generated based on machine credentials and can be accessed by all processes running on the machine. For the same reason, the DPAPI provider is not ideal to protect sections in a Web farm scenario where the same encrypted *web.config* file will be deployed to several servers. In this case, either you manually encrypt all *web.config* files on each machine or you copy the same container key to all servers. To accomplish this, you create a key container for the application, export it to an XML file, and import it on each server that will need to decrypt the encrypted *web.config* file. To create a key container, you do as follows:

```
aspnet_regiis.exe -pc YourContainerName -exp
```

Next, you export the key container to an XML file:

```
aspnet_regiis.exe -px YourContainerName YourXmlFile.xml
```

Next, you move the XML file to each server and import it as follows:

```
aspnet_regiis.exe -pi YourContainerName YourXmlFile.xml
```

As a final step, grant the ASP.NET account permission to access the container.

> **Note**   We won't cover the .NET Framework configuration API in this book. You can find deep coverage of the structure of configuration files and related APIs in my other recent book, *Programming Microsoft ASP.NET 2.0 Applications: Advanced Topics* (Microsoft Press, 2005).

Connection Pooling

Connection pooling is a fundamental aspect of high-performance, scalable applications. For local or intranet desktop applications that are not multithreaded, connection pooling is no big deal—you'll get nearly the same performance with and without pooling. Furthermore, using a nonpooled connection gives you more control over the lifetime. For multithreaded applications, the use of connection pooling is a necessity for performance reasons and to avoid nasty, hardware-dependent bugs. Finally, if ASP.NET applications are involved, every millisecond that the connection is idle steals valuable resources from other requests. Not only should you rely on connection pooling, but you should also open the connection as late as possible and close it as soon as you can.

Using connection pooling makes it far less expensive for the application to open and close the connection to the database, even if that is done frequently. (We'll cover this topic in more detail later.) All standard .NET data providers have pooling support turned on by default. The .NET data providers for SQL Server and Oracle manage connection pooling internally using ad hoc classes. For the OLE DB data provider, connection pooling is implemented through the OLE DB service infrastructure for session pooling. Connection-string arguments (for example, *OLE DB Service*) can be used to enable or disable various OLE DB services, including pooling. A similar situation occurs with ODBC, in which pooling is controlled by the ODBC driver manager.

Configuring Pooling

Some settings in the connection string directly affect the pooling mechanism. The parameters you can control to configure the SQL Server environment are listed in Table 7-9.

Table 7-9   SQL Server Connection Pooling Keywords

Keyword	Description
Connection Lifetime	Sets the maximum duration in seconds of the connection object in the pool. This keyword is checked only when the connection is returned to the pool. If the time the connection has been open is greater than the specified lifetime, the connection object is destroyed. (We'll cover this topic in more detail later.)
Connection Reset	Determines whether the database connection is reset when being drawn from the pool. Default is *true*.
Enlist	Indicates that the pooler automatically enlists the connection in the creation thread's current transaction context. Default is *true*.
Max Pool Size	Maximum number of connections allowed in the pool. Default is 100.
Min Pool Size	Minimum number of connections allowed in the pool. Default is 0.
Pooling	Indicates that the connection object is drawn from the appropriate pool or, if necessary, is created and added to the appropriate pool. Default is *true*.

With the exception of *Connection Reset*, all the keywords listed in Table 7-9 are acceptable to the Oracle managed provider, too.

As far as SQL Server and Oracle providers are concerned, connection pooling is automatically enabled; to disable it, you need to set *Pooling* to *false* in the connection string. To control pooling for an ODBC data source, you use the ODBC Data Source Administrator in the Control Panel. The Connection Pooling tab allows you to specify connection pooling parameters for each ODBC driver installed. Note that any changes to a specific driver affect all applications that make use of it. The .NET data provider for OLE DB automatically pools connections using OLE DB session pooling. You can disable pooling by setting the *OLE DB Services* keyword to −4.

In ADO.NET 2.0, auto enlistment (the *Enlist* keyword) works in the connection strings of all standard data providers, including providers for OLE DB and ODBC. In ADO.NET 1.x, only managed providers for SQL Server and Oracle support auto-enlistment because they are made of native managed code instead of being wrappers around existing code. The new *EnlistTransaction* method on connection classes allows you to enlist a connection object programmatically, be it pooled or not.

Getting and Releasing Objects

Each connection pool is associated with a distinct connection string and the transaction context. When a new connection is opened, if the connection string does not exactly match an existing pool, a new pool is created. Once created, connection pools are not destroyed until the process ends. This behavior does not affect the system performance because maintenance of inactive or empty pools requires only minimal overhead.

When a pool is created, multiple connection objects are created and added so that the minimum size is reached. Next, connections are added to the pool on demand, up to the maximum pool size. Adding a brand-new connection object to the pool is the really expensive operation here, as it requires a roundtrip to the database. Next, when a connection object is requested, it is drawn from the pool as long as a usable connection is available. A usable connection must currently be unused, have a matching or null transaction context, and have a valid link to the server. If no usable connection is available, the pooler attempts to create a new connection object. When the maximum pool size is reached, the request is queued and served as soon as an existing connection object is released to the pool.

Connections are released when you call methods such as *Close* or *Dispose*. Connections that are not explicitly closed might not be returned to the pool unless the maximum pool size has been reached and the connection is still valid.

A connection object is removed from the pool if the lifetime has expired (which will be explained further in a moment) or if a severe error has occurred. In these cases, the connection is marked as invalid. The pooler periodically scavenges the various pools and permanently removes invalid connection objects.

> **Important**   Unlike in ADO, connection pools in ADO.NET are created based on the connection string applying an exact match algorithm. In other words, to avoid the creation of an additional connection pool you must ensure that two connection strings carrying the same set of parameters are expressed by two byte-per-byte identical strings. A different order of keywords, or blanks interspersed in the text, is not ignored and ends up creating additional pools and therefore additional overhead.

To make connection pooling work effectively, it is extremely important that connection objects are returned to the pool as soon as possible. It is even more important, though, that connections are returned. Note that a connection object that goes out of scope is not closed and, therefore, not immediately returned. For this reason, it is highly recommended that you work with connection objects according to the following pattern:

```
SqlConnection conn = new SqlConnection(connString);
try {
    conn.Open();
    // Do something here
}
catch {
    // Trap errors here
}
finally {
    conn.Close();
}
```

Alternately, you can resort to the C# *using* statement, as follows:

```
using (SqlConnection conn = new SqlConnection(connString))
{
    // Do something here
    // Trap errors here
}
```

The *using* statement is equivalent to the preceding *try/catch/finally* block in which *Close* or *Dispose* is invoked in the *finally* block. You can call either *Close* or *Dispose* or even both—they do the same thing. *Dispose* cleans the connection string information and then calls *Close*. In addition, note that calling each multiple times doesn't result in run-time troubles, as closing or disposing an already closed or disposed connection is actually a no-operation.

> **Note** Before the .NET Framework 2.0, there was no sort of *using* statement in Visual Basic .NET. Starting with Visual Studio .NET 2005, you can rely on a shortcut keyword for *try/catch/finally* blocks also in Visual Basic .NET. The keyword is *Using ... End Using*:
>
> ```
> Using conn As New SqlConnection()
>    ...
> End Using
> ```

Detecting Connections Leaks

In ADO.NET 2.0, you can more easily figure out whether you're leaking connections, thanks to some new performance counters. In particular, you can monitor the *Number-OfReclaimedConnections* counter; if you see it going up, you have the evidence that your application is making poor use of connection objects. A good symptom of connection leaking is when you get an invalid operation exception that claims the timeout period elapsed prior to obtaining a connection from the pool. You can make this exception disappear or, more exactly, become less frequent by tweaking some parameters in the connection string. Needless to say, this solution doesn't remove the leak; it simply changes run-time conditions to make it happen less frequently. Here's a quick list of things you should not do that relate to connection management:

- **Do not turn connection pooling off.** With pooling disabled, a new connection object is created every time. No timeout can ever occur, but you lose a lot in performance and, more important, you are still leaking connections.

- **Do not shrink the connection lifetime.** Reducing the lifetime of the connection will force the pooler to renew connection objects more frequently. A short lifetime (a few seconds) will make the timeout exception extremely unlikely, but it adds significant overhead and doesn't solve the real problem. Let's say that it is only a little better than turning pooling off.

- **Do not increase the connection timeout.** You tell the pooler to wait a longer time before throwing the timeout exception. Whatever value you set here, ASP.NET aborts the thread after three minutes. In general, this option worsens performance without alleviating the problem.

- **Do not increase the pool size.** If you set the maximum pool size high enough (how high depends on the context), you stop getting timeout exceptions while keeping pooling enabled. The drawback is that you greatly reduce your application's scalability because you force your application to use a much larger number of connections than is actually needed.

To avoid leaking connections, you need to guarantee *only* that the connection is closed or disposed of when you're done, and preferably soon after.

In the previous section, I emphasized the importance of writing code that guarantees the connection is always closed. However, there might be nasty cases in which your code places a call to *Close*, but it doesn't get called. Let's see why. Consider the following code:

```
SqlConnection conn = new SqlConnection(connString);
conn.Open();
SqlCommand cmd = new SqlCommand(cmdText, conn);
cmd.ExecuteNonQuery();
conn.Close();
```

What if the command throws an exception? The *Close* method is not called, and the connection is not returned to the pool. Wrapping the code in a *using* statement would do the trick because it ensures that *Dispose* is always invoked on the object being used. Here's the correct version of the code:

```
using (SqlConnection conn = new SqlConnection(connString))
{
    conn.Open();
    SqlCommand cmd = new SqlCommand(cmdText, conn);
    cmd.ExecuteNonQuery();
    conn.Close();  // Not called in case of exception
} // Dispose always called
```

That's the only way to avoid connection leaking.

Managing Connection Lifetime

The *Connection Lifetime* keyword indicates in seconds the time a connection object is considered valid. When the time has elapsed, the connection object should be disposed of. But why on earth should you get rid of a perfectly good connection object? This keyword is useful only in a well-known situation, and it should never be used otherwise. Imagine that you have a cluster of servers sharing the workload. At some point, you realize the load is too high and you turn on an additional server. With good reason, you expect the workload to be distributed among all servers. However, this might not happen—the newly added server is idle.

A plausible and common reason for this is that middle-tier components cache the connections and never open new ones. By disposing of working connections, you force the middle-tier applications to create new connections. Needless to say, new connections will be assigned to the least loaded server. In the end, you should set *Connection Lifetime* only if you're in a cluster scenario. Finally, note that in ADO.NET 2.0 the connection builder classes use a different (and more intuitive) name to address the keyword—*LoadBalanceTimeout*.

> **Note**   The *LoadBalanceTimeout* is not a newly supported attribute for a connection string. If you use the *SqlConnectionStringBuilder* class to programmatically build the connection string, you'll find a *LoadBalanceTimeout* property to set the *Connection Lifetime* attribute.

Clearing the Connection Pool

Until ADO.NET 2.0, there was no way to programmatically clear the pool of open connections. Admittedly, this is not an operation you need to perform often, but it becomes essential in case the database server goes down for whatever reason. Consider the following scenario: your ASP.NET pages open and then successfully close some connections out of the same pool. Next, the server suddenly goes down and is restarted. As a result, all connection objects in the pool are now invalid because each of them holds a reference to a server connection that no longer exists. What happens when a new page request is issued?

The answer is that the pooler returns an apparently valid connection object to the page, and the page runs the command. Unfortunately, the connection object is not recognized by the database server, resulting in an exception. The connection object is removed from the pool and replaced. The exception will be raised for each command as long as there are connection objects in the pool. In summary, shutting down the server without shutting down the application brings the connection pool into an inconsistent, corrupted state.

This situation is common for applications that deal with server reboots, like a failover cluster. Only one solution is possible—flushing the connection pool. It is not as easy to implement as it might seem at first, though. An easier workaround is catching the exception and changing the connection string slightly to force the use of a new connection pool.

In ADO.NET 2.0, the solution to this issue comes with the framework. ADO.NET 2.0 is smart enough to recognize when an exception means that the pool is corrupted. When an exception is thrown during the execution of a command, ADO.NET 2.0 determines if the exception means that the pool is corrupted. In this case, it walks down the pool and marks each connection as obsolete. When does an exception indicate pool corruption? It has to be a fatal exception raised from the network layer on a previously opened connection. All other exceptions are ignored and bubble up as usual.

Two new static methods—*ClearPool* and *ClearAllPools,* defined for both *SqlConnection* and *OracleConnection*—can be used to programmatically clear the pool, if you know that the server has been stopped and restarted. These methods are used internally by ADO.NET 2.0 to clear the pool as described earlier.

Executing Commands

Once you have a physical channel set up between your client and the database, you can start preparing and executing commands. The ADO.NET object model provides two types of command objects—the traditional one-off command and the data adapter. The one-off command executes a SQL command or a stored procedure and returns a sort of cursor. Using that, you then scroll through the rows and read data. While the cursor is in use, the connection is busy and open. The data adapter, on the other hand, is a more powerful object that internally uses a command and a cursor. It retrieves and loads the data into a data container class—*DataSet* or *DataTable*. The client application can then process the data while disconnected from the source.

We'll cover container classes and data adapters in the next chapter. Let's focus on one-off commands, paying particular attention to SQL Server commands.

The *SqlCommand* Class

The *SqlCommand* class represents a SQL Server statement or stored procedure. It is a cloneable and sealed class that implements the *IDbCommand* interface. In ADO.NET 2.0, it derives from *DbCommand* which, in turn, implements the interface. A command executes in the context of a connection and, optionally, a transaction. This situation is reflected by the constructors available in the *SqlCommand* class:

```
public SqlCommand();
public SqlCommand(string);
public SqlCommand(string, SqlConnection);
public SqlCommand(string, SqlConnection, SqlTransaction);
```

The string argument denotes the text of the command to execute (and it can be a stored procedure name), whereas the *SqlConnection* parameter is the connection object to use. Finally, if specified, the *SqlTransaction* parameter represents the transactional context in which the command has to run. ADO.NET command objects never implicitly open a connection. The connection must be explicitly assigned to the command by the programmer and opened and closed with direct operations. The same holds true for the transaction.

Properties of the *SqlCommand* Class

Table 7-10 shows the attributes that make up a command in the .NET data provider for SQL Server.

Table 7-10   Properties of the _SqlCommand_ Class

Property	_IDbCommand_ Interface	Description
CommandText	Yes	Gets or sets the statement or the stored procedure name to execute.
CommandTimeout	Yes	Gets or sets the seconds to wait while trying to execute the command. The default is 30.
CommandType	Yes	Gets or sets how the _CommandText_ property is to be interpreted. Set to _Text_ by default, which means the _CommandText_ property contains the text of the command.
Connection	Yes	Gets or sets the connection object used by the command. It is null by default.
Notification		Gets or sets the _SqlNotificationRequest_ object bound to the command. _This property requires SQL Server 2005._
NotificationAutoEnlist		Indicates whether the command will automatically enlist the SQL Server 2005 notification service. _This property requires SQL Server 2005._
Parameters	Yes	Gets the collection of parameters associated with the command.
Transaction	Yes	Gets or sets the transaction within which the command executes. The transaction must be connected to the same connection as the command.
UpdatedRowSource	Yes	Gets or sets how query command results are applied to the row being updated. The value of this property is used only when the command runs within the _Update_ method of the data adapter. Acceptable values are in the _UpdateRowSource_ enumeration.

Commands can be associated with parameters, and each parameter is rendered using a provider-specific object. For the SQL Server managed provider, the parameter class is _SqlParameter_. The command type determines the role of the _CommandText_ property. The possible values for _CommandType_ are:

- **Text.**   The default setting, which indicates the property contains Transact-SQL text to execute directly.

- **StoredProcedure.**   Indicates that the content of the property is intended to be the name of a stored procedure contained in the current database.

- **TableDirect.**   Indicates the property contains a comma-separated list containing the names of the tables to access. All rows and columns of the tables will be returned. It is supported only by the data provider for OLE DB.

To execute a stored procedure, you need the following:

```
using (SqlConnection conn = new SqlConnection(ConnString))
{
    SqlCommand cmd = new SqlCommand(sprocName, conn);
    cmd.CommandType = CommandType.StoredProcedure;
    cmd.Connection.Open();
    cmd.ExecuteNonQuery();
}
```

In ADO.NET 2.0, commands have two main new features—asynchronous executors and support for notification services. We'll cover both later.

Methods of the *SqlCommand* Class

Table 7-11 details the methods available for the *CommandText* class.

Table 7-11 Methods of the *CommandText* Class

Property	IDbCommand Interface	Description
BeginExecuteNonQuery		Executes a nonquery command in a nonblocking manner. *Not supported in ADO.NET 1.x.*
BeginExecuteReader		Executes a query command in a nonblocking manner. *Not supported in ADO.NET 1.x.*
BeginExecuteXmlReader		Executes an XML query command in a nonblocking manner. *Not supported in ADO.NET 1.x.*
Cancel	Yes	Attempts to cancel the execution of the command. No exception is generated if the attempt fails.
CreateParameter	Yes	Creates a new instance of a *SqlParameter* object.
EndExecuteNonQuery		Completes a nonquery command executed asynchronously. *Not supported in ADO.NET 1.x.*
EndExecuteReader		Completes a query command executed asynchronously. *Not supported in ADO.NET 1.x.*
EndExecuteXmlReader		Completes an XML query command executed asynchronously. *Not supported in ADO.NET 1.x.*
ExecuteNonQuery	Yes	Executes a nonquery command, and returns the number of rows affected.
ExecuteReader	Yes	Executes a query, and returns a read-only cursor—the data reader—to the data.
ExecuteScalar	Yes	Executes a query, and returns the value in the 0,0 position (first column of first row) in the result set. Extra data is ignored.
ExecuteXmlReader		Executes a query that returns XML data and builds an *XmlReader* object.
Prepare	Yes	Creates a prepared version of the command in an instance of SQL Server.
ResetCommandTimeout		Resets the command timeout to the default.

Parameterized commands define their own arguments using instances of the *SqlParameter* class. Parameters have a name, value, type, direction, and size. In some cases, parameters can also be associated with a source column. A parameter is associated with a command by using the *Parameters* collection:

```
SqlParameter parm = new SqlParameter();
parm.ParameterName = "@employeeid";
parm.DbType = DbType.Int32;
parm.Direction = ParameterDirection.Input;
cmd.Parameters.Add(parm);
```

The following SQL statement uses a parameter:

```
SELECT * FROM employees WHERE employeeid=@employeeid
```

The .NET data provider for SQL Server identifies parameters by name, using the @ symbol to prefix them. In this way, the order in which parameters are associated with the command is not critical.

> **Note**   Named parameters are supported by the managed provider for Oracle but not by the providers for OLE DB and ODBC data sources. The OLE DB and ODBC data sources use positional parameters identified with the question mark (?) placeholder. The order of parameters is important.

Ways to Execute

As Table 7-11 shows, a *SqlCommand* object can be executed either synchronously or asynchronously. Let's focus on synchronous execution, which is supported on all .NET platforms. Execution can happen in four different ways: *ExecuteNonQuery*, *ExecuteReader*, *ExecuteScalar*, and *ExecuteXmlReader*. The various executors work in much the same way, but they differ in the return values. Typically, you use the *ExecuteNonQuery* method to perform update operations such as those associated with UPDATE, INSERT, and DELETE statements. In these cases, the return value is the number of rows affected by the command. For other types of statements, such as SET or CREATE, the return value is −1.

The *ExecuteReader* method is expected to work with query commands, and returns a data reader object—an instance of the *SqlDataReader* class. The data reader is a sort of read-only, forward-only cursor that client code scrolls and reads from. If you execute an update statement through *ExecuteReader*, the command is successfully executed but no affected rows are returned. We'll return to data readers in a moment.

The *ExecuteScalar* method helps considerably when you have to retrieve a single value. It works great with SELECT COUNT statements or for commands that retrieve aggregate values. If you call the method on a regular query statement, only the value in the first column of the first row is read and all the rest is discarded. Using *ExecuteScalar* results in more compact code than you'd get by executing the command and manually retrieving the value in the top-left corner of the rowset.

These three executor methods are common to all command objects. The *SqlCommand* class also features the *ExecuteXmlReader* method. It executes a command that returns XML data and builds an XML reader so that the client application can easily navigate through the XML tree. The *ExecuteXmlReader* method is ideal to use with query commands that end with the FOR XML clause or with commands that query for text fields filled with XML data. Note that while the *XmlReader* object is in use, the underlying connection is busy.

ADO.NET Data Readers

The data reader class is specific to a DBMS and works like a firehose-style cursor. It allows you to scroll through and read one or more result sets generated by a command. The data reader operates in a connected way and moves in a forward-only direction. A data reader is instantiated during the execution of the *ExecuteReader* method. The results are stored in a buffer located on the client and are made available to the reader.

By using the data reader object, you access data one record at a time as soon as it becomes available. An approach based on the data reader is effective both in terms of system overhead and performance. Only one record is cached at any time, and there's no wait time to have the entire result set loaded in memory.

Table 7-12 shows the properties of the *SqlDataReader* class—that is, the data reader class for SQL Server.

Table 7-12   Properties of the *SqlDataReader* Class

Property	Description
Depth	Indicates the depth of nesting for the current row. For the *SqlDataReader* class, it always returns 0.
FieldCount	Gets the number of columns in the current row.
HasRows	Gets a value that indicates whether the data reader contains one or more rows. *Not supported in ADO.NET 1.0.*
IsClosed	Gets a value that indicates whether the data reader is closed.
Item	Indexer property, gets the value of a column in the original format.
RecordsAffected	Gets the number of rows modified by the execution of a batch command.

The *Depth* property is meant to indicate the level of nesting for the current row. The depth of the outermost table is always 0; the depth of inner tables grows by one. Most data readers, including the *SqlDataReader* and *OracleDataReader* classes, do not support multiple levels of nesting so that the *Depth* property always returns 0.

The *RecordsAffected* property is not set until all rows are read and the data reader is closed. The default value of *RecordsAffected* is –1. Note that *IsClosed* and *RecordsAffected* are the only properties you can invoke on a closed data reader.

Table 7-13 lists the methods of the SQL Server data reader class.

Table 7-13   Methods of the *SqlDataReader* Class

Methods	Description
Close	Closes the reader object. Note that closing the reader does not automatically close the underlying connection.
GetBoolean	Gets the value of the specified column as a Boolean.
GetByte	Gets the value of the specified column as a byte.
GetBytes	Reads a stream of bytes from the specified column into a buffer. You can specify an offset both for reading and writing.
GetChar	Gets the value of the specified column as a single character.
GetChars	Reads a stream of characters from the specified column into a buffer. You can specify an offset both for reading and writing.
GetDataTypeName	Gets the name of the back-end data type in the specified column.
GetDateTime	Gets the value of the specified column as a *DateTime* object.
GetDecimal	Gets the value of the specified column as a decimal.
GetDouble	Gets the value of the specified column as a double-precision floating-point number.
GetFieldType	Gets the *Type* object for the data in the specified column.
GetFloat	Gets the value of the specified column as a single-precision floating-point number.
GetGuid	Gets the value of the specified column as a globally unique identifier (GUID).
GetInt16	Gets the value of the specified column as a 16-bit integer.
GetInt32	Gets the value of the specified column as a 32-bit integer.
GetInt64	Gets the value of the specified column as a 64-bit integer.
GetName	Gets the name of the specified column.
GetOrdinal	Given the name of the column, returns its ordinal number.
GetSchemaTable	Returns a *DataTable* object that describes the metadata for the columns managed by the reader.
GetString	Gets the value of the specified column as a string.
GetValue	Gets the value of the specified column in its original format.
GetValues	Copies the values of all columns in the supplied array of objects.
IsDbNull	Indicates whether the column contains null values. The type for a null column is *System.DBNull*.
NextResult	Moves the data reader pointer to the beginning of the next result set, if any.
Read	Moves the data reader pointer to the next record, if any.

The SQL Server data reader also features a variety of other DBMS-specific get methods. They include methods such as *GetSqlDouble*, *GetSqlMoney*, *GetSqlDecimal*, and so on. The difference between the *GetXXX* and *GetSqlXXX* methods is in the return type. With the *GetXXX* methods, a base .NET Framework type is returned; with the *GetSqlXXX* methods, a .NET Framework wrapper for a SQL Server type is returned—such as *SqlDouble*, *SqlMoney*, or *SqlDecimal*. The SQL Server types belong to the *SqlDbType* enumeration.

All the *GetXXX* methods that return a value from a column identify the column through a 0-based index. Note that the methods don't even attempt a conversion; they simply return data as is and just make a cast to the specified type. If the actual value and the type are not compatible, an exception is thrown.

> **Note**   The *GetBytes* method is useful to read large fields one step at a time. However, the method can also be used to obtain the length in bytes of the data in the column. To get this information, pass a buffer that is a null reference and the return value of the method will contain the length.

Reading Data with the Data Reader

The key thing to remember when using a data reader is that you're working while connected. The data reader represents the fastest way to read data out of a source, but you should read your data as soon as possible and then release the connection. One row is available at a time, and you must move through the result set by using the *Read* method. The following code snippet illustrates the typical loop you implement to read all the records of a query:

```
using (SqlConnection conn = new SqlConnection(connString))
{
    string cmdText = "SELECT * FROM customers";
    SqlCommand cmd = new SqlCommand(cmdText, conn);
    cmd.Connection.Open();
    SqlDataReader reader = cmd.ExecuteReader();
    while (reader.Read())
        CustomerList.Items.Add(reader["companyname"].ToString());
    reader.Close();
}
```

You have no need to explicitly move the pointer ahead and no need to check for the end of the file. The *Read* method returns *false* if there are no more records to read. A data reader is great if you need to consume data by processing the records in some way. If you need to cache values for later use, the data reader is not appropriate. You need a container object in this case, as we'll see in Chapter 8.

> **Note**   Although accessing row fields by name is easy to read and understand, it is not the
> fastest approach. Internally, in fact, the data reader needs to resolve the name to a 0-based
> index. If you provide the index directly, you get slightly faster code:
>
> ```
> const int Customers_CustomerID = 0;
> ...
> Response.Write(reader[Customers_CustomerID].ToString());
> ```
>
> The preceding code shows that using constants turns out to be a good compromise between
> speed and readability.

Command Behaviors

When calling the *ExecuteReader* method on a command object—on any command object,
regardless of the underlying DBMS—you can require a particular working mode known as a
command behavior. *ExecuteReader* has a second overload that takes an argument of type
CommandBehavior:

```
cmd.ExecuteReader(CommandBehavior.CloseConnection);
```

CommandBehavior is an enumeration. Its values are listed in Table 7-14.

Table 7-14   Command Behaviors for the Data Reader

Behavior	Description
CloseConnection	Automatically closes the connection when the data reader is closed.
Default	No special behavior is required. Setting this option is functionally equivalent to calling *ExecuteReader* without parameters.
KeyInfo	The query returns only column metadata and primary key information. The query is executed without any locking on the selected rows.
SchemaOnly	The query returns only column metadata and does not put any lock on the database rows.
SequentialAccess	Enables the reader to load data as a sequential stream. This behavior works in conjunction with methods such as *GetBytes* and *GetChars*, which can be used to read bytes or characters having a limited buffer size for the data being returned.
SingleResult	The query is expected to return only the first result set.
SingleRow	The query is expected to return a single row.

The sequential access mode applies to all columns in the returned result set. This means you
can access columns only in the order in which they appear in the result set. For example, you
cannot read column 2 before column 1. More exactly, if you read or move past a given location, you can no longer read or move back. Combined with the *GetBytes* method, sequential
access can be helpful in cases in which you must read BLOBs with a limited buffer.

> **Note** You can also specify *SingleRow* when executing queries that are expected to return multiple result sets. In this case, all the generated result sets are correctly returned, but each result set has a single row. *SingleRow* and *SingleResult* serve the purpose of letting the underlying provider machinery know about the expected results so that some internal optimization can optionally be made.

Closing the Reader

The data reader is not a publicly creatable object. It does have a constructor, but not one that is callable from within user applications. The data reader constructor is marked as internal and can be invoked only from classes defined in the same assembly—*System.Data*. The data reader is implicitly instantiated when the *ExecuteReader* method is called. Opening and closing the reader are operations distinct from instantiation and must be explicitly invoked by the application. The *Read* method advances the internal pointer to the next readable record in the current result set. The *Read* method returns a Boolean value indicating whether more records can be read. While records are being read, the connection is busy and no operation—other than closing—can be performed on the connection object.

The data reader and the connection are distinct objects and should be managed and closed independently. Both objects provide a *Close* method that should be called twice—once on the data reader (first) and once on the connection. When the *CloseConnection* behavior is required, closing the data reader also closes the underlying connection. In addition, the data reader's *Close* method fills in the values for any command output parameters and sets the *RecordsAffected* property.

> **Tip** Because of the extra work *Close* always performs on a data reader class, closing a reader with success can sometimes be expensive, especially in cases of long-running and complicated queries. In situations in which you need to squeeze out every bit of performance, and where the return values and number of records affected are not significant, you can invoke the *Cancel* method of the associated *SqlCommand* object instead of closing the reader. *Cancel* aborts the operation and closes the reader faster. Aside from this, you're still responsible for properly closing the underlying connection.

Accessing Multiple Result Sets

Depending on the syntax of the query, multiple result sets can be returned. By default, the data reader is positioned on the first of them. You use the *Read* method to scroll through the various records in the current result set. When the last record is found, the *Read* method returns *false* and does not advance further. To move to the next result set, you should use the *NextResult* method. The method returns *false* if there are no more result sets to read. The following code shows how to access all records in all returned result sets:

```
using (SqlConnection conn = new SqlConnection(connString))
{
    string cmdText = Query.Text;
```

```
SqlCommand cmd = new SqlCommand(cmdText, conn);
cmd.Connection.Open();
SqlDataReader reader = cmd.ExecuteReader();

do {
    // Move through the first result set
    while (reader.Read())
        sb.AppendFormat("{0}, {1}<br/>", reader[0], reader[1]);

    // Separate result sets
    sb.Append("<hr />");
} while (reader.NextResult());

    reader.Close();
}

// Display results in the page
Results.Text = sb.ToString();
```

Figure 7-7 shows the output generated by the sample page based on this code.

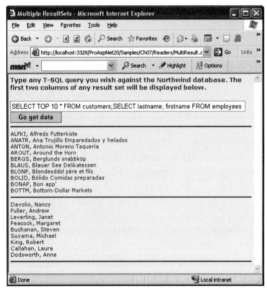

Figure 7-7   Processing multiple result sets.

> **Note**   The .NET Framework version 1.1 extends the programming interface of data readers by adding the *HasRows* method, which returns a Boolean value indicating whether there are more rows to read. However, the method does not tell anything about the number of rows available. Similarly, there is no method or trick for knowing in advance how many result sets have been returned.

Asynchronous Commands

A database operation is normally a synchronous operation—the caller regains control of the application only after the interaction with the database is completed. This approach can lead to performance and scalability issues in lengthy operations—a common scenario when you interact with a DBMS. The .NET Framework 1.x supports asynchronous operations, but the model is implemented around user-level code. In other words, you can implement your own procedures asynchronously and connect to databases and run commands as part of the code, but connection management and command execution remain atomic operations that execute synchronously.

The .NET data provider for SQL Server in ADO.NET 2.0 provides true asynchronous support for executing commands. This offers a performance advantage because you can perform other actions until the command completes. However, this is not the only benefit. The support for asynchronous operations is built into the *SqlCommand* class and is limited to executing non-query commands and getting a reader or an XML reader. You can use three different approaches to build commands that work asynchronously: nonblocking, polling, and callback.

Setting Up Asynchronous Commands

To enable asynchronous commands, you must set the new *Async* attribute to *true* in the connection string. You'll receive an exception if any of the asynchronous methods are called over a connection that doesn't have asynchronous capabilities explicitly turned on. Enabling asynchronous commands does have a cost in terms of overall performance; for this reason, you're better off using the *Async* keyword only with connection objects that execute asynchronous operations only.

If you need both synchronous and asynchronous commands, employ different connections wherever possible. Note, though, that you can still call synchronous methods over connections enabled to support asynchronous operations. However, you'll only end up using more resources than needed and experience a performance degradation.

> **Note**   Asynchronous commands are not implemented by creating a new thread and blocking execution on it. Among other things, ADO.NET is not thread-safe and blocking threads would be a serious performance hit. When asynchronous commands are enabled, ADO.NET opens the TCP socket to the database in overlapped mode and binds it to the I/O completion port. In light of this, synchronous operations execute as the emulation of asynchronous operations, and this explains why they're more expensive than asynchronous-enabled connections.

Nonblocking Commands

Nonblocking commands are the simplest case of asynchronous commands. The code starts the operation and continues executing other unrelated methods; then it comes back to get the results. Whatever the model of choice happens to be, the first step of an asynchronous command is calling one of the *BeginExecuteXXX* methods. For example, if you want to execute a reading command, you call *BeginExecuteReader*:

```
// Start a non-blocking execution
IAsyncResult iar = cmd.BeginExecuteReader();

// Do something else meanwhile
...

// Block the execution until done
SqlDataReader reader = cmd.EndExecuteReader(iar);

// Process data here ...
ProcessData(reader);
```

The *BeginExecuteReader* function returns an *IAsyncResult* object you will use later to complete the call. Note that *EndExecuteReader* is called to finish the operation and will block execution until the ongoing command terminates. The *EndExecuteReader* function will automatically sync up the command with the rest of the application, blocking the code whenever the results of the command are not ready.

As an alternative to the aforementioned approach, the client code might want to check the status of a running asynchronous operation and poll for completion. The following code illustrates the polling option with a query statement:

```
// Executes a query statement
IAsyncResult iar = cmd.BeginExecuteReader();
do {
    // Do something here
} while (!iar.IsCompleted);

// Sync up
SqlDataReader reader = cmd.EndExecuteReader(iar);
ProcessData(reader);
```

It is important to note that if *iar.IsCompleted* returns *true*, the *EndExecuteReader* method will not block the application.

The third option for nonblocking commands has the client code start the database operation and continue without waiting. Later on, when the operation is done, it receives a call. In this case, you pass a delegate to a *BeginExecuteXXX* method and any information that constitutes the state of the particular call. The state is any information you want to pass to the callback function. In this case, you pass the command object:

```
// Begin executing the command
IAsyncResult ar = cmd.BeginExecuteReader(
    new AsyncCallback(ProcessData), cmd);
```

After initiating the asynchronous operation, you can forget about it and do any other work. The specified callback function is invoked at the end of the operation. The callback must have the following layout:

```
public void ProcessData(IAsyncResult ar)
{
    // Retrieve the context of the call
    SqlCommand cmd = (SqlCommand) iar.AsyncState;

    // Complete the async operation
    SqlDataReader reader = cmd.EndExecuteReader(iar);
    ...
}
```

The context of the call you specified as the second argument to *BeingExecuteReader* is packed in the *AsyncState* property of the *IAsyncResult* object.

> **Note** The callback will be called in a thread-pool thread, which is likely to be different from the thread that initiated the operation. Proper thread synchronization might be needed, depending on the application. This also poses a problem with the user interface of applications, especially Windows Forms applications. Ensuring that the UI is refreshed in the right thread is up to you. Windows Forms controls and forms provide mechanisms for deciding if the correct thread is currently executing and for accessing the correct thread if it isn't. You should consult the MSDN documentation or a good Windows Forms programming book for more information regarding multithreaded Windows Forms programming. Note that if you fail to use the threading model correctly, your application will almost certainly lock up and quite possibly even crash.

Executing Parallel Commands in an ASP.NET Page

Having asynchronous commands available is not necessarily a good reason for using them without due forethought. Let's examine a couple of scenarios where asynchronous commands are useful for building better Web pages. The first scenario we'll consider is the execution of multiple SQL statements in parallel, either against the same or different database servers.

Imagine that your page displays information about a particular customer—both personal and accounting data. The former block of data comes from the client's database; the latter is excerpted from the accounting database. You can fire both queries at the same time and have them execute in parallel on distinct machines—thus benefiting from true parallelism. Here's an example:

```
protected void QueryButton_Click(object sender, EventArgs e)
{
  string custID = CustomerList.SelectedValue;
```

```
using (SqlConnection conn1 = new SqlConnection(ConnString1))
using (SqlConnection conn2 = new SqlConnection(ConnString2))
{
  // Fire the first command: get customer info
  SqlCommand cmd1 = new SqlCommand(CustomerInfoCmd, conn1);
  cmd1.Parameters.Add("@customerid", SqlDbType.Char, 5).Value = custID;
  conn1.Open();
  IAsyncResult arCustomerInfo = cmd1.BeginExecuteReader();

  // Fire the second command: get order info
  SqlCommand cmd2 = new SqlCommand(CustomerOrderHistory, conn2);
  cmd2.CommandType = CommandType.StoredProcedure;
  cmd2.Parameters.Add("@customerid", SqlDbType.Char, 5).Value = custID;
  conn2.Open();
  IAsyncResult arOrdersInfo = cmd2.BeginExecuteReader();

  // Prepare wait objects to sync up
  WaitHandle[] handles = new WaitHandle[2];
  handles[0] = arCustomerInfo.AsyncWaitHandle;
  handles[1] = arOrdersInfo.AsyncWaitHandle;
  SqlDataReader reader;

  // Wait for all commands to terminate (no longer than 5 secs)
  for (int i=0; i<2; i++)
  {
    StringBuilder builder = new StringBuilder();
    int index = WaitHandle.WaitAny(handles, 5000, false);
        if (index == WaitHandle.WaitTimeout)
              throw new Exception("Timeout expired");

    if (index == 0) {     // Customer info
      reader = cmd1.EndExecuteReader(arCustomerInfo);
      if (!reader.Read())
        continue;

      builder.AppendFormat("{0}<br>", reader["companyname"]);
      builder.AppendFormat("{0}<br>", reader["address"]);
      builder.AppendFormat("{0}<br>", reader["country"]);
      Info.Text = builder.ToString();
      reader.Close();
    }
    if (index == 1) {     // Orders info
      reader = cmd2.EndExecuteReader(arOrdersInfo);
      gridOrders.DataSource = reader;
      gridOrders.DataBind();
      reader.Close();
    }
  }
}
}
```

The page fires the two commands and then sits waiting for the first command to terminate. The *AsyncWaitHandle* object of each *IAsyncResult* is stored in an array and passed to the *WaitAny* method of the *WaitHandle* class. *WaitAny* signals out when any of the commands terminates, but the surrounding *for* statement reiterates the wait until all pending commands terminate. You could have more easily opted for the *WaitAll* method. In this case, though, you can process results as they become available. This fact ensures a performance gain, especially for long-running stored procedures.

> **Note**   You can implement the same behavior in ADO.NET 1.x without asynchronous commands by simply assigning each command to a different thread—either a user-defined one or one from the thread pool. In this case, though, each command would have blocked a thread. Blocking threads is fine for client-side applications, but it might compromise scalability in server-side applications such as ASP.NET applications.

Nonblocking Data-Driven ASP.NET Pages

Imagine a data-driven ASP.NET page that employs long-running, synchronous commands. The more the page is requested, the more likely it is that a large share of system threads are blocked while waiting for the database to return results. The paradoxical effect of this is that the Web server is virtually idle (with almost no CPU and network usage) but can't accept new requests because it has very few threads available.

To address this problem, since version 1.0 ASP.NET supports asynchronous HTTP handlers—that is, a special breed of page classes that implement the *IHttpAsyncHandler* interface instead of *IHttpHandler*. Asynchronous HTTP handlers take care of a request and produce a response in an asynchronous manner. In the .NET Framework 2.0, asynchronous handlers can combine with asynchronous commands to boost data-driven pages.

The *IHttpAsyncHandler* interface counts *BeginProcessRequest* and *EndProcessRequest* methods. In the former method, you connect to the database and kick off the query. *BeginProcessRequest* receives a callback function directly from ASP.NET; the same callback is used to detect the completion of the asynchronous command.

When *BeginProcessRequest* returns, the page gives the control back to ASP.NET as if it was served. ASP.NET is now free to reuse the thread to process another request while the database server proceeds. When the query is complete, the signaling mechanism ends up invoking the *EndProcessRequest* method, although not necessarily on the same thread as the rest of the page, so to speak. The *EndProcessRequest* method is where you simply collect the data and render the page out.

We'll cover asynchronous handlers in my other book on this subject, *Programming Microsoft ASP.NET 2.0 Applications: Advanced Topics*.

> **Note**   A fair number of methods work synchronously even in the context of asynchronous commands. The list includes *BeginXXX* methods and most methods of the data reader class, such as *GetXXX* methods *Read*, *Close*, and *Dispose*.

Working with Transactions

In ADO.NET, you can choose between two types of transactions: local and distributed. A local transaction involves a single resource—typically, the database you're connected to. You begin the transaction, you attach one or more commands to its context, and decide whether the whole operation was successful or whether it failed. The transaction is then committed or rolled back accordingly. This approach is functionally similar to simply running a SQL stored procedure that groups a few commands under the same transaction. Using ADO.NET code makes it more flexible but doesn't change the final effect.

A distributed transaction spans multiple heterogeneous resources and ensures that if the entire transaction is committed or rolled back, all modifications made at the various steps are committed or rolled back as well. A distributed transaction requires a Transaction Processing (TP) monitor. The Distributed Transaction Coordinator (DTC) is the TP monitor for Microsoft Windows 2000 and later.

In ADO.NET 1.x, you manage a local transaction through a bunch of database-specific transaction objects—for example, *SqlTransaction* for SQL Server transactions. You begin the transaction, associate commands to it, and decide the outcome. For distributed transactions, you need Enterprise Services and serviced components. You can enlist database connections to Enterprise Services DTC managed transactions by using the aforementioned *EnlistDistributedTransaction* method on the connection class.

In ADO.NET 2.0, local and distributed transactions can also be managed (more easily, actually) through the new classes defined in the *System.Transactions* namespace—specifically, with the *TransactionScope* class.

Managing Local Transactions as in ADO.NET 1.x

You start a new local transaction through the *BeginTransaction* method of the connection class. You can give the transaction a name and an isolation level. The method maps to the SQL Server implementation of *BEGIN TRANSACTION*. The following code snippet shows the typical flow of a transactional piece of code:

```
SqlTransaction tran;
tran = conn.BeginTransaction();
SqlCommand cmd1 = new SqlCommand(cmdText1);
cmd1.Connection = conn;
cmd1.Transaction = tran;
...
SqlCommand cmd2 = new SqlCommand(cmdText2);
cmd2.Connection = conn;
cmd2.Transaction = tran;
...
try {
  cmd1.ExecuteNonQuery();
  cmd2.ExecuteNonQuery();
```

```
  tran.Commit();
}
catch {
  tran.Rollback();
}
finally {
  conn.Close();
}
```

The newly created transaction object operates on the same connection represented by the connection object you used to create it. To add commands to the transaction, you set the *Transaction* property of command objects. Note that if you set the *Transaction* property of a command to a transaction object that is not connected to the same connection, an exception will be thrown as you attempt to execute a statement. Once all the commands have terminated, you call the *Commit* method of the transaction object to complete the transaction, or you call the *Rollback* method to cancel the transaction and undo all changes.

The isolation level of a transaction indicates the locking behavior for the connection. Common values are: *ReadCommitted* (default), *ReadUncommitted*, *RepeatableRead*, and *Serializable*. Imagine a situation in which one transaction changes a value that a second transaction might need to read. *ReadCommitted* locks the row and prevents the second transaction from reading until the change is committed. *ReadUncommitted* doesn't hold locks, thus improving the overall performance. In doing so, though, it allows the second transaction to read a modified row before the original change is committed or rolled back. This is a "dirty read" because if the first transaction rolls the change back, the read value is invalid and there's nothing you can do about it. (Of course, you set *ReadUncommitted* only if dirty reads are not a problem in your scenario.) Note also that disallowing dirty reads also decreases overall system concurrency.

Imagine one transaction reads a committed row; next, another transaction modifies or deletes the row and commits the change. At this point, if the first transaction attempts to read the row again, it will obtain different results. To prevent this, you set the isolation level to *RepeatableRead*, which prevents further updates and dirty reads but not other operations that can generate phantom rows. Imagine that a transaction runs a query; next, another transaction does something that modifies the results of the previous query. When the first transaction ends, it returns an inconsistent result to the client. The *Serializable* level prevents concurrent transactions from updating or inserting rows until a given transaction is complete. Table 7-15 summarizes the isolation levels.

Table 7-15   Isolation Levels

Level	Dirty Reads	Nonrepeatable	Phantom Rows
ReadUncommitted	Yes	Yes	Yes
ReadCommitted	No	Yes	Yes
RepeatableRead	No	No	Yes
Serializable	No	No	No

The highest isolation level, *Serializable*, provides a high degree of protection against concurrent transactions, but it requires that each transaction complete before any other transaction is allowed to work on the database.

The isolation level can be changed at any time and remains in effect until explicitly changed. If changed during a transaction, the server is expected to apply the new locking level to all statements remaining.

You terminate a transaction explicitly by using the *Commit* or *Rollback* method. The *SqlTransaction* class supports named savepoints in the transaction that can be used to roll back a portion of the transaction. Named savepoints exploit a specific SQL Server feature—the SAVE TRANSACTION statement.

This approach to local transactions is only possible in ADO.NET 1.x and is, of course, fully supported in ADO.NET 2.0. Let's explore alternative approaches.

Introducing the *TransactionScope* Object

The preceding code based on *BeginTransaction* ties you to a specific database and requires you to start a new transaction to wrap a few database commands. What if you need to work with distinct databases and then, say, send a message to a message queue? In ADO.NET 1.x, you typically create a distributed transaction in Enterprise Services. In ADO.NET 2.0, you can perform both local and distributed transactions through a new object—*TransactionScope*. Here's the code:

```
using (TransactionScope ts = new TransactionScope())
{
  using (SqlConnection conn = new SqlConnection(ConnString))
  {
    SqlCommand cmd = new SqlCommand(cmdText, conn);
    cmd.Connection.Open();
    try {
      cmd.ExecuteNonQuery();
    }
    catch (SqlException ex) {
      // Error handling code goes here
      lblMessage.Text = ex.Message;
    }
  }

  // Must call to complete; otherwise abort
  ts.Complete();
}
```

The connection object is defined within the scope of the transaction, so it automatically participates in the transaction. The only thing left to do is commit the transaction, which you do by placing a call to the method *Complete*. If you omit that call, the transaction fails and rolls back no matter what really happened with the command or commands. Needless to say, any exceptions will abort the transaction.

> **Important**   You must guarantee that the *TransactionScope* object will be disposed of. By design, the transaction scope commits or rolls back on disposal. Waiting for the garbage collector to kick in and dispose of the transaction scope can be expensive because distributed transactions have a one-minute timeout by default. Keeping multiple databases locked for up to a minute is an excellent scalability killer. Calling *TransactionScope.Dispose* manually in the code might not be enough, as it won't be called in case of exceptions. You should either opt for a *using* statement or a *try/catch/finally* block.

Distributed Transactions with *TransactionScope*

Let's consider a transaction that includes operations on different databases—the Northwind database of SQL Server 2000 and a custom *MyData.mdf* file managed through SQL Server 2005 Express. The file is available in the *app_Data* directory of the sample project. The sample table we're interested in here can be created with the following command:

```
CREATE TABLE Numbers (ID int, Text varchar(50))
```

You create a unique and all-encompassing *TransactionScope* instance and run the various commands, even on different connections. You track the outcome of the various operations and call *Complete* if all went fine. Here's an example:

```
bool canCommit = true;

using (TransactionScope ts = new TransactionScope())
{
    // ************************************************************
    // Update Northwind on SQL Server 2000
    using (SqlConnection conn = new SqlConnection(ConnString))
    {
        SqlCommand cmd = new SqlCommand(UpdateCmd, conn);
        cmd.Connection.Open();
        try {
            cmd.ExecuteNonQuery();
        }
        catch (SqlException ex) {
            canCommit &= false;
        }
    }

    // ************************************************************
    // Update Numbers on SQL Server 2005
    using (SqlConnection conn = new SqlConnection(ConnString05))
    {
        SqlCommand cmd = new SqlCommand(InsertCmd, conn);
        cmd.Connection.Open();
        try {
            cmd.ExecuteNonQuery();
        }
        catch (SqlException ex) {
            canCommit &= false;
```

```
        }
    }

    // Must call to complete; otherwise abort
    if (canCommit)
        ts.Complete();
}
```

If an error occurs, say, on the SQL Server 2005 database, any changes successfully entered on the SQL Server 2000 database are automatically rolled back.

TransactionScope is a convenience class that supports the dispose pattern, and internally it simply sets the current transaction, plus it has some state to track scoping. By wrapping everything in a *TransactionScope* object, you're pretty much done, as the object takes care of everything else for you. For example, it determines whether you need a local or distributed transaction, enlists any necessary distributed resources, and proceeds with local processing otherwise. As the code reaches a point where it won't be running locally, *TransactionScope* escalates to DTC as appropriate.

Which objects can be enlisted with a transaction? Anything that implements the required interface—*ITransaction*—can be enlisted. ADO.NET 2.0 ships all standard data providers with support for *System.Transactions*. MSMQ works in compatibility mode.

When some code invokes the *Complete* method, it indicates that all operations in the scope are completed successfully. Note that the method does not physically terminate the distributed transaction, as the commit operation will still happen on *TransactionScope* disposal. However, after calling the method, you can no longer use the distributed transaction.

> **Note**   There are a number of differences between *System.Transactions* and Enterprise Services as far as distributed transactions are concerned. First, *System.Transactions* is a transaction framework designed specifically for the managed environment, so it fits more naturally into .NET applications. Of course, internally the classes of the *System.Transactions* namespace might end up delegating some work to DTC and COM+, but that is nothing more than an implementation detail. Another important difference between the two is the existence of a lightweight transaction manager implemented on the managed side that allows for a number of optimizations, including presenting several enlistments as only one for DTC and support for promotable transactions.

Enlisting in a Distributed Transaction in ADO.NET 1.x

If your code uses *TransactionScope*, there's no need for a connection object to explicitly enlist in a transaction. However, if needed, the *EnlistTransaction* method provides you with exactly that capability.

Manually enlisting connections into distributed transactions is a feature already available in ADO.NET 1.1 through the *EnlistDistributedTransaction* method of the connection class. The method manually enlists the connection into a transaction being managed by the Enterprise Services DTC. In this case, you work with a distributed transaction that is defined elsewhere and takes direct advantage of the DTC.

> **Note**   *EnlistDistributedTransaction* is useful when you have pooled business objects with an open connection. In this case, enlistment occurs only when the connection is opened. If the object participates in multiple transactions, the connection for that object is not reopened and therefore has no way to automatically enlist in new transactions. In this case, you can disable automatic transaction enlistment and enlist the connection explicitly by using *EnlistDistributed-Transaction*.

SQL Server 2005–Specific Enhancements

The .NET data provider for SQL Server also has new features that are tied to the enhancements in SQL Server 2005. SQL Server 2005 introduces significant enhancements in various areas, including data-type support, query dependency and notification, and multiple active result sets (MARS).

Support for CLR Types

SQL Server 2005 supports any CLR types. In addition to default types, you can store into and retrieve from SQL Server tables any object that is a valid .NET type. This includes both system types—such as a *Point*—and user-defined classes. This extended set of capabilities is reflected in the ADO.NET 2.0 provider for SQL Server.

CLR types appear as objects to the data reader, and parameters to commands can be instances of CLR types. The following code snippet demonstrates how to retrieve a value from the MyCustomers table that corresponds to an instance of user-defined *Customer* class:

```
string cmdText = "SELECT CustomerData FROM MyCustomers";
SqlConnection conn = new SqlConnection(connStr);
SqlCommand cmd = new SqlCommand(cmdText, conn);
cmd.Connection.Open();
SqlDataReader reader = cmd.ExecuteReader();
while(reader.Read())
{
  Customer cust = (Customer) reader[0];
  // Do some work
}
cmd.Connection.Close();
```

A SQL Server 2005 user-defined type is stored as a binary stream of bytes. The *get* accessor of the data reader gets the bytes and deserializes them to a valid instance of the original class. The reverse process (serialization) takes place when a user-defined object is placed in a SQL Server column.

Support for XML as a Native Type

SQL Server 2005 natively supports the XML data type, which means you can store XML data in columns. At first glance, this feature seems to be nothing new because XML data is plain text and to store XML data in a column you only need the column to accept text. Native XML support in SQL Server 2005, however, means something different—you can declare the type of a given column as native XML, not plain text adapted to indicate markup text.

In ADO.NET 1.x, the *ExecuteXmlReader* method allows you to process the results of a query as an XML stream. The method builds an *XmlTextReader* object on top of the data coming from SQL Server. Therefore, for the method to work, the entire result set must be XML. Scenarios in which this method is useful include when the FOR XML clause is appended or when you query for a scalar value that happens to be XML text.

In ADO.NET 2.0, when SQL Server 2005 is up and running, you can obtain an *XmlTextReader* object for each table cell (row, column) whose type is XML. You obtain a *SqlDataReader* object and have it return XML to you using the new *GetSqlXml* method. The following code snippet provides a useful example:

```
string cmdText = " SELECT * FROM MyCustomers";
SqlCommand cmd = new SqlCommand(cmdText, conn);
SqlDataReader reader = cmd.ExecuteReader();
while(reader.Read())
{
  // Assume that field #3 contains XML data

  // Get data and do some work
  SqlXml xml = reader.GetSqlXml(3);
  ProcessData(xml.Value);
}
```

The *SqlXml* class represents the XML data type. The *Value* property of the class returns the XML text as a string.

SQL Notifications and Dependencies

Applications that display volatile data or maintain a cache would benefit from friendly server notification whenever their data changes. SQL Server 2005 offers this feature—it notifies client applications about dynamic changes in the result set generated by a given query. Suppose your application manages the results of a query. If you register for a notification, your application is informed if something happens at the SQL Server level that modifies the result set generated by that query. This means that if a record originally selected by your query is updated or deleted, or if a new record is added that meets the criteria of the query, you're notified. Note, though, that the notification reaches your application only if it is still up and running—which poses a clear issue with ASP.NET pages. But let's move forward one step at a time.

The SQL Server provider in ADO.NET 2.0 provides two ways to use this notification feature and two related classes—*SqlDependency* and *SqlNotificationRequest*. *SqlNotificationRequest* is a lower-level class that exposes server-side functionality, allowing you to execute a command with a notification request. When a T-SQL statement is executed in SQL Server 2005, the notification mechanism keeps track of the query, and if it detects a change that might cause the result set to change, it sends a message to a queue. A queue is a new SQL Server 2005 database object that you create and manage with a new set of T-SQL statements. How the queue is polled and how the message is interpreted is strictly application-specific.

The *SqlDependency* class provides a high-level abstraction of the notification mechanism and allows you to set an application-level dependency on the query so that changes in the server can be immediately communicated to the client application through an event. The following code binds a command to a SQL dependency:

```
SqlCommand cmd = new SqlCommand("SELECT * FROM Employees", conn);
SqlDependency dep = new SqlDependency(cmd);
dep.OnChange += new OnChangeEventHandler(OnDependencyChanged);
SqlDataReader reader = cmd.ExecuteReader();
```

The *OnChange* event on the *SqlDependency* class fires whenever the class detects a change that affects the result set of the command. Here's a typical handler:

```
void OnDependencyChanged(object sender, SqlNotificationsEventArgs e)
{
    ...
}
```

When the underlying machinery detects a change, it fires the event to the application.

As mentioned, using notifications in this way is not particularly interesting from an ASP.NET perspective because the page returns immediately after running the query. However, the caching API of ASP.NET 2.0 provides a similar feature that automatically tracks the results of a query via the ASP.NET cache. What you have in ASP.NET 2.0 is a custom type of cache dependency that monitors the results of a query for both SQL Server 2000 and SQL Server 2005, although in radically different ways. You create a dependency on a command or a table, and place it in the ASP.NET *Cache* object. The cache item will be invalidated as soon as a change in the monitored command or table is detected. If a SQL Server 2000 instance is involved, you can detect changes to only one of the tables touched by the query; if SQL Server 2005 is involved, you get finer control and can track changes to the result set of the query. We'll cover ASP.NET caching in great detail in Chapter 14.

Multiple Active Result Sets

Version 1.x of the SQL Server managed provider, along with the SQL Server ODBC driver, supports only one active result set per connection. The (unmanaged) OLE DB provider and the outermost ADO library appear to support multiple active result sets, but this is an illusion. In OLE DB, the effect is obtained by opening additional and nonpooled connections.

In SQL Server 2005, the multiple active result set (MARS) feature is natively implemented and allows an application to have more than one *SqlDataReader* open on a connection, each started from a separate command. Having more than one data reader open on a single connection offers a potential performance improvement because multiple readers are much less expensive than multiple connections. At the same time, MARS adds some hidden per-operation costs that are a result of its implementation. Considering the tradeoffs and making a thoughtful decision is up to you.

The canonical use of MARS is when you get a data reader to walk through a result set while using another command on the same connection to issue update statements to the database. The following code demonstrates a sample page that walks through a data reader and updates the current record using a second command. If you try this approach in ADO.NET 1.x, or in ADO.NET 2.0 with MARS disabled, you get an exception complaining that the data reader associated with this connection is open and should be closed first.

```
using (SqlConnection conn = new SqlConnection(connString))
{
  SqlCommand cmd1 = new SqlCommand("SELECT * FROM employees", conn);
  cmd1.Connection.Open();
  SqlDataReader reader = cmd1.ExecuteReader();

  // Walks the data reader
  while (reader.Read())
  {
    // Reverses the first name
    string firstNameReversed = reader["firstname"].ToString();
    char[] buf = firstNameReversed.ToCharArray();
    Array.Reverse(buf);
    firstNameReversed = new string(buf);

    // Set the new first name on the same connection
    int id = (int)reader["employeeid"];
    SqlCommand cmd2 = new SqlCommand(
           "UPDATE employees SET firstname=@newFirstName WHERE
            employeeid=@empID", conn);
    cmd2.Parameters.AddWithValue("@newFirstName", firstNameReversed);
    cmd2.Parameters.AddWithValue("empID", id);
    cmd2.ExecuteNonQuery();
  }
  reader.Close();

  // Get a new reader to refresh the UI
  grid.DataSource = cmd1.ExecuteReader();
  grid.DataBind();
  cmd1.Connection.Close();
}
```

Note that for MARS to work, you must use a distinct *SqlCommand* object, as shown in the following code. If you use a third command object to re-execute the query to get up-to-date records, there's no need to close the reader explicitly.

Another big benefit of MARS is that, if you're engaged in a transaction, it lets you execute code in the same isolation-level scope of the original connection. You won't get this benefit if you open a second connection under the covers.

In ADO.NET 2.0, the MARS feature is enabled by default when SQL Server 2005 is the database server. To disable MARS, you set the *MultipleActiveResultSets* attribute to *false* in the connection string. There are some hidden costs associated with MARS. First, MARS requires the continuous creation of *SqlCommand* objects. To deal with this issue, a pool of command objects is constituted and maintained. Second, there is a cost in the network layer as a result of multiplexing the I/O stream of data. Most of these costs are structural, and you should not expect a great performance improvement by disabling the MARS feature. So what's the purpose of the *MultipleActiveResultSets* attribute? The attribute appears mostly for backward compatibility. In this way, applications that expect an exception when more than one result set is used can continue working.

> **Note**   MARS-like behavior is available in the .NET Framework 2.0 versions of the OLE DB and Oracle managed providers. The Oracle provider doesn't support the MARS attribute on the connection string, but it enables the feature automatically. The OLE DB provider doesn't support the connection string attribute either—it simulates multiple result sets when you connect to earlier versions of SQL Server or when the MDAC 9.0 library is not available. When you operate through OLE DB on a version of SQL Server 2005 equipped with MDAC 9.0, multiple result sets are active and natively implemented.

Conclusion

The .NET data access subsystem is made of two main subtrees—the managed providers and the database-agnostic container classes. ADO.NET managed providers are a new type of data source connectors and replace the COM-based OLE DB providers of ADO and ASP. As of this writing, the .NET Framework includes two native providers—one for SQL Server and one for Oracle—and support for all OLE DB providers and ODBC drivers. Third-party vendors also support MySQL, DB2, and Sybase, and they have alternate providers for Oracle.

A managed provider is faster and more appropriate than any other database technology for data-access tasks in .NET. Especially effective with SQL Server, a managed provider hooks up at the wire level and removes any sort of abstraction layer. In this way, a managed provider makes it possible for the ADO.NET to return to callers the same data types they would use to refresh the user interface. A managed provider supplies objects to connect to a data source, execute a command, start a transaction, and then grab or set some data.

In this chapter, we focused on establishing a connection to the data source and setting up commands and transactions. In the next chapter, we'll complete our look at ADO.NET by exploring data container classes such as *DataSet* and *DataTable*.

Just the Facts

- ADO.NET is a data-access subsystem in the Microsoft .NET Framework and is made of two distinct but closely related sets of classes—data providers and data containers.

- The functionalities supplied by a .NET data provider fall into a couple of categories: the capability of populating container classes, and the capability of setting up a connection and executing commands.

- The .NET Framework comes with data providers for SQL Server, Oracle, and all OLE DB and ODBC data sources.

- A data provider is faster and more appropriate than any other database technology for data-access tasks in .NET. Especially effective with SQL Server, a managed data provider hooks up at the wire level and removes any sort of abstraction layer.

- The data provider supplies an object to establish and manage the connection to a data source. This object implements connection pooling.

- In .NET applications, connection strings can be stored in a special section of the configuration file and encrypted if required.

- The data provider supplies an object to execute commands on an open connection and optionally within a transaction. The command object lists various execute methods to account for query and nonquery commands. Commands can execute either synchronously or asynchronously.

- Data returned by a query command are cached in a data reader object, which is a kind of optimized read-only, forward-only cursor.

- Local and distributed transactions can be managed through the *TransactionScope* class introduced with ADO.NET 2.0.

Chapter 9

The Data-Binding Model

To write effective ASP.NET 1.x data-driven applications, you need a deep understanding of ADO.NET objects. You have to be familiar with connections, commands, transactions, parameters, and all the objects we dealt with in the previous two chapters. In ASP.NET 2.0, the role of ADO.NET object is more blurred because of the introduction of a new family of data-related and more programmer-friendly components—the data source objects. In ASP.NET 2.0, you use ADO.NET objects directly much less frequently. You also use them in relatively standard data-driven pages belonging to relatively simple or prototype Web sites. Does this mean that ADO.NET objects have suddenly become unnecessary? Will ASP.NET 2.0 magically let you write data applications without having to really know about databases? Of course not.

Complex and sophisticated enterprise systems typically isolate ADO.NET code in the data tier, and they often have it wrapped up by an additional layer of helper libraries such as the Microsoft Data Access Application Block. Realistic pages belonging to similar systems never call ADO.NET objects directly, like we did in the demonstration pages of the past two chapters. In ASP.NET 2.0, ADO.NET objects are still essential pieces of the .NET Framework, but they have been pushed into the back-end infrastructure of most common data-binding operations. ASP.NET 2.0 offers the possibility of writing data access code that hides many essential steps from view and buries them in the framework's code. Basically, what many ASP.NET 1.x developers called "that boring ADO.NET boilerplate code" is now packed into a bunch of new data source controls.

Overall, the data-binding model of ASP.NET is founded on three pillars: data-binding expressions, classic data source–based binding, and data source controls, which are limited to ASP.NET 2.0. Let's start with data source–based binding, which is probably the most common form.

Data Source–Based Data Binding

Web applications are, for the most part, just data-driven applications. For this reason, the ability to bind HTML elements such as drop-down lists or tables to structured data is a key feature for any development platform. Data binding is the process that retrieves data from a fixed source and dynamically associates this data to properties on server controls. Valid target controls are those that have been specifically designed to support data binding—that is, data-bound controls. Data-bound controls are not another family of controls; they're simply server controls that feature a few well-known data-related properties and feed them using a well-known set of collection objects.

Feasible Data Sources

Many .NET classes can be used as data sources—and not just those that have to do with data-base content. In ASP.NET, any object that exposes the *IEnumerable* interface is a valid bindable data source. The *IEnumerable* interface defines the minimal API to enumerate the contents of the data source:

```
public interface IEnumerable
{
    IEnumerator GetEnumerator();
}
```

Many bindable objects, though, actually implement more advanced versions of *IEnumerable*, such as *ICollection* and *IList*. In particular, you can bind a Web control to the following classes:

- ADO.NET container classes such as *DataSet*, *DataTable*, and *DataView*
- Data readers
- Custom collections, dictionaries, and arrays

To be honest, I should note that the *DataSet* and *DataTable* classes don't actually implement *IEnumerable* or any other interfaces that inherit from it. However, both classes do store collections of data internally. These collections are accessed using the methods of an intermediate interface—*IListSource*—which performs the trick of making *DataSet* and *DataTable* classes look like they implement a collection.

ADO.NET Classes

As we saw in Chapter 8, ADO.NET provides a bunch of data container classes that can be filled with any sort of data, including results of a database query. These classes represent excellent resources for filling data-bound controls such as lists and grids. If having memory-based classes such as the *DataSet* in the list is no surprise, it's good to find data readers there, too. An open data reader can be passed to the data-binding engine of a control. The control will then walk its way through the reader and populate the user interface while keeping the connection to the database busy.

> **Note**   Data binding works differently for Web pages and Microsoft Windows desktop appli-
> cations. Aside from the internal implementations, both Web and Windows Forms can share the
> same data source objects with the exception of the data reader. You can bind a data reader
> only to ASP.NET controls. Likewise, only Windows Forms controls can be bound to instances of
> the *DataViewManager* class that we briefly mentioned in Chapter 8.

The *DataSet* class can contain more than one table; however, only one table at a time can be
associated with standard ASP.NET data-bound controls. If you bind the control to a *DataSet*,
you need to set an additional property to select a particular table within the *DataSet*. Be aware
that this limitation is not attributable to ASP.NET as a platform; it is a result of the implementation of the various data-bound controls. In fact, you could write a custom control that
accepts a *DataSet* as its sole data-binding parameter.

DataSet and *DataTable* act as data sources through the *IListSource* interface; *DataView* and data
readers, on the other hand, implement *IEnumerable* directly.

Collection-Based Classes

At the highest level of abstraction, a collection serves as a container for instances of other
classes. All collection classes implement the *ICollection* interface, which in turn implements
the *IEnumerable* interface. As a result, all collection classes provide a basic set of functionalities. All collection classes have a *Count* property to return the number of cached items; they
have a *CopyTo* method to copy their items, in their entirety or in part, to an external array; they
have a *GetEnumerator* method that instantiates an enumerator object to loop through the
child items. *GetEnumerator* is the method behind the curtain whenever you call the *foreach*
statement in C# and the *For...Each* statement in Microsoft Visual Basic .NET.

IList and *IDictionary* are two interfaces that extend *ICollection*, giving a more precise character-
ization to the resultant collection class. *ICollection* provides only basic and minimal functionality for a collection. For example, *ICollection* does not have any methods to add or remove
items. Add and remove functions are exactly what the *IList* interface provides. In the *IList*
interface, the *Add* and *Insert* methods place new items at the bottom of the collection or at the
specified index. The *Remove* and *RemoveAt* methods remove items, while *Clear* empties the
collection. Finally, *Contains* verifies whether an item with a given value belongs to the collection, and *IndexOf* returns the index of the specified item. Commonly used container classes
that implement both *ICollection* and *IList* are *Array*, *ArrayList*, and *StringCollection*.

The *IDictionary* interface defines the API that represents a collection of key/value pairs. The
interface exposes methods similar to *IList*, but with different signatures. Dictionary classes
also feature two extra properties: *Keys* and *Values*. They return collections of keys and values,
respectively, found in the dictionary. Typical dictionary classes are *ListDictionary*, *Hashtable*,
and *SortedList*.

You'll likely use custom collection classes in ASP.NET data-binding scenarios more often than you'll use predefined collection classes. The simplest way to code a custom collection in .NET 1.x is to derive a new class from *CollectionBase* and override at least the *Add* method and the *Item* property, as shown in the following code snippet:

```
public class OrderCollection : CollectionBase
{
    public OrderCollection()
    {
    }

    // Add method
    public void Add(OrderInfo o)
    {
        InnerList.Add(o);
    }

    // Indexer ("Item") property
    public OrderInfo this[int index]
    {
        get { return (OrderInfo) InnerList[index]; }
        set { InnerList[index] = value; }
    }
}
public class OrderInfo
{
    private int _id;
    public int ID
    {
        get { return _id; }
        set { _id = value; }
    }
    private DateTime _date;
    public DateTime Date
    {
        get { return _date; }
        set { _date = value; }
    }
    ...
}
```

It is important that the element class—*OrderInfo*, in the preceding code—implements data members as properties, instead of fields, as shown below:

```
public class OrderInfo
{
    public int ID;
    public DateTime Date;
}
```

Data members coded as fields are certainly faster to write, but they are not discovered at run time unless the class provides a custom type descriptor (in other words, it implements the *ICustomTypeDescriptor* interface) that exposes fields as properties.

In ASP.NET 2.0, the advent of generics greatly simplifies the development of custom collections. In some cases, the code to write reduces to the following:

```
public class OrderCollection : List<OrderInfo>
{
}
```

Data-Binding Properties

In ASP.NET, there are two main categories of data-bound controls—list controls and iterative controls. As we'll see in more detail later on, list controls repeat a fixed template for each item found in the data source. Iterative controls are more flexible and let you define the template to repeat explicitly, as well as other templates that directly influence the final layout of the control.

All data-bound controls implement the *DataSource* and *DataSourceID* properties, plus a few more, as detailed in Figure 9-1.

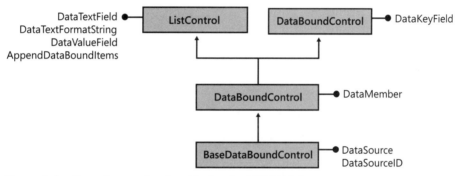

Figure 9-1   Class diagram for data binding in ASP.NET 2.0.

Note that the figure refers to the ASP.NET 2.0 object model. In ASP.NET 1.x, there's no *DataSourceID* property. Likewise, no intermediate classes exist such as *BaseDataBoundControl* and *DataBoundControl*. *ListControl* and *BaseDataList* form the common base for list and iterative controls.

> **Note**   Both in ASP.NET 1.x and ASP.NET 2.0 the *Repeater* control—a low-level iterative control—doesn't inherit from either of the classes in the diagram. It inherits directly from the *Control* class.

The *DataSource* Property

The *DataSource* property lets you specify the data source object the control is linked to. Note that this link is logical and does not result in any overhead or underlying operation until you explicitly order to bind the data to the control. As mentioned, you activate data binding on a control by calling the *DataBind* method. When the method executes, the control actually loads data from the associated data source, evaluates the data-bound properties (if any), and generates the markup to reflect changes:

```
public virtual object DataSource {get; set;}
```

The *DataSource* property is declared of type *object* and can ultimately accept objects that implement either *IEnumerable* (including data readers) or *IListSource*. By the way, only *DataSet* and *DataTable* implement the *IListSource* interface.

The *DataSource* property of a data-bound control is generally set programmatically. However, nothing prevents you from adopting a kind of declarative approach, as follows:

```
<asp:DropDownList runat="server" id="theList"
    DataSource="<%# GetData() %>"
    ...
/>
```

GetData is a public or protected member of the host page class that returns a bindable object.

> **Note**   How can a data-bound control figure out which actual object it is bound to? Will it be a collection, a data reader, or perhaps a *DataTable*? All standard data-bound controls are designed to work only through the *IEnumerable* interface. For this reason, any object bound to *DataSource* is normalized to an object that implements *IEnumerable*. In some cases, the normalization is as easy (and fast) as casting the object to the *IEnumerable* interface. In other cases—specifically, when *DataTable* and *DataSet* are involved—an extra step is performed to locate a particular named collection of data that corresponds to the value assigned to the *DataMember* property. We'll return to this point and discuss some code in my other recent book, *Programming Microsoft ASP.NET 2.0 Applications: Advanced Topics* (Microsoft Press, 2005), while developing custom data-bound controls.

The *DataSourceID* Property

Introduced with ASP.NET 2.0, the *DataSourceID* property gets or sets the ID of the data source component from which the data-bound control retrieves its data. This property is the point of contact between ASP.NET 2.0 data-bound controls and the new family of data source controls that includes *SqlDataSource* and *ObjectDataSource*. (I'll cover these controls in more detail later in the chapter.)

```
public virtual string DataSourceID {get; set;}
```

By setting *DataSourceID*, you tell the control to turn to the associated data source control for any needs regarding data–retrieval, paging, sorting, counting, or updating.

Like *DataSource*, *DataSourceID* is available on all data-bound controls. The two properties are mutually exclusive. If both are set, you get an invalid operation exception at run time. Note, though, that you also get an exception if *DataSourceID* is set to a string that doesn't correspond to an existing data source control.

The *DataMember* Property

The *DataMember* property gets or sets the name of the data collection to extract when data binding to a data source:

```
public virtual string DataMember {get; set;}
```

You use the property to specify the name of the *DataTable* to use when the *DataSource* property is bound to a *DataSet* object:

```
DataSet data = new DataSet();
SqlDataAdapter adapter = new SqlDataAdapter(cmdText, connString);
adapter.Fill(data);

// Table is the default name of the first table in a
// DataSet filled by an adapter
grid.DataMember = "Table";
grid.DataSource = data;
grid.DataBind();
```

DataMember and *DataSource* can be set in any order, provided that both are set before *DataBind* is invoked. *DataMember* has no relevance if you bind to data using *DataSourceID* with standard data source components.

> **Note** This is not a limitation of the binding technology, but rather a limitation of standard data source components, which don't support multiple views. We'll return to this point later when discussing data source components.

The *DataTextField* Property

Typically used by list controls, the *DataTextField* property specifies which property of a databound item should be used to define the display text of the nth element in a list control:

```
public virtual string DataTextField {get; set;}
```

For example, for a drop-down list control the property feeds the displayed text of each item in the list. The following code creates the control shown in Figure 9-2:

```
CountryList.DataSource = data;
CountryList.DataTextField = "country";
CountryList.DataBind();
```

The same happens for *ListBox*, *CheckBoxList*, and other list controls. Unlike *DataMember*, the *DataTextField* property is necessary also in case the binding is operated by data source components.

Figure 9-2 A drop-down list control filled with the country column of a database table.

> **Note** List controls can automatically format the content of the field bound through the *DataTextField* property. The format expression is indicated via the *DataTextFormatString* property.

The *DataValueField* Property

Similar to *DataTextField*, the *DataValueField* property specifies which property of a data-bound item should be used to identify the nth element in a list control:

```
public virtual string DataValueField {get; set;}
```

To understand the role of this property, consider the markup generated for a drop-down list, set as in the code snippet shown previously:

```
<select name="CountryList" id="CountryList">
    <option selected="selected" value="[All]">[All]</option>
    <option value="Argentina">Argentina</option>
    <option value="Austria">Austria</option>
    ...
</select>
```

The text of each *<option>* tag is determined by the field specified through *DataTextField*; the value of the value attribute is determined by *DataValueField*. Consider the following code filling a *ListBox* with customer names:

```
CustomerList.DataMember = "Table";
CustomerList.DataTextField = "companyname";
CustomerList.DataValueField = "customerid";
CustomerList.DataSource = data;
CustomerList.DataBind();
```

If *DataValueField* is left blank, the value of the *DataTextField* property is used instead. Here's the corresponding markup:

```
<select size="4" name="CustomerList" id="CustomerList">
    <option value="BOTTM">Bottom-Dollar Markets</option>
    <option value="LAUGB">Laughing Bacchus Wine Cellars</option>
    ...
</select>
```

As you can see, the *value* attribute now is set to the customer ID—the unique, invisible value determined by the *customerid* field. The content of the *value* attribute for the currently selected item is returned by the *SelectedValue* property of the list control. If you want to access programmatically the displayed text of the current selection, use the *SelectedItem.Text* expression.

The *AppendDataBoundItems* Property

Introduced in ASP.NET 2.0, *AppendDataBoundItems* is a Boolean property that indicates whether the data-bound items should be appended to or whether they should overwrite the existing contents of the control. By default, *AppendDataBoundItems* is set to *false*, meaning that data-bound contents replace any existing contents. This behavior is the same as you have in ASP.NET 1.x, where this property doesn't exist:

```
public virtual bool AppendDataBoundItems {get; set;}
```

AppendDataBoundItems is useful when you need to combine constant items with data-bound items. For example, imagine you need to fill a drop-down list with all the distinct countries in which you have a customer. The user will select a country and see the list of customers who live there. To let users see all the customers in any country, you add an unbound element, such as *[All]*:

```
<asp:DropDownList runat="server" ID="CountryList"
    AppendDataBoundItems="true">
    <asp:ListItem Text="[All]" />
</asp:DropDownList>
```

With *AppendDataBoundItems* set to *false* (which is the default behavior in ASP.NET 1.x), the *[All]* item will be cleared before data-bound items are added. In ASP.NET 1.x, you need to add it programmatically after the binding operation completes.

The *DataKeyField* Property

The *DataKeyField* property gets or sets the key field in the specified data source. The property serves the needs of ASP.NET 1.x grid-like controls (*DataList* and *DataGrid*) and lets them (uniquely) identify a particular record. Note that the identification of the record is univocal only if the original data source has a unique-constrained field:

```
public virtual string DataKeyField {get; set;}
```

The *DataKeyField* property is coupled with the *DataKeys* array property. When *DataKeyField* is set, *DataKeys* contains the value of the specified key field for all the control's data items currently displayed in the page. We'll cover this in more detail in the next chapter when we talk about *DataGrid* controls.

The new grid control of ASP.NET (the *GridView* control) extends the *DataKeyField* to an array of strings and renames it *DataKeyNames*. The *DataKeys* property is maintained, though defined differently, as we'll see in the next chapter.

List Controls

List controls display (or at least need to have in memory) many items at the same time—specifically, the contents of the data source. Depending on its expected behavior, the control will pick the needed items from memory and properly format and display them. List controls include *DropDownList*, *CheckBoxList*, *RadioButtonList*, *ListBox*, and, in ASP.NET 2.0, also the *BulletedList* control. All list controls inherit from the base *ListControl* class both in ASP.NET 1.x and 2.0.

The *DropDownList* Control

The *DropDownList* control enables users to select one item from a single-selection drop-down list. You can specify the size of the control by setting its height and width in pixels, but you can't control the number of items displayed when the list drops down. Table 9-1 lists the most commonly used properties of the control.

Table 9-1   Properties of the *DropDownList* Control

Property	Description
AppendDataBoundItems	Indicates whether statically defined items should be maintained or cleared when adding data-bound items. *Not supported in ASP.NET 1.x.*
AutoPostBack	Indicates whether the control should automatically post back to the server when the user changes the selection.
DataMember	The name of the table in the *DataSource* to bind.
DataSource	The data source that populates the items of the list.
DataSourceID	ID of the data source component to provide data. *Not supported in ASP.NET 1.x.*
DataTextField	Name of the data source field to supply the text of list items.
DataTextFormatString	Formatting string used to control list items are displayed.
DataValueField	Name of the data source field to supply the value of a list item.
Items	Gets the collection of items in the list control.
SelectedIndex	Gets or sets the index of the selected item in the list.
SelectedItem	Gets the selected item in the list.
SelectedValue	Gets the value of the selected item in the list.

The programming interface of the *DropDownList* control also features three properties to configure the border of the drop-down list: *BorderColor*, *BorderStyle*, and *BorderWidth*. Although the properties are correctly transformed by style properties, most browsers won't use them to change the appearance of the drop-down list.

The *DataTextField* and *DataValueField* properties don't accept expressions, only plain column names. To combine two or more fields of the data source, you can use a calculated column. You can either use a column computed by the database or exploit the power of the ADO.NET object model and add an in-memory column. The following SQL query returns a column obtained by concatenating *lastname* and *firstname*:

```
SELECT lastname + ', ' + firstname AS 'EmployeeName'
FROM Employees
```

The same result can also be obtained without the involvement of the database. Once you've filled a *DataTable* object with the result of the query, you add a new column to its *Columns* collection. The content of the column is based on an expression. The following code adds an EmployeeName column to the data source that concatenates the last name and first name:

```
dataTable.Columns.Add("EmployeeName",
    typeof(string),
    "lastname + ', ' + firstname");
```

An expression-based column does not need to be filled explicitly. The values for all the cells in the column are calculated and cached when the column is added to the table. The table tracks any dependencies and updates the calculated column whenever any of the constituent columns are updated.

The *CheckBoxList* Control

The *CheckBoxList* control is a single monolithic control that groups a collection of checkable list items, each of which is rendered through an individual *CheckBox* control. The properties of the child check boxes are set by reading the associated data source. You insert a check box list in a page as follows:

```
<asp:CheckBoxList runat="server" id="employeesList">
```

Table 9-2 lists the specific properties of the *CheckBoxList* control.

Table 9-2   Properties of the *CheckBoxList* Control

Property	Description
AppendDataBoundItems	Indicates whether statically defined items should be maintained or cleared when adding data-bound items. *Not supported in ASP.NET 1.x.*
AutoPostBack	Indicates whether the control should automatically post back to the server when the user changes the selection.
CellPadding	Indicates pixels between the border and contents of the cell.

Table 9-2 Properties of the *CheckBoxList* Control

Property	Description
CellSpacing	Indicates pixels between cells.
DataMember	The name of the table in the *DataSource* to bind.
DataSource	The data source that populates the items of the list.
DataSourceID	ID of the data source component to provide data. *Not supported in ASP.NET 1.x.*
DataTextField	Name of the data source field to supply the text of list items.
DataTextFormatString	Formatting string used to control list items are displayed.
DataValueField	Name of the data source field to supply value of a list item.
Items	Gets the collection of items in the list control.
RepeatColumns	Gets or sets the number of columns to display in the control.
RepeatDirection	Gets or sets a value that indicates whether the control displays vertically or horizontally.
RepeatLayout	Gets or sets the layout of the check boxes (table or flow).
SelectedIndex	Gets or sets the index of the first selected item in the list—the one with the lowest index.
SelectedItem	Gets the first selected item.
SelectedValue	Gets the value of the first selected item.
TextAlign	Gets or sets the text alignment for the check boxes.

The *CheckBoxList* control does not supply any properties that know which items have been selected. But this aspect is vital for any Web application that uses checkable elements. The *CheckBoxList* control can have any number of items selected, but how can you retrieve them?

Any list control has an *Items* property that contains the collection of the child items. The *Items* property is implemented through the *ListItemCollection* class and makes each contained item accessible via a *ListItem* object. The following code loops through the items stored in a *CheckBoxList* control and checks the *Selected* property of each of them:

```
foreach(ListItem item in chkList.Items)
{
    if (item.Selected) {
        // this item is selected
    }
}
```

Figure 9-3 shows a sample page that lets you select some country names and composes an ad hoc query to list all the customers from those countries.

Note that the *SelectedXXX* properties work in a slightly different manner for a *CheckBoxList* control. The *SelectedIndex* property indicates the lowest index of a selected item. By setting *SelectedIndex* to a given value, you state that no items with a lower index should be selected any longer. As a result, the control automatically deselects all items with an index lower than the new value of *SelectedIndex*. Likewise, *SelectedItem* returns the first selected item, and *SelectedValue* returns the value of the first selected item.

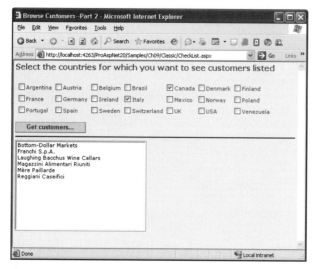

Figure 9-3   A horizontally laid out *CheckBoxList* control in action.

The *RadioButtonList* Control

The *RadioButtonList* control acts as the parent control for a collection of radio buttons. Each of the child items is rendered through a *RadioButton* control. By design, a *RadioButtonList* control can have zero or one item selected. The *SelectedItem* property returns the selected element as a *ListItem* object. Note, though, that there is nothing to guarantee that only one item is selected at any time. For this reason, be extremely careful when you access the *SelectedItem* of a *RadioButtonList* control—it could be null:

```
if (radioButtons.SelectedValue != null)
{
    // Process the selection here
    ...
}
```

The *RadioButtonList* control supports the same set of properties as the *CheckBoxList* control and, just like it, accepts some layout directives. In particular, you can control the rendering process of the list with the *RepeatLayout* and *RepeatDirection* properties. By default, the list items are rendered within a table, which ensures the vertical alignment of the companion text. The property that governs the layout is *RepeatLayout*. The alternative is displaying the items as free HTML text, using blanks and breaks to guarantee some sort of minimal structure. *RepeatDirection* is the property that controls the direction in which—with or without a tabular structure—the items flow. Feasible values are *Vertical* (the default) and *Horizontal*. *RepeatColumns* is the property that determines how many columns the list should have. By default, the value is 0, which means all the items will be displayed in a single row, vertical or horizontal, according to the value of *RepeatDirection*.

The *ListBox* Control

The *ListBox* control represents a vertical sequence of items displayed in a scrollable window. The *ListBox* control allows single-item or multiple-item selection and exposes its contents through the usual *Items* collection, as shown in the following code:

```
<asp:listbox runat="server" id="theListBox"
    rows="5" selectionmode="Multiple" />
```

You can decide the height of the control through the *Rows* property. The height is measured in number of rows rather than pixels or percentages. When it comes to data binding, the *ListBox* control behaves like the controls discussed earlier in the chapter.

Two properties make this control slightly different from other list controls—the *Rows* property, which represents the number of visible rows in the control, and the *SelectionMode* property, which determines whether one or multiple items can be selected. The programming interface of the list box also contains the set of *SelectedXXX* properties we considered earlier. In this case, they work as they do for the *CheckBoxList* control—that is, they returns the selected item with the lowest index.

> **Note**   All the list controls examined so far support the *SelectedIndexChanged* event, which is raised when the selection from the list changes and the page posts back to the server. You can use this event to execute server-side code whenever a control is selected or deselected.

The *BulletedList* Control

The *BulletedList* control is a programming interface built around the <ul> and <ol> HTML tags, with some extra features such as the bullet style, data binding, and support for custom images. The *BulletedList* control is not supported in ASP.NET 1.x. The following example uses a custom bullet object:

```
<asp:bulletedlist runat="server" bulletstyle="Square">
    <asp:listitem>One</asp:listitem>
    <asp:listitem>Two</asp:listitem>
    <asp:listitem>Three</asp:listitem>
</asp:bulletedlist>
```

The bullet style lets you choose the style of the element that precedes the item. You can use numbers, squares, circles, and uppercase and lowercase letters. The child items can be rendered as plain text, hyperlinks, or buttons. Table 9-3 details the main properties of a *BulletedList* control.

Table 9-3   Properties of the *BulletedList* Control

Property	Description
AppendDataBoundItems	Indicates whether statically defined items should be maintained or cleared when adding data-bound items
BulletImageUrl	Gets or sets the path to the image to use as the bullet
BulletStyle	Determines the style of the bullet
DataMember	The name of the table in the *DataSource* to bind
DataSource	The data source that populates the items of the list
DataSourceID	ID of the data source component to provide data
DataTextField	Name of the data source field to supply text of list items
DataTextFormatString	Formatting string used to control list items are displayed
DataValueField	Name of the data source field to supply value of a list item
DisplayMode	Determines how to display the items: plain text, link buttons, or hyperlinks
FirstBulletNumber	Gets or sets the value that starts the numbering
Items	Gets the collection of items in the list control
Target	Indicates the target frame in case of hyperlink mode

The items of a *BulletedList* control supports a variety of graphical styles—disc, circle, and custom image, plus a few numberings including roman numbering. The initial number can be programmatically set through the *FirstBulletNumber* property. The *DisplayMode* property determines how to display the content of each bullet—plain text (the default), link button, or hyperlink. In the case of link buttons, the *Click* event is fired on the server to let you handle the event when the page posts back. In the case of hyperlinks, the browser will display the target page in the specified frame—the *Target* property. The target URL coincides with the contents of the field specified by *DataValueField*.

Figure 9-4 shows a sample page that includes a *RadioButtonList* and a *BulletedList* control. The radio-button list is bound to the contents of a system enumerated type—*BulletStyle*—and displays as selectable radio buttons the various bullet styles. To bind the contents of an enumerated type to a data-bound control, you do as follows:

```
BulletOptions.DataSource = Enum.GetValues(typeof(BulletStyle));
BulletOptions.SelectedIndex = 0;
BulletOptions.DataBind();
```

To retrieve and set the selected value, use the following code:

```
BulletStyle style = (BulletStyle) Enum.Parse(typeof(BulletStyle), BulletOptions.SelectedValue);
BulletedList1.BulletStyle = style;
```

Figure 9-4   A sample page to preview the style of a *BulletedList* control.

Iterative Controls

Iterative controls are a special type of data-bound controls that supply a template-based mechanism to create free-form user interfaces. Iterative controls take a data source, loop through the items, and iteratively apply user-defined HTML templates to each row. This basic behavior is common to all three ASP.NET iterators—*Repeater*, *DataList*, and *DataGrid*. Beyond that, iterative controls differ from each other in terms of layout capabilities and functionality.

Iterative controls differ from list controls because of their greater rendering flexibility. An iterative control lets you apply an ASP.NET template to each row in the bound data source. A list control, on the other hand, provides a fixed and built-in template for each data item. List controls are customizable to some extent, but you can't change anything other than the text displayed. No changes to layout are supported. On the other hand, using a list control is considerably easier than setting up an iterative control, as we'll see in a moment. Defining templates requires quite a bit of declarative code, and if accomplished programmatically, it requires that you write a class that implements the *ITemplate* interface. A list control only requires you to go through a few data-binding properties.

We'll take a look at *DataGrid* controls in Chapter 10 and reserve more space for lower-level iterators such as *Repeater* and *DataList* in my other recent book, *Programming Microsoft ASP.NET 2.0 Applications: Advanced Topics*. When they are properly customized and configured, there's no graphical structure—be it flat or hierarchical—that the *Repeater* and *DataList* controls can't generate. Let's briefly meet each control.

The *Repeater* Control

The *Repeater* control displays data using user-provided layouts. It works by repeating a specified ASP.NET template for each item displayed in the list. The *Repeater* is a rather basic templated data-bound control. It has no built-in layout or styling capabilities. All formatting and layout information must be explicitly declared and coded using HTML tags and ASP.NET classes.

The *Repeater* class acts as a naming container by implementing the marker interface *INamingContainer*. (See Chapter 3.) Table 9-4 lists the main properties exposed by the control, not including those inherited from the base class.

Table 9-4   Properties of the *Repeater* Control

Property	Description
AlternatingItemTemplate	Template to define how every other item is rendered.
DataMember	The name of the table in the *DataSource* to bind.
DataSource	The data source that populates the items of the list.
DataSourceID	ID of the data source component to provide data. *Not supported in ASP.NET 1.x.*
FooterTemplate	Template to define how the footer is rendered.
HeaderTemplate	Template to define how the header is rendered.
Items	Gets a *RepeaterItemCollection* object—that is, a collection of *RepeaterItem* objects. Each element of the collection represents a displayed data row in the *Repeater*.
ItemTemplate	Template to define how items are rendered.
SeparatorTemplate	Template to define how the separator between items is to be rendered.

For the most part, properties are the template elements that form the control's user interface. The *Repeater* populates the *Items* collection by enumerating all the data items in the bound data source. For each data-bound item (for example, a table record), it creates a *RepeaterItem* object and adds it to the *Items* collection. The *RepeaterItemCollection* class is a plain collection class with no special or peculiar behavior. The *RepeaterItem* class represents a displayed element within the overall structure created by the *Repeater*. The *RepeaterItem* contains properties to point to the bound data item (such as a table record), the index, and the type of the item (regular item, alternating item, header, footer, and so on). Here's a quick example of a *Repeater*:

```
<asp:Repeater ID="Repeater1" runat="server">
    <HeaderTemplate>
        <h2>We have customers in the following cities</h2>
        <hr />
    </HeaderTemplate>
    <SeparatorTemplate>
        <hr noshade style="border:dashed 1px blue" />
    </SeparatorTemplate>
    <ItemTemplate>
        <%# Eval("City")%>   <b><%# Eval("Country")%></b>
    </ItemTemplate>
    <FooterTemplate>
        <hr />
```

```
      <%# CalcTotal() %> cities
    </FooterTemplate>
</asp:Repeater>
```

Bound to the output of the following query, the structure produces what is shown in Figure 9-5:

```
SELECT DISTINCT country, city FROM customers WHERE country=@TheCountry
```

The *@TheCountry* parameter is the name of the country picked from the drop-down list:

```
data = new DataTable();
SqlDataAdapter adapter = new SqlDataAdapter(cmdText, connString);
adapter.SelectCommand.Parameters.AddWithValue("@TheCountry",
Countries.SelectedValue);
adapter.Fill(data);
Repeater1.DataSource = data;
Repeater1.DataBind();
```

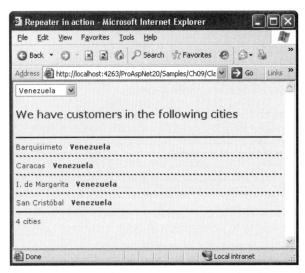

Figure 9-5   A sample *Repeater* control in action. No predefined list control can generate
such free-form output.

Of all templates, only *ItemTemplate* and *AlternatingItemTemplate* are data-bound, meaning that
they are repeated for each item in the data source. You need a mechanism to access public
properties on the data item (such as a table record) from within the template. The *Eval*
method takes the name of the property (for example, the name of the table column) and
returns the content. We'll learn more about *Eval* and <%# ... %> code blocks in a moment
when discussing data-binding expressions.

The *DataList* Control

The *DataList* is a data-bound control that begins where the *Repeater* ends and terminates a
little before the starting point of the *DataGrid* control. In some unrealistically simple cases,

you could even take some code that uses a *Repeater*, replace the control, and not even notice any difference. The *DataList* overtakes the *Repeater* in several respects, mostly in the area of graphical layout. The *DataList* supports directional rendering, meaning that items can flow horizontally or vertically to match a specified number of columns. Furthermore, it provides facilities to retrieve a key value associated with the current data row and has built-in support for selection and in-place editing. (I discuss these features in *Programming Microsoft ASP.NET 2.0 Applications: Advanced Topics.*)

In addition, the *DataList* control supports more templates and can fire some extra events beyond those of the *Repeater* control. Data binding and the overall behavior are nearly identical for the *Repeater* and *DataList* controls.

The *DataList* works by making some assumptions about the expected results. This is both good and bad news for you as a programmer. It means that in some cases much less code is needed to accomplish the same effect; on the other hand, it also indicates that you should know the behavior of the control very well to govern it. For example, the *DataList* assumes that no HTML tag is split across templates. This fact isn't a problem per se, but it can result in badly formed or totally unexpected HTML output. In addition, by default the *DataList* renders its entire output as an HTML table, meaning that if this is exactly what you want, there's no need for you to comply with *<table>* or *<td>* elements.

In addition to being a naming container, the *DataList* class implements the *IRepeatInfoUser* interface. The *IRepeatInfoUser* interface defines the properties and methods that must be implemented by any list control that repeats a list of items. This interface is also supported by the *CheckBoxList* and *RadioButtonList* controls and is the brains behind the *RepeatXXX* properties we met earlier. Here's how to rewrite the previous example to get stricter control over the output:

```
<asp:DataList ID="DataList1" runat="server" RepeatColumns="5"
    GridLines="Both">
  <FooterStyle Font-Bold="true" ForeColor="blue" />
  <HeaderTemplate>
     <h2>We have customers in the following cities</h2>
  </HeaderTemplate>
  <ItemTemplate>
     <%# Eval("City") %>   <b><%# Eval("Country")%></b>
  </ItemTemplate>
  <FooterTemplate>
     <%# CalcTotal() %> cities
  </FooterTemplate>
</asp:DataList>
```

The output is shown in Figure 9-6. Note the *FooterStyle* tag; the *DataList* also lets you explicitly style the content of each supported template. In this case, we're going to get boldface and blue text in the footer panel.

Figure 9-6   A sample *DataList* control in action. Note the extended layout capabilities that let you divide by columns by simply setting a property.

The *DataGrid* Control

The *DataGrid* is an extremely versatile data-bound control that is a fixed presence in any real-world ASP.NET 1.x application. While fully supported, in ASP.NET 2.0, the *DataGrid* is pushed into the background by the introduction of a new and much more powerful grid control—the *GridView*. We'll cover both in the next chapter.

The *DataGrid* control renders a multicolumn, fully templated grid and provides a highly customizable, Microsoft Office Excel–like user interface. In spite of the rather advanced programming interface and the extremely rich set of attributes, the *DataGrid* simply generates an HTML table with interspersed hyperlinks to provide interactive functionalities such as sorting, paging, selection, and in-place editing.

The *DataGrid* is a column-based control and supports various types of data-bound columns, including text columns, templated columns, and command columns. You associate the control with a data source using the *DataSource* property. Just as for other data-bound controls, no data will be physically loaded and bound until the *DataBind* method is called. The simplest way of displaying a table of data using the ASP.NET grid is as follows:

```
<asp:DataGrid runat="server" id="grid" />
```

The control will then automatically generate an HTML table column for each property available in the bound data source. This is only the simplest scenario, however. If needed, you can specify which columns should be displayed and style them at will:

```
grid.DataSource = data;
grid.DataBind();
```

Figure 9-7 demonstrates the grid's output for a sample that returns three fields. As mentioned, we'll cover the *DataGrid* control in much greater detail in the next chapter.

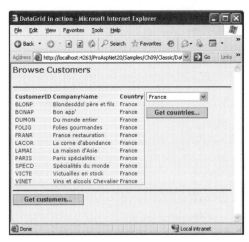

Figure 9-7   A sample *DataGrid* control in action.

Data-Binding Expressions

What we have examined so far is the most common form of data binding that involves list and iterative controls and collections of data. Note that any ASP.NET controls support some minimal form of data binding, including text boxes and labels, through the *DataBind* method. In its simplest form, a binding is a connection between one piece of data and a server control property. This simple form of binding is established through a special expression that gets evaluated when the code in the page calls the *DataBind* method on the control.

Simple Data Binding

A data-binding expression is any executable code wrapped by <% ... %> and prefixed by the symbol #. Typically, you use data-binding expressions to set the value of an attribute in the opening tag of a server control. A data-binding expression is programmatically managed via an instance of the *DataBoundLiteralControl* class.

> **Note**   The binding expression is really any executable code that can be evaluated at run time. Its purpose is to generate data that the control can use to bind for display or editing. Typically, the code retrieves data from the data source, but there is no requirement that this be the case. Any executable code is acceptable as long as it returns data for binding.

The following code snippet shows how to set the text of a label with the current time:

```
<asp:label runat="server" Text='<%# DateTime.Now %>' />
```

Within the delimiters, you can invoke user-defined page methods, static methods, and properties and methods of any other page components. The following code demonstrates a label bound to the name of the currently selected element in a drop-down list control:

```
<asp:label runat="server" Text='<%# dropdown.SelectedItem.Text %>' />
```

Note that if you're going to use quotes within the expression, you should wrap the expression itself with single quotes. The data-binding expression can accept a minimal set of operators, mostly for concatenating subexpressions. If you need more advanced processing and use external arguments, resort to a user-defined method. The only requirement is that the method is declared public or protected.

> **Important**   Any data-bound expression you define in the page is evaluated only after *DataBind* is called. You can either call *DataBind* on the page object or on the specific control. If you call *DataBind* on the page object, it will recursively call *DataBind* on all controls defined in the page. If *DataBind* is not called, no < %# …% > expressions will ever be evaluated.

Binding in Action

Data-binding expressions are particularly useful to update, in a pure declarative manner, properties of controls that depend on other controls in the same page. For example, suppose you have a drop-down list of colors and a label, and you want the text of the label to reflect the selected color:

```
<asp:DropDownList ID="SelColors" runat="server" AutoPostBack="True">
    <asp:ListItem>Orange</asp:ListItem>
    <asp:ListItem>Green</asp:ListItem>
    <asp:ListItem>Red</asp:ListItem>
    <asp:ListItem>Blue</asp:ListItem>
</asp:DropDownList>
<asp:Label runat="server" ID="lblColor"
    Text='<%# "<b>You selected: </b>" + SelColors.SelectedValue %>' />
```

Note that in the <%# … %> expression you can use any combination of methods, constants, and properties as long as the final result matches the type of the bound property. Also note that the evaluation of the expression requires a postback and a call to *DataBind*. We set the *AutoPostBack* property to *true* just to force a postback when the selection changes in the drop-down list. At the same time, a call to the page's or label's *DataBind* method is required for the refresh to occur:

```
protected void Page_Load(object sender, EventArgs e) {
    DataBind();
}
```

You can bind to expressions virtually any control properties regardless of the type. Let's see how to bind the *ForeColor* property of the *Label* control to the color string picked from the drop-down list:

```
ForeColor='<%# Color.FromName(SelColors.SelectedValue) %>'
```

Note that you can't just set *ForeColor* to an expression that evaluates to a color string, such as "orange":

```
ForeColor='<%# SelColors.SelectedValue %>'
```

The preceding code won't compile because of the impossible automatic conversion between a string (your expression) and a color (the type of the *ForeColor* property). Interestingly enough, of the two following statements only the second will work fine:

```
ForeColor='<%# "orange" %>'
ForeColor="orange"
```

The upshot is that a data-binding expression requires that the return type match the type of the property represented via an attribute. Using a plain constant string is fine, on the other hand, because the page parser recognizes the expression and seamlessly inserts proper conversion code, if such a conversion is possible. Figure 9-8 shows the sample page in action.

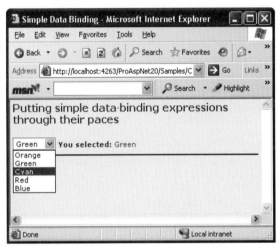

Figure 9-8   A drop-down list and a label tied up together using a data-binding expression.

Implementation of Data-Binding Expressions

What really happens when a data-binding expression is found in a Web page? How does the ASP.NET runtime process it? Let's consider the following code:

```
<asp:label runat="server" id="today" text='<%# DateTime.Now %>' />
```

When the page parser takes care of the *.aspx* source code, it generates a class where each server control has a factory method. The factory method simply maps the tag name to a server-side control class and transforms attributes on the tag into property assignments. In addition, if a data-binding expression is found, the parser adds a handler for the *DataBinding* event of the control—a *Label* in this case. Here's some pseudocode to illustrate the point:

```
private Control __BuildControlToday() {
    Label __ctrl = new Label();
```

```
    this.today = __ctrl;
    __ctrl.ID = "today";

    __ctrl.DataBinding += new EventHandler(this.__DataBindToday);
    return __ctrl;
}
```

The handler assigns the data-binding expression verbatim to the property:

```
public void __DataBindToday(object sender, EventArgs e) {
    Label target;
    target = (Label) sender;
    target.Text = Convert.ToString(DateTime.Now);
}
```

If the value returned by the data-binding expression doesn't match the expected type, you generally get a compile error. However, if the expected type is *string*, the parser attempts a standard conversion through the *Convert.ToString* method. (All .NET Framework types are convertible to a string because they inherit the *ToString* method from the root *object* type.)

The *DataBinder* Class

Earlier in this chapter, we met <%# ... %> expressions in the context of templates along with the *Eval* method. The *Eval* method is a kind of tailor-made operator you use in data-binding expressions to access a public property on the bound data item. The *Eval* method as used earlier is an ASP.NET 2.0–only feature and will generate a compile error if used in ASP.NET 1.x applications. For all versions of ASP.NET, you can use a functionally equivalent method, also named *Eval*, but from another class—*DataBinder*.

> **Important**   Through the *Eval* method—even if it comes from *DataBinder* or *Page*—you can access public properties on the bound data item. Let me clarify what public properties are in this context and why I insist on calling them properties. Any class that implements *IEnumerable* can be bound to a control. The list of actual classes certainly includes *DataTable* (where a data item logically corresponds to table record), but it also includes custom collections (where a data item corresponds to an instance of a given class). The *Eval* method ends up querying the data item object for its set of properties. The object that represents a table record will return descriptors for its columns; other objects will return their set of public properties.

The *DataBinder* class supports generating and parsing data-binding expressions. Of particular importance is its overloaded static method *Eval*. The method uses reflection to parse and evaluate an expression against a run-time object. Clients of the *Eval* method include RAD tools such as Microsoft Visual Studio .NET designers and Web controls that declaratively place calls to the method to feed properties dynamically changing values.

The *Eval* Method

The syntax of *DataBinder.Eval* typically looks like this:

```
<%# DataBinder.Eval(Container.DataItem, expression) %>
```

A third, optional parameter is omitted in the preceding snippet. This parameter is a string that contains formatting options for the bound value. The *Container.DataItem* expression references the object on which the expression is evaluated. The expression is typically a string with the name of the field to access on the data item object. It can be an expression that includes indexes and property names. The *DataItem* property represents the object within the current container context. Typically, a container is the current instance of the item object—for example, a *DataGridItem* object—that is about to be rendered.

The code shown earlier is commonly repeated, always in the same form. Only the expression and the format string change from page to page.

A More Compact *Eval*

The original syntax of *DataBinder.Eval* can be simplified in ASP.NET 2.0, as we already saw earlier in the *Repeater* example. In ASP.NET 2.0, you can use

```
<%# Eval(expression) %>
```

wherever the following expression is accepted in ASP.NET 1.x:

```
<%# DataBinder.Eval(Container.DataItem, expression) %>
```

It goes without saying that the *DataBinder* object is also fully supported in ASP.NET 2.0.

Any piece of code that appears within the <%# ... %> delimiters enjoys special treatment from the ASP.NET runtime. Let's briefly look at what happens with this code. When the page is compiled for use, the *Eval* call is inserted in the source code of the page as a standalone call. The following code gives an idea of what happens:

```
object o = Eval("lastname");
string result = Convert.ToString(o);
```

The result of the call is converted to a string and is assigned to a data-bound literal control—an instance of the *DataBoundLiteralControl* class. Then the data-bound literal is inserted in the page's control tree.

In ASP.NET 2.0, the *TemplateControl* class—the parent of *Page*—is actually enriched with a new, protected (but not virtual) method named *Eval*. The following pseudocode illustrates how the method works:

```
protected object Eval(string expression)
{
    if (Page == null)
```

```
        throw new InvalidOperationException(…);
    return DataBinder.Eval(Page.GetDataItem(), expression);
}
```

As you can see, *Eval* is a simple wrapper built around the *DataBinder.Eval* method. The *DataBinder.Eval* method is invoked using the current container's data item. Quite obviously, the current container's data is null outside a data-binding operation—that is, in the stack of calls following a call to *DataBind*. This fact brings up a key difference between *Eval* and *DataBinder.Eval*.

> **Important**   The *TemplateControl*'s *Eval* is a data-binding method and can be used only in the context of a data-bound control during a data-binding operation. On the other hand, *DataBinder.Eval* is a fully fledged method that can be used anywhere in the code. Typically, you use it in the implementation of custom data-bound controls. I'll show this in the companion volume, *Programming Microsoft ASP.NET 2.0 Applications: Advanced Topics*.

Getting the Default Data Item

The pseudocode that illustrates the behavior of the page's *Eval* method shows a *GetDataItem* method off the *Page* class. What is it? As mentioned, the simplified syntax assumes a default *Container.DataItem* context object. *GetDataItem* is simply the function that returns that object.

More precisely, *GetDataItem* is the endpoint of a stack-based mechanism that traces the current binding context for the page. Each control in the control tree is pushed onto this stack at the time the respective *DataBind* method is called. When the *DataBind* method returns, the control is popped from the stack. If the stack is empty, and you attempt to call *Eval* programmatically, *GetDataItem* throws an invalid operation exception. In summary, you can use the Eval shortcut only in templates; if you need to access properties of a data item anywhere else in the code, resort to *DataBinder.Eval* and indicate the data item object explicitly.

> **Tip**   As mentioned, you generally need to call *DataBinder.Eval* directly only in the code of custom data-bound controls. (I cover custom controls in *Programming Microsoft ASP.NET 2.0 Applications: Advanced Topics*.) When this happens, though, you might want to save a few internal calls and CPU cycles by calling *DataBinder.GetPropertyValue* instead. This is exactly what *DataBinder.Eval* does in the end.

Other Data-Binding Methods

In ASP.NET 2.0, data-binding expressions go far beyond read-only evaluation of enumerable and tabular data. In addition to *DataBinder*, ASP.NET 2.0 provides a class that can bind to the result of XPath expressions that are executed against an object that implements the *IXPathNavigable* interface. This class is named *XPathBinder*; it plays the same role as *DataBinder*, except it works on XML data. The *XPathBinder* class backs up a new data-binding method named *XPath*.

ASP.NET 2.0 also supports declarative two-way data binding, meaning that you can read and write data item properties through a new data-binding method named *Bind*.

Finally, ASP.NET 2.0 supports user-defined expressions that operate outside the boundaries of data-binding operations. It might seem weird that I discuss non-data-binding expressions in a section explicitly dedicated to data-binding expressions. The reason I mention this option here is to avoid confusion, as the syntax for custom expressions is nearly identical.

The *XPath* Method

In ASP.NET 2.0, data-bound controls can be associated with raw XML data. You can bind XML data in version 1.x, but you have to first fit XML data into a relational structure such as a *DataSet*. When a templated control such as *DataList* or *Repeater* is bound to an XML data source (such as the new *XmlDataSource* control, which we'll cover in the next section), individual XML fragments can be bound inside the template using the *XPathBinder* object.

The *XPathBinder.Eval* method accepts an *XmlNode* object along with an XPath expression, and it evaluates and returns the result. The output string can be formatted if a proper format string is specified. *XPathBinder.Eval* casts the container object to *IXPathNavigable*. This is a prerequisite to applying the XPath expression. If the object doesn't implement the interface, an exception is thrown. The *IXPathNavigable* interface is necessary because in the .NET Framework the whole XPath API is built for, and works only with, objects that provide a navigator class. The goal of the interface is creating an XPath navigator object for the query to run.

Like *DataBinder*, the *XPathBinder* class supports a simplified syntax for its evaluator method. The syntax assumes a default container context that is the same object that is tracked for the data binder. The following example demonstrates using the simplified XPath data-binding syntax:

```
<%# XPath("Orders/Order/Customer/LastName") %>
```

The output value is the object returned by *XPathBinder.Eval* converted to a string. Internally, *XPathBinder.Eval* gets a navigator object from the data source and evaluates the expression. The managed XPath API is used.

> **Note** In this book, we don't cover XML classes in the .NET Framework. A good reference is my book *Applied XML with the .NET Framework* (Microsoft Press, 2003). The book covers .NET Framework 1.x, but as far as XPath is concerned, what you can learn from that source is exactly what you need to know.

The *XPathSelect* Method

The *XPathBinder* class also features a *Select* method. The method executes an XPath query and retrieves a nodeset—an enumerable collection of XML nodes. This collection can be assigned as a late-bound value to data-bound controls (such as the *Repeater* control). An equivalent simplified syntax exists for this scenario, too:

```
<asp:Repeater runat="server"
    DataSource='<%# XPathSelect("orders/order/summary") %>'>
...
</asp:Repeater>
```

XPathSelect is the keyword you use in data-binding expressions to indicate the results of an XPath query run on the container object. If the container object does not implement *IXPathNavigable*, an exception is thrown. Like *Eval* and *XPath*, *XPathSelect* assumes a default data item context object.

The *Bind* Method

As we'll see in Chapter 11, ASP.NET 2.0 supports two-way data binding—that is, the capability to bind data to controls and submit changes back to the database. The *Eval* method is representative of a one-way data binding that automates data reading but not data writing. The new *Bind* method can be used whenever *Eval* is accepted and through a similar syntax:

```
<asp:TextBox Runat="server" ID="TheNotes" Text='<%# Bind("notes") %>' />
```

The big difference is that *Bind* works in both directions—reading and writing. For example, when the *Text* property is being set, *Bind* behaves exactly like *Eval*. In addition, when the *Text* property is being read, *Bind* stores the value into a collection. Enabled ASP.NET 2.0 data-bound controls (for example, the new *FormView* control and other templated controls) automatically retrieve these values and use them to compose the parameter list of the insert or edit command to run against the data source. The argument passed to *Bind* must match the name of a parameter in the command. For example, the text box shown earlier provides the value for the *@notes* parameter.

User-Defined Dynamic Expressions

Data-binding expressions are not really dynamic expressions because they are evaluated only within the context of a data-binding call. ASP.NET 2.0 provides a made-to-measure infrastructure for dynamic expressions based on a new breed of components—the expression builders. (I cover expression builders in *Programming Microsoft ASP.NET 2.0 Applications: Advanced Topics*.)

Dynamic expressions have a syntax that is similar to data binding, except that they use the $ prefix instead of #. Dynamic expressions are evaluated when the page compiles. The content of the expression is extracted, transformed into code, and injected into the code created for the page. A few predefined expression builders exist, as listed in Table 9-5.

Table 9-5 Custom Expressions

Syntax	Description
AppSettings:XXX	Returns the value of the specified setting from the *<appSettings>* section of the configuration file.
ConnectionStrings:XXX[.YYY]	Returns the value of the specified XXX string from the *<connectionStrings>* section of the configuration file. The optional YYY parameter indicates which attribute is read from the section. It can be either *connectionString* (default) or *providerName*.
Resources:XXX, YYY	Returns the value of the YYY global resource read from the XXX resource file (*.resx*).

To declaratively bind a control property to the value of the expression, you follow the schema shown here:

```
<%$ expression %>
```

The exact syntax is defined by the builder associated with each expression. Note, though, that literal expressions are not permitted in the body of the page. In other words, you can use expression only to set a control property. You can't have the following:

```
<h1><%$ AppSettings:AppVersionNumber %></h1>
```

Instead, you should wrap the expression in a server control, the simplest of which would be the *Literal* control. The following code generates the page in Figure 9-9:

```
<h1><asp:Literal runat="server"
        Text="<%$ Resources:Resource, AppWelcome %>" /></h1>
<hr />
<b>Code version <asp:Literal runat="server"
      Text="<%$ AppSettings:AppVersionNumber %>" /></b>
```

Needless to say, you need to have an *AppVersionNumber* string resource in the *App_GlobalResource* and an *AppWelcome* setting in the *web.config* file:

```
<appSettings>
    <add key="AppVersionNumber" value="8.2.2001" />
</appSettings>
```

Figure 9-9 The heading text and the version number are obtained through declarative expressions.

The remaining expression—*ConnectionStrings*—is extremely helpful with data source controls to avoid hard-coding the connection string in the *.aspx* file.

> **Note**   Microsoft provides the few built-in expression builders listed in Table 9-5. Developers can define others by simply writing new classes that inherit from *ExpressionBuilder*. To be recognized and properly handled, custom expression builders must be registered in the *web.config* file. I'll touch on this topic in *Programming Microsoft ASP.NET 2.0 Applications: Advanced Topics*.

Data Source Components

ASP.NET 1.x has an extremely flexible and generic data-binding architecture that gives developers full control of the page life cycle. Developers can link data-bound controls such as the *DataGrid* to any enumerable collection of data. While this approach represents a quantum leap from classic ASP, it still requires page developers to learn a lot of architectural details to create even relatively simple read-only pages. This is a problem for Web developers with limited skills because they soon get into trouble if left alone to decide how (or whether) to implement paging, sorting, updates, or perhaps a master/detail view. But this is a (different) problem for experienced developers, as they have to continually reimplement the same pattern to access data sources, get data, and make the data consistent with the programming interface of data controls.

The key issue with ASP.NET 1.x data binding is a lack of a higher-level and possibly declarative model for data fetching and data manipulation. As a result, an ASP.NET 1.x data access layer is boring to write and requires hundreds of lines of code even for relatively simple scenarios. Enter ASP.NET 2.0 data source components.

Overview of Data Source Components

A data source component is a server control designed to interact with data-bound controls and hide the complexity of the manual data-binding pattern. Data source components not only provide data to controls, but they also support data-bound controls in the execution of other common operations such as insertions, deletions, sorting, and updates. Each data source component wraps a particular data provider—relational databases, XML documents, or custom classes. The support for custom classes means that you can now directly bind your controls to existing classes—for example, classes in your business or data access layer. (I'll say more about this later.)

Existing ASP.NET 1.x controls have been extended in ASP.NET 2.0 to support binding to data source controls as far as data retrieval is concerned. The *DataSourceID* property represents the point of contact between old-style data-bound controls and the new data source components. In ASP.NET 2.0, you can successfully bind a *DataGrid* to a data source control without writing a single line of code—not even the ritual call to *DataBind*. However, achieving codeless programming is not the primary goal of data source controls. Think of data source controls as the natural tool to achieve a less complex and semi-automatic interaction between a variety of data sources and controls.

Existing controls such as *DataGrid* and *Repeater* don't take full advantage of data source components. Only ASP.NET 2.0–specific controls such as *GridView*, *FormView*, and *DetailsView* benefit from the true power of data source controls. This is because new controls have a different internal structure specifically designed to deal with data source controls and share with them the complexity of the data-binding pattern.

A Click in the Life of *DataGrid*

To understand the primary goal of data source components, consider what happens when the user performs an action on some data displayed through a *DataGrid*. Imagine that you display an editable grid—that is, a grid that contains an edit column. Users click a cell to edit the corresponding row; the *DataGrid* posts back and fires an event. Page authors handle the event by writing some code to turn on the control in edit mode. A pair of OK/Cancel buttons replaces the edit button. The user edits the contents of the row and then clicks to save or cancel changes. What happens at this point?

The *DataGrid* control captures the event, validates, and then fires the *UpdateCommand* event. The page author is in charge of handling the event, collecting new data, and building and running any required command against the data source. All these steps require code. The same happens if you need to sort data, view a new page, or drill down into the currently selected record.

A Click in the Life of *GridView*

Let's see what happens if you use the successor to the *DataGrid* control—the *GridView* control—which is specifically designed to adhere to the data source model. Let's assume the same scenario: the user clicks, and the control enters edit mode. The first difference is that you don't need to write any code to turn on edit mode. If you click on a cell within an edit column, the control "knows" what you want to do and intelligently takes the next step and executes the requested action—turning on the edit mode.

When the user clicks to save changes, again the *GridView* control anticipates the user's next action and talks to the data source control to have it perform the requested operation (update) on the data source. All this requires no code from the page author; only a few settings, such as the command text and the connection string, are required and can be set declaratively.

The combination of data source controls and new, smarter data-bound controls demonstrates its true power when your code addresses relatively common scenarios, which is probably 70 to 80 percent of the time. If you need to have things done in a particular way, just work the old way and take full control of the page life cycle. This said, in data source controls you find much more than just a deep understanding of the page life cycle. Data source controls support declarative parameters, transparent data caching, server-side paging ability, hierarchical data support, and the ability to work asynchronously. Implementing all these features manually would require quite a bit of code.

Internals of Data Source Controls

A data source control represents one or more named views of data. Each view manages a collection of data. The data associated with a data source control is managed through SQL-like operations such as SELECT, INSERT, DELETE, and COUNT and through capabilities such as sorting and paging. Data source controls come in two flavors—tabular and hierarchical. Tabular controls are described in Table 9-6.

Table 9-6   Tabular Data Source Controls

Class	Description
AccessDataSource	Represents a connection to a Microsoft Office Access database. Inherits from the SqlDataSource control but points to an MDB file and uses the Jet 4.0 OLE DB provider to connect to the database.
ObjectDataSource	Allows binding to a custom .NET business object that returns data. The class is expected to follow a specific design pattern and include, for example, a parameterless constructor and methods that behave in a certain way.
SqlDataSource	Represents a connection to an ADO.NET data provider that returns SQL data, including data sources accessible through OLE DB and ODBC. The name of the provider and the connection string are specified through properties.

Note that the SqlDataSource class is not specific to SQL Server. It can connect to any ADO.NET provider that manages relational data. Hierarchical data source controls are listed in Table 9-7.

Table 9-7   Hierarchical Data Source Controls

Class	Description
SiteMapDataSource	Allows binding to any provider that supplies site map information. The default provider supplies site map data through an XML file in the root folder of the application.
XmlDataSource	Allows binding to XML files and strings with or without schema information.

Note that data source controls have no visual rendering. They are implemented as controls to allow for "declarative persistence" (automatic instantiation during the request processing) as a native part of the .aspx source code and to gain access to the page view state.

Data Source Views

A named view is represented by a data source view object—an instance of the DataSourceView class. These classes represent a customized view of data in which special settings for sorting, filtering, and other data operations have been defined. The DataSourceView class is the base class for all views associated with a data source control. The number of views in a data source control depends on the connection string, characteristics, and actual contents of the underlying data source. In ASP.NET 2.0, built-in controls support only one view, the default view. Table 9-8 lists the properties of the *DataSourceView* class.

Table 9-8   Properties of the *DataSourceView* Class

Property	Description
CanDelete	Indicates whether deletions are allowed on the underlying data source. The deletion is performed by invoking the *Delete* method.
CanInsert	Indicates whether insertions are allowed on the underlying data source. The insertion is performed by invoking the *Insert* method.
CanPage	Indicates whether the data in the view can be paged.
CanRetrieveTotalRowCount	Indicates whether information about the total row count is available.
CanSort	Indicates whether the data in the view can be sorted.
CanUpdate	Indicates whether updates are allowed on the underlying data source. The update is performed by invoking the *Update* method.
Name	Returns the name of the current view.

The *CanXXX* properties indicate not only whether the data source control is capable of performing the specified operation but also whether that operation is appropriate given the current status of the data. Table 9-9 lists all the methods supported by the class.

Table 9-9   Methods of the *DataSourceView* Class

Method	Description
Delete	Performs a delete operation on the data associated with the view
Insert	Performs an insert operation on the data associated with the view
Select	Returns an enumerable object filled with the data contained in the underlying data storage
Update	Performs an update operation on the data associated with the view

All data source view objects support data retrieval through the *Select* method. The method returns an object that implements the *IEnumerable* interface. The real type of the object depends on the data source control and the attributes set on it.

Interaction with Data-Bound Controls

Figure 9-10 shows the interaction between a data source control and data-bound control in ASP.NET 2.0.

ASP.NET 2.0 controls are aware of the full potential of the data source control and, through the data source control, they use the methods of *IDataSource* to connect to the underlying data repository. Implementing the interface is the only official requirement for a control that intends to behave like a data source control. Once it gets hold of a data source view object, the control can call the properties and methods shown in Table 9-8 and Table 9-9 to perform required tasks.

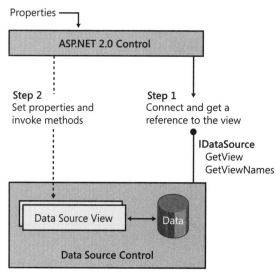

Figure 9-10   The data-bound control gets a view object and talks about capabilities and operations.

Hierarchical Data Source Views

Unlike tabular data source controls, which typically have only one named view, hierarchical data source controls support a view for each level of data that the data source control represents. Hierarchical and tabular data source controls share the same conceptual specification of a consistent and common programming interface for data-bound controls. The only difference is the nature of the data they work with—hierarchical versus flat and tabular.

The view class is different and is named *HierarchicalDataSourceView*. The class features only one method—*Select*—which returns an enumerable hierarchical object. Hierarchical data source controls are, therefore, read-only.

The *SqlDataSource* Control

The *SqlDataSource* control is a data source control that represents a connection to a relational data store such as SQL Server or Oracle or any data source accessible through OLE DB and ODBC bridges.

You set up the connection to the data store using two main properties, *ConnectionString* and *ProviderName*. The former represents the connection string and contains enough information to open a session with the underlying engine. The latter specifies the namespace of the ADO.NET managed provider to use for the operation. The *ProviderName* property defaults to *System.Data.SqlClient*, which means that the default data store is SQL Server. For example, to target an OLE DB provider, use the *System.Data.OleDb* string instead.

The control can retrieve data using either a data adapter or a command object. Depending on your choice, fetched data will be packed in a *DataSet* object or a data reader. The following code snippet shows the minimal code necessary to activate a SQL data source control bound to a SQL Server database:

```
<asp:SqlDataSource runat="server" ID="MySqlSource"
    ProviderName='<%$ ConnectionStrings:LocalNWind.ProviderName %>'
    ConnectionString='<%$ ConnectionStrings:LocalNWind %>'
    SelectCommand="SELECT * FROM employees" />
<asp:DataGrid runat="server" ID="grid" DataSourceID="MySqlSource" />
```

Programming Interface of *SqlDataSource*

The data operations supported by the associated view class are provided by the property groups listed in Table 9-10.

Table 9-10   Properties for Configuring Data Operations

Property Group	Description
DeleteCommand, DeleteParameters, DeleteCommandType	Gets or sets the SQL statement, related parameters, and type (text or stored procedure) used to delete rows in the underlying data store.
FilterExpression, FilterParameters	Gets or sets the string (and related parameters) to create a filter on top of the data retrieved using the *Select* command. Only works if the control manages data through a *DataSet*.
InsertCommand, InsertParameters, InsertCommandType	Gets or sets the SQL statement, related parameters, and type (text or stored procedure) used to insert new rows in the underlying data store.
SelectCommand, SelectParameters, SelectCommandType	Gets or sets the SQL statement, related parameters, and type (text or stored procedure) used to retrieve data from the underlying data store.
SortParameterName	Gets or sets the name of an input parameter that a command's stored procedure will use to sort data. (The command in this case must be a stored procedure.) It raises an exception if the parameter is missing.
UpdateCommand, UpdateParameters, UpdateCommandType	Gets or sets the SQL statement, related parameters, and type (text or stored procedure) used to update rows in the underlying data store.

Each command property is a string that contains the SQL text to be used. The command can optionally contain the parameters listed in the associated parameter collection. The managed provider and its underlying relational engine determine the exact syntax of the SQL to use and the syntax of the embedded parameters. For example, if the data source control points to SQL Server, command parameter names must be prefixed with the @ symbol. If the target data source is an OLE DB provider, parameters are unnamed, identified with a ? placeholder symbol, and located by position. The following code snippet shows a more complex data source control in which parametric delete and update commands have been enabled:

```
<asp:SqlDataSource runat="server" ID="MySqlSource"
    ConnectionString='<%$ ConnectionStrings:LocalNWind %>'
    SelectCommand="SELECT * FROM employees"
    UpdateCommand="UPDATE employees SET lastname=@lname"
    DeleteCommand="DELETE FROM employees WHERE employeeid=@TheEmp"
    FilterExpression="employeeid > 3">
    <!-- parameters go here -->
</asp:SqlDataSource>
```

The syntax used for the *FilterExpression* property is the same as the syntax used for the *RowFilter* property of the *DataView* class, which in turn is similar to that used with the SQL WHERE clause. If the *FilterExpression* property needs to be parametric, you can indicate parameters through the *FilterParameters* collection. Filtering is enabled only when *DataSourceMode* is set to *DataSet*.

> **Note**   Note the difference between filter expressions and parameters on the *Select* command. Parameters on the command influence the result set returned by the data store; a filter expression restricts for display the result set returned through the *Select* command.

Table 9-11 details other operational properties defined on the *SqlDataSource* class. The list doesn't include cache-related properties, which we'll cover in a moment.

Table 9-11   Other Properties on *SqlDataSource*

Property	Description
CancelSelectOnNullParameter	Indicates whether a data-retrieval operation is cancelled if a parameter evaluates to *null*. The default value is *true*.
ConflictDetection	Determines how the control should handle data conflicts during a delete or update operation. By default, changes that occurred in the meantime are overwritten.
ConnectionString	The connection string to connect to the database.
DataSourceMode	Indicates how data should be returned—via a *DataSet* or data reader.
OldValuesParameterFormatString	Gets or sets a format string to apply to the names of any parameters passed to the *Delete* or *Update* method.
ProviderName	Indicates the namespace of the ADO.NET managed provider to use.

It is interesting to note that many of these properties mirror identical properties defined on the actual view class, as illustrated earlier in Figure 9-10.

The *SqlDataSource* object features a few methods and events, which in most cases are common to all data source components. The methods are *Delete*, *Insert*, *Select*, and *Update*, and they're implemented as mere wrappers around the corresponding methods of the underlying data source view class. Events exist in pairs—*Deleting/Deleted*, *Inserting/Inserted*, *Selecting/Selected*, and *Updating/Updated*—and fire before and after any of the methods just mentioned. The beginning of a filtering operation is signaled through the *Filtering* event.

As mentioned, ASP.NET 2.0–specific controls are the only ones to really take advantage of the capabilities of data source controls. For this reason, in the next two chapters devoted to *GridView*, *DetailsView*, and *FormView* controls, we'll see a lot of sample code showing how to use the *SqlDataSource* control for selecting, updating, paging, and sorting. In this chapter, we'll need to spend more time discussing other features of the control that can be particularly useful in real-world applications.

Declarative Parameters

Each command property has its own collection of parameters—an instance of a collection class named *ParameterCollection*. ASP.NET 2.0 supports quite a few parameter types, which are listed in Table 9-12.

Table 9-12   Parameter Types in ASP.NET 2.0

Parameter	Description
ControlParameter	Gets the parameter value from any public property of a server control
CookieParameter	Sets the parameter value based on the content of the specified HTTP cookie
FormParameter	Gets the parameter value from the specified input field in the HTTP request form
Parameter	Gets the parameter value assigned by the code
ProfileParameter	Gets the parameter value from the specified property name in the profile object created from the application's personalization scheme
QueryStringParameter	Gets the parameter value from the specified variable in the request query string
SessionParameter	Sets the parameter value based on the content of the specified session state slot

Each parameter class has a *Name* property and a set of properties specific to its role and implementation. To understand declarative parameters in data source controls, take a look at the following code:

```
<asp:SqlDataSource runat="server" ID="MySource"
    ConnectionString='<%$ ConnectionStrings:LocalNWind %>'
    SelectCommand="SELECT * FROM employees WHERE employeeid > @MinID">
    <SelectParameters>
        <asp:ControlParameter Name="MinID" ControlId="EmpID"
            PropertyName="Text" />
    </SelectParameters>
</asp:SqlDataSource>
```

The query contains a placeholder named *@MinID*. The data source control automatically populates the placeholder with the information returned by the *ControlParameter* object. The value of the parameter is determined by the value of a given property on a given control. The name of the property is specified by the *PropertyName* attribute. The ID of the control is in the *ControlId* attribute. For the previous code to work, page developers must guarantee that the page contains a control with a given ID and property; otherwise, an exception is thrown. In the example, the value of the property *Text* on the *EmpID* control is used as the value for the matching parameter.

The binding between formal parameters (the placeholders in the command text) and actual values depends on how the underlying managed provider handles and recognizes parameters. If the provider type supports named parameters—as is the case with SQL Server and Oracle—the binding involves matching the names of placeholders with the names of the parameters. Otherwise, the matching is based on the position. Hence, the first placeholder is bound to the first parameter, and so on. This is what happens if OLE DB is used to access the data.

Conflicts Detection

The *SqlDataSource* control can optionally perform database-intrusive operations (deletions and updates) in either of two ways. The data source control is associated with a data-bound control, so it is not a far-fetched idea that data is read at the same time, perhaps modified on the client, and then updated. In a situation in which multiple users have read/write access to the database, what should be the behavior of the update/delete methods if the record they attempt to work on has been modified in the meantime?

The *SqlDataSource* control uses the *ConflictDetection* property to determine what to do when performing update and delete operations. The property is declared as type *ConflictOptions*—an enum type. The default value is *OverwriteChanges*, which means that any intrusive operation happens regardless of whether values in the row have changed since they were last read. The alternative is the *CompareAllValues* value, which simply ensures that the *SqlDataSource* control passes the original data read from the database to the *Delete* or *Update* method of the underlying view class.

It is important to note that changing the value of *ConflictDetection* doesn't produce any significant effect unless you write your delete or update statements in such a way that the command fails if the data in the row doesn't match the data that was initially read. To get this, you should define the command as follows:

```
UPDATE employees SET firstname=@firstname
WHERE employeeid=@employeeid AND firstname=@original_firstname
```

In other words, you must explicitly add to the command an extra clause to check whether the current value of the field being modified still matches the value initially read. In this way, intermediate changes entered by concurrent users make the WHERE clause fail and make the command fail. You are in charge of tweaking the command text yourself; setting *ConflictDetection* to *CompareAllValues* is not enough.

How would you format the name of the parameters that represent old values? The *SqlDataSource* control uses the *OldValuesParameterFormatString* property to format these parameter names. The default value is *original_{0}*.

When you use the *CompareAllValues* option, you can handle the *Deleted* or *Updated* event on the data source control to check how many rows are affected. If no rows are affected by the operation, a concurrency violation might have occurred:

```
void OnUpdated(object sender, SqlDataSourceStatusEventArgs e)
{
    if (e.AffectedRows == 0) {
        ...
    }
}
```

Caching Behavior

The data binding between a data-bound control and its data source component is automatic and takes place on each postback caused by the data-bound control. Imagine a page with grid, a data source control, and a button. If you turn on the grid in edit mode, the *Select* command is run; if you click the button (outside the boundaries of the data-bound control) the UI of the grid is rebuilt from the view state and no *Select* statement is run.

To save a query on each postback, you can ask the data source control to cache the result set for a given duration. While data is cached, the *Select* method retrieves data from the cache rather than from the underlying database. When the cache expires, the *Select* method retrieves data from the underlying database, and stores the fresh data back to the cache. The caching behavior of the *SqlDataSource* control is governed by the properties in Table 9-13.

Table 9-13   Caching Properties on *SqlDataSource*

Property	Description
CacheDuration	Indicates in seconds how long the data should be maintained in the cache.
CacheExpirationPolicy	Indicates if the cache duration is absolute or sliding. If absolute, data is invalidated after the specified number of seconds. If sliding, data is invalidated if not used for the specified duration.
CacheKeyDependency	Indicates the name of a user-defined cache key that is linked to all cache entries created by the data source control. By expiring the key, you can clear the control's cache.
EnableCaching	Enables or disables caching support.
SqlCacheDependency	Gets or sets a semicolon-delimited string that indicates which databases and tables to use for the SQL Server cache dependency.

A single cache entry is created for each distinct combination of *SelectCommand*, *ConnectionString*, and *SelectParameters*. Multiple *SqlDataSource* controls can share the same cache entries if they happen to load the same data from the same database. You can take control of cache entries managed by the data source control through the *CacheKeyDependency* property. If set to a non-null string, the property forces the *SqlDataSource* control to create a dependency between that key and all cache entries created by the control. At this point, to clear the control's cache, you only have to assign a new value to the dependency key:

```
Cache["ClearAll"] = anyInitializationValue;
SqlDataSource1.CacheKeyDependency = "ClearAll";
...
Cache["ClearAll"] = anyOtherValue;
```

The *SqlDataSource* control can cache data only when working in *DataSet* mode. You get an exception if *DataSourceMode* is set to *DataReader* and caching is enabled.

Finally, the *SqlCacheDependency* property links the *SqlDataSource* cached data with the contents of the specified database table (typically, the same table where the cached data comes from):

```
<asp:SqlDataSource ID="SqlDataSource1" runat="server"
  CacheDuration="1200"
  ConnectionString="<%$ ConnectionStrings:LocalNWind %>"
  EnableCaching="true"
  SelectCommand="SELECT * FROM employees"
  SqlCacheDependency="Northwind:Employees">
</asp:SqlDataSource>
```

Whenever the underlying table changes, the cached data is automatically flushed. We'll cover SQL cache dependencies in detail in Chapter 14.

The *AccessDataSource* Class

The *AccessDataSource* control is a data source control that represents a connection to an Access database. It is based on the *SqlDataSource* control and provides a simpler, made-to-measure programming interface. As a derived class, *AccessDataSource* inherits all members defined on its parent and overrides a few of them. In particular, the control replaces the *ConnectionString* and *ProviderName* properties with a more direct *DataFile* property. You set this property to the *.mdb* database file of choice. The data source control resolves the file path at run time and uses the Microsoft Jet 4 OLE DB provider to connect to the database.

> **Note**   *AccessDataSource* actually inherits from *SqlDataSource* and for this reason can't make base members disappear, as hinted at earlier. *AccessDataSource* doesn't really replace the *ConnectionString* and *ProviderName* properties; it overrides them so that an exception is thrown whenever someone attempts to set their value. Another property overridden only to throw exceptions is *SqlCacheDependency*. This feature, of course, is not supported.

Working with an Access Database

The following code shows how to use the *AccessDataSource* control to open an *.mdb* file and bind its content to a drop-down list control. Note that the control opens Access database files in read-only mode by default:

```
<asp:AccessDataSource runat="server" ID="MyAccessSource"
    DataFile="nwind.mdb"
    SelectCommand="SELECT * FROM Customers" />
Select a Customer:
<asp:DropDownList runat="server" DataSourceId="MyAccessSource" />
```

Several features of the *AccessDataSource* control are inherited from the base class, *SqlDataSource*. In fact, the Access data source control is basically a SQL data source control optimized to work with Access databases. Like its parent control, the *AccessDataSource* control supports two distinct data source modes—*DataSet* and *DataReader*, depending on the ADO.NET classes used to retrieve data. Filtering can be applied to the selected data only if the fetch operation returns a *DataSet*. Caching works as on the parent class except for the *SqlCacheDependency* feature.

Updating an Access Database

The *AccessDataSource* can also be used to perform insert, update, or delete operations against the associated database. This is done using ADO.NET commands and parameter collections. Updates are problematic for Access databases when performed from within an ASP.NET application because an Access database is a plain file and the default account of the ASP.NET process (ASPNET or NetworkService, depending on the host operating system) might not have sufficient permission to write to the database file. For the data source updates to work, you should grant write permission to the ASP.NET account on the database file. Alternatively, you can use a different account with adequate permission.

> **Note** Most Internet service providers (ISPs) normally give you one directory in which ASPNET and NetworkService accounts have been granted write permission. In this case, you just place your Access file in this directory and you can read and write seamlessly. In general, though, Access databases are plain files and, as such, are subject to the security rules of ASP.NET.

The *ObjectDataSource* Control

The *ObjectDataSource* class enables user-defined classes to associate the output of their methods to data-bound controls. Like other data source controls, *ObjectDataSource* supports declarative parameters to allow developers to pass page-level variables to the object's methods. The *ObjectDataSource* class makes some assumptions about the objects it wraps. As a consequence, an arbitrary class can't be used with this data source control. In particular, bindable classes are expected to have a default constructor, to be stateless, and to have methods that easily map to select, update, insert, and delete semantics. Also, the object must perform updates one item at a time; objects that update their states using batch operations are not supported. The bottom line is that managed objects that work well with *ObjectDataSource* are designed with this data source class in mind.

Programming Interface of *ObjectDataSource*

The *ObjectDataSource* component provides nearly the same programmatic interface (events, methods, and properties, and associated behaviors) as the *SqlDataSource*, with the addition of three new events and a few properties. The events are related to the lifetime of the underlying business object—*ObjectCreating*, *ObjectCreated*, and *ObjectDisposing*. Table 9-14 lists other key properties of *ObjectDataSource*.

Table 9-14   Main Properties of *ObjectDataSource*

Property	Description
ConvertNullToDBNull	Indicates whether null parameters passed to insert, delete, or update operations are converted to *System.DBNull*. False by default.
DataObjectTypeName	Gets or sets the name of a class that is to be used as a parameter for a *Select*, *Insert*, *Update*, or *Delete* operation.
DeleteMethod, DeleteParameters	Gets or sets the name of the method and related parameters used to perform a delete operation.
EnablePaging	Indicates whether the control supports paging.
FilterExpression, FilterParameters	Indicates the filter expression (and parameters) to filter the output of a select operation.
InsertMethod, InsertParameters	Gets or sets the name of the method and related parameters used to perform an insert operation.
MaximumRowsParameterName	If the *EnablePaging* property is set to *true*, indicates the parameter name of the *Select* method that accepts the value for the number of records to retrieve.
OldValuesParameterFormatString	Gets or sets a format string to apply to the names of any parameters passed to the *Delete* or *Update* methods.
SelectCountMethod	Gets or sets the name of the method used to perform a select count operation.
SelectMethod, SelectParameters	Gets or sets the name of the method and related parameters used to perform a select operation.
SortParameterName	Gets or sets the name of an input parameter used to sort retrieved data. It raises an exception if the parameter is missing.
StartRowIndexParameterName	If the *EnablePaging* property is set to *true*, indicates the parameter name of the *Select* method that accepts the value for the starting record to retrieve.
UpdateMethod, UpdateParameters	Gets or sets the name of the method and related parameters used to perform an update operation.

The *ObjectDataSource* control uses reflection to locate and invoke the method to handle the specified operation. The *TypeName* property returns the fully qualified name of the assembly that defines the class to call. If the class is defined in the *App_Code* directory, you don't need to indicate the assembly name. Otherwise, you use a comma-separated string in the form of *[classname, assembly]*. Let's see an example.

> **Warning**   Having too many classes in the *App_Code* directory can become a nightmare at development time because any changes to any files will cause Visual Studio .NET to recompile the whole set of files in the project.

Implementing Data Retrieval

The following code snippet illustrates a class that can be used with an object data source. Architected according to the Table Data Gateway (TDG) pattern, the class represents employees and takes advantage of two other helper classes (at the very minimum): *Employee* and *Employee-Collection*. The class *Employee* contains information about the entity being represented; the class *EmployeeCollection* represents a collection of employees. The behavior of the entity "employee" is codified in a bunch of methods exposed out of the gateway class—*Employees*:

```
public class Employees
{
    public static string ConnectionString {
        ...
    }
    public static void Load(int employeeID) {
        ...
    }
    public static EmployeeCollection LoadAll() {
        ...
    }
    public static EmployeeCollection LoadByCountry(string country) {
        ...
    }
    public static void Save(Employee emp) {
        ...
    }
    public static void Insert(Employee emp) {
        ...
    }
    public static void Delete(int employeeID) {
        ...
    }
    ...
}
```

The TDG pattern requires the gateway to be shared among instances of the entity class—in the following example, I implemented the class with static methods. If you don't use static methods, the worker class you use with *ObjectDataSource* must have a default parameterless constructor. Furthermore, the class should not maintain any state.

> **Warning**   Using static methods in the context of a TDG pattern is fine from an architectural viewpoint, but it might pose practical problems with unit testing. What if you test a business class that calls the Data Access Layer (DAL) internally and the DAL fails? Can you figure out what really happened? Does the business class work or not? To effectively test a business layer that calls into a DAL, you need to focus on the object under test. Mock objects come to the rescue. Mock objects are programmable polymorphic objects that present themselves as others and can wrap DAL anomalies and signal them out clearly, making the test succeed if nothing else happens. The point is that mocking toolkits typically don't like static methods. That's why instance methods might be preferable in real-world implementations of the TDG pattern.

The worker class must be accessible from within the *.aspx* page and can be bound to the *ObjectDataSource* control, as shown here:

```
<asp:ObjectDataSource runat="server" ID="MyObjectSource"
    TypeName="ProAspNet20.DAL.Employees"
    SelectMethod="LoadAll" />
```

When the HTTP runtime encounters a similar block in a Web page, it generates code that calls the *LoadAll* method on the specified class. The returned data—an instance of the *EmployeeCollection*—is bound to any control that links to *MyObjectSource* via the *DataSourceID* property. Let's take a brief look at the implementation of the *LoadAll* method:

```
public static EmployeeCollection LoadAll()
{
    EmployeeCollection coll = new EmployeeCollection();

    using (SqlConnection conn = new SqlConnection(ConnectionString))
    {
        SqlCommand cmd = new SqlCommand("SELECT * FROM employees", conn);
        conn.Open();
        SqlDataReader reader = cmd.ExecuteReader();
        HelperMethods.FillEmployeeList(coll, reader);
        reader.Close();
        conn.Close();
    }
    return coll;
}
```

A bit oversimplified to fit in the section, the preceding code remains quite clear: you execute a command, fill in a custom collection class, and return it to the data-bound control. The only piece of code you need to write is the worker class—you don't need to put any code in the code-behind class of the page:

```
<asp:DataGrid ID="grid" runat="server" DataSourceID="MyObjectSource" />
```

The *DataGrid* receives a collection of *Employee* objects defined as follows:

```
public class EmployeeCollection : List<Employee>
{
}
```

Binding is totally seamless, even without ADO.NET container objects. (See the companion code for full details.)

The method associated with the *SelectMethod* property must return any of the following: an *IEnumerable* object such as a collection, *DataSet*, *DataTable*, or *Object*. Preferably, the *Select* method is not overloaded, although *ObjectDataSource* doesn't prevent you from using overloading in your business classes.

Using Parameters

In most cases, methods require parameters. *SelectParameters* is the collection you use to add input parameters to the select method. Imagine you have a method to load employees by country. Here's the code you need to come up with:

```
<asp:ObjectDataSource ID="ObjectDataSource1" runat="server"
    TypeName="ProAspNet20.DAL.Employees"
    SelectMethod="LoadByCountry">
    <SelectParameters>
        <asp:ControlParameter Name="country" ControlID="Countries"
            PropertyName="SelectedValue" />
    </SelectParameters>
</asp:ObjectDataSource>
```

The preceding code snippet is the declarative version of the following pseudocode, where *Countries* is expected to be a drop-down list filled with country names:

```
string country = Countries.SelectedValue;
EmployeeCollection coll = Employees.LoadByCountry(country);
```

The *ControlParameter* class automates the retrieval of the actual parameter value and the binding to the parameter list of the method. What if you add an *[All Countries]* entry to the drop-down list? In this case, if the *All Countries* option is selected, you need to call *LoadAll* without parameters; otherwise, if a particular country is selected, you need to call *LoadByCountry* with a parameter. Declarative programming works great in the simple scenarios; otherwise, you just write code:

```
void Page_Load(object sender, EventArgs e)
{
    // Must be cleared every time (or disable the viewstate)
    ObjectDataSource1.SelectParameters.Clear();

    if (Countries.SelectedIndex == 0)
        ObjectDataSource1.SelectMethod = "LoadAll";
    else
    {
        ObjectDataSource1.SelectMethod = "LoadByCountry";
        ControlParameter cp = new ControlParameter("country",
            "Countries", "SelectedValue");
        ObjectDataSource1.SelectParameters.Add(cp);
    }
}
```

Note that data source controls are like ordinary server controls and can be programmatically configured and invoked. In the code just shown, you first check the selection the user made and if it matches the first option (*All Countries*), configure the data source control to make a parameterless call to the *LoadAll* method.

You must clean up the content of the *SelectParameters* collection upon page loading. The data source control (more precisely, the underlying view control) caches most of its properties to the view state. As a result, *SelectParameters* is not empty when you refresh the page after changing the drop-down list selection. The preceding code clears only the *SelectParameters* collection; performance-wise, it could be preferable to disable the view state altogether on the data source control. However, if you disable the view state, all collections will be empty on the data source control upon loading.

> **Important**   *ObjectDataSource* allows data retrieval and update while keeping data access and business logic separate from user interface. The use of the *ObjectDataSource* class doesn't automatically transform your system into a well-designed, effective n-tiered system. Data source controls are mostly a counterpart to data-bound controls so that the latter can work more intelligently. To take full advantage of *ObjectDataSource*, you need to have your DAL already in place. It doesn't work the other way around. *ObjectDataSource* doesn't necessarily have to be bound to the root of the DAL, which could be on a remote location and perhaps behind a firewall. In this case, you write a local intermediate object and connect it to *ObjectDataSource* on one end and to the DAL on the other end. The intermediate object acts as an application-specific proxy and works according to the application's specific rules. *ObjectDataSource* doesn't break n-tiered systems, nor does it transform existing systems into truly n-tier systems. It greatly benefits, instead, from existing business and data layers.

Caching Data and Object Instances

The *ObjectDataSource* component supports caching only when the specified select method returns a *DataSet* or *DataTable* object. If the wrapped object returns a custom collection (as in the example we're considering), an exception is thrown.

ObjectDataSource is designed to work with classes in the business layer of the application. An instance of the business class is created for each operation performed and destroyed shortly after the operation is complete. This model is the natural offspring of the stateless programming model that ASP.NET promotes. In case of business objects that are particularly expensive to initialize, you can resort to static classes or static methods in instance classes. (If you do so, bear in mind what we said earlier regarding unit testing classes with static methods.)

Instances of the business object are not automatically cached or pooled. Both options, though, can be manually implemented by properly handling the *ObjectCreating* and *Object-Disposing* events on an *ObjectDataSource* control. The *ObjectCreating* event fires when the data source control needs to get an instance of the business class. You can write the handler to retrieve an existing instance of the class and return that to the data source control:

```
// Handle the ObjectCreating event on the data source control
public void BusinessObjectBeingCreated(object sender,
        ObjectDataSourceEventArgs e)
{
    BusinessObject bo = RetrieveBusinessObjectFromPool();
    if (bo == null)
        bo = new BusinessObject();
    e.ObjectInstance = bo;
}
```

Likewise, in *ObjectDisposing* you store the instance again and cancel the disposing operation being executed:

```
// Handle the ObjectDisposing event on the data source control
public void BusinessObjectBeingDisposed(object sender,
        ObjectDataSourceDisposingEventArgs e)
{
    ReturnBusinessObjectToPool(e.ObjectInstance);
    e.Cancel = true;
}
```

It is not only object instances that aren't cached. In some cases, even retrieved data is not persisted in memory for the specified duration. More precisely, the *ObjectDataSource* control does support caching just as *SqlDataSource* does, except that caching is enabled only if the select method returns a *DataTable* or *DataSet* object. A *DataView*, and in general a simple enumerable collection of data, isn't cached; if you enable caching in this scenario, an exception will be thrown.

> **Note**   Just as with caching, filtering is also not permitted when the return value is not an ADO.NET container class

Setting Up for Paging

Unlike *SqlDataSource*, *ObjectDataSource* also supports paging. Three properties in Table 9-14 participate in paging—*EnablePaging*, *StartRowIndexParameterName*, and *MaximumRowsParameterName*.

As the name clearly suggests, *EnablePaging* toggles support for paging on and off. The default value is *false*, meaning that paging is not turned on automatically. *ObjectDataSource* provides an infrastructure for paging, but actual paging must be implemented in the class bound to *ObjectDataSource*. In the following code snippet, the *Customers* class has a method, *LoadByCountry*, that takes two additional parameters to indicate the page size and the index of the first record in the page. The names of these two parameters must be assigned to *MaximumRowsParameterName* and *StartRowIndexParameterName*, respectively:

```
<asp:ObjectDataSource ID="ObjectDataSource1" runat="server"
    TypeName="ProAspNet20.DAL.Customers"
    StartRowIndexParameterName="firstRow"
    MaximumRowsParameterName="totalRows"
    SelectMethod="LoadByCountry">
  <SelectParameters>
    <asp:ControlParameter Name="country" ControlID="Countries"
        PropertyName="SelectedValue" />
    <asp:ControlParameter Name="totalRows" ControlID="PageSize"
        PropertyName="Text" />
    <asp:ControlParameter Name="firstRow" ControlID="FirstRow"
        PropertyName="Text" />
  </SelectParameters>
</asp:ObjectDataSource>
```

The implementation of paging is up to the method and must be coded manually. *LoadByCountry* provides two overloads, one of which supports paging. Internally, paging is actually delegated to *FillCustomerList*:

```
public static CustomerCollection LoadByCountry(string country)
{
    return LoadByCountry(country, -1, 0);
}
public static CustomerCollection LoadByCountry(string country,
        int totalRows, int firstRow)
{
    CustomerCollection coll = new CustomerCollection();

    using (SqlConnection conn = new SqlConnection(ConnectionString))
    {
        SqlCommand cmd;
        cmd = new SqlCommand(CustomerCommands.cmdLoadByCountry, conn);
        cmd.Parameters.AddWithValue("@country", country);

        conn.Open();
        SqlDataReader reader = cmd.ExecuteReader();
        HelperMethods.FillCustomerList(coll, reader, totalRows, firstRow);
        reader.Close();
        conn.Close();
    }

    return coll;
}
```

As you can see in the companion source code, *FillCustomerList* doesn't use a particularly smart approach. It simply scrolls the whole result set using a reader and discards all the records that don't belong in the requested range. You could improve upon this approach to make paging smarter. What's important here is that paging is built into your business object and exposed by data source controls to the pageable controls through a well-known interface.

Updating and Deleting Data

To update underlying data using *ObjectDataSource*, you need to define an update/insert/delete method. All the actual methods you use must have semantics that are well-suited to implement such operations. Again, this requirement is easily met if you employ the TDG pattern in the design of your DAL. Here are some good prototypes for the update operations:

```
public static void Save(Employee emp)
public static void Insert(Employee emp)
public static void Delete(int id)
```

More than select operations, update operations require parameters. To update a record, you need to pass new values and one or more old values to make sure the right record to update is located and to take into account the possibility of data conflicts. To delete a record, you need to identify it by matching a supplied primary key parameter. To specify input parameters, you can use command collections such as *UpdateParameters*, *InsertParameters*, or *DeleteParameters*. Let's examine update/insert scenarios first.

To update an existing record or insert a new one, you need to pass new values. This can be done in either of two ways—listing parameters explicitly or aggregating all parameters in an all-encompassing data structure. The prototypes shown previously for *Save* and *Insert* follow the latter approach. An alternative might be the following:

```
public static void Save(int id, string firstName, string lastName, ...)

public static void Insert(string firstName, string lastName, ...)
```

You can use command parameter collections only if the types involved are simple types—numbers, strings, dates. If your DAL implements the TDG pattern (or a similar one, such as Data Mapper), your update/insert methods are likely to accept a custom aggregate data object as a parameter—the *Employee* class seen earlier. To make a custom class such as *Employee* acceptable to the *ObjectDataSource* control, you need to set the *DataObjectTypeName* property:

```
<asp:ObjectDataSource ID="RowDataSource" runat="server"
    TypeName="ProAspNet20.DAL.Employees"
    SelectMethod="Load"
    UpdateMethod="Save"
    DataObjectTypeName="ProAspNet20.DAL.Employee">
  <SelectParameters>
      <asp:ControlParameter Name="id" ControlID="GridView1"
          PropertyName="SelectedValue" />
  </SelectParameters>
</asp:ObjectDataSource>
```

The preceding *ObjectDataSource* control saves rows through the *Save* method, which takes an *Employee* object. Note that when you set the *DataObjectTypeName* property, the *UpdateParameters* collection is ignored. The *ObjectDataSource* instantiates a default instance of the object before the operation is performed and then attempts to fill its public members with the values of any matching input fields found around the bound control. Because this work is performed using reflection, the names of the input fields in the bound control must match the names of public properties exposed by the object in the *DataObjectTypeName* property. A practical limitation you must be aware of is that you can't define the *Employee* class using complex data types, as follows:

```
public class Employee {
    public string LastName {…}
    public string FirstName {…}
    ...
    public Address HomeAddress {…}
}
```

Representing individual values (*strings* in the sample), the *LastName* and *FirstName* members have good chances to match an input field in the bound control. The same can't be said for the *HomeAddress* member, which is declared of a custom aggregate type like *Address*. If you go with this schema, all the members in *Address* will be ignored; any related information won't be carried into the *Save* method, with resulting null parameters. All the members in the *Address* data structure should become members of the *Employee* class.

> **Note**   Recall that data source controls work at their fullest only with a few ASP.NET 2.0 controls, such as *GridView* (Chapter 10) and *DetailsView* (Chapter 11). We'll return to the topic of the internal mechanism of parameter binding later in the book. For now, it suffices to say that as a page author you're responsible for making input fields and member names match in the following way: columns in *GridView* and rows in *DetailsView* have a *DataField* attribute pointing to the data source field to use (that is, *lastname*, where *lastname* is typically a database column retrieved by the select operation). The data field name must match (case-insensitive) a public property in the class used as a parameter in the update/insert operation—in this case, the *Employee* class.

Unlike the insert operation, the update operation also requires a primary key value to identify uniquely the record being updated. If you use an explicit parameter listing, you just append an additional parameter to the list to represent the ID, as follows:

```
<asp:ObjectDataSource runat="server" ID="MyObjectSource"
    TypeName="ProAspNet20.SimpleBusinessObject"
    SelectMethod="GetEmployees"
    UpdateMethod="SetEmployee">
  <UpdateParameters>
      <asp:Parameter Name="employeeid" Type="Int32" />
      <asp:Parameter Name="firstname" Type="string" />
      <asp:Parameter Name="lastname" Type="string" />
      <asp:Parameter Name="country" Type="string" DefaultValue="null" />
  </UpdateParameters>
</asp:ObjectDataSource>
```

Note that by setting the *DefaultValue* attribute to *null*, you can make a parameter optional. A null value for a parameter must then be gracefully handled by the method to implement the update.

There's an alternative method to set the primary key—through the *DataKeyNames* property of *GridView* and *DetailsView* controls. I'll briefly mention it here and cover it in much greater detail in the next two chapters:

```
<asp:GridView runat="server" ID="grid1"
    DataKeyNames="employeeid"
    DataSourceId="MyObjectSource"
    AutoGenerateEditButton="true">
  ...
</asp:GridView>
```

When *DataKeyNames* is set on the bound control, data source controls automatically add a parameter to the list of parameters for update and delete commands. The default name of the parameter is *original_XXX*, where *XXX* stands for the value of *DataKeyNames*. For the operation to succeed, the method (or the SQL command if you're using *SqlDataSource*) must handle a parameter with the same name. Here's an example:

```
UPDATE employees SET lastname=@lastname
       WHERE employeeid=@original_employeeid
```

The name format of the key parameter can be changed at will through the *OldValues-ParameterFormatString* property. For example, a value of "{0}" assigned to the property would make the following command acceptable:

```
UPDATE employees SET lastname=@lastname
       WHERE employeeid=@employeeid
```

Setting the *DataKeyNames* property on the bound control (hold on, it's *not* a property on the data source control) is also the simplest way to configure a delete operation. For a delete operation, in fact, you don't need to specify a whole record with all its fields; the key is sufficient.

> **Note**   In ASP.NET 2.0 data-bound controls such as *GridView* and *DetailsView*, the *DataKey-Names* property replaces *DataKeyField*, which we found on *DataGrid* and *DataList* controls in ASP.NET 1.x. The difference between the two lies in the fact that *DataKeyNames* support keys based on multiple fields. If *DataKeyNames* is set to multiple fields (for example, *id,name*), two parameters are added: *original_id* and *original_name*.

Configuring Parameters at Run Time

When using *ObjectDataSource* with an ASP.NET 2.0 made-to-measure control (for example, *GridView*), most of the time the binding is totally automatic and you don't have to deal with it. If you need it, though, there's a back door you can use to take control of the update process—the *Updating* event:

```
protected void Updating(object sender, ObjectDataSourceMethodEventArgs e)
{
    Employee emp = (Employee) e.InputParameters[0];
    emp.LastName = "whosthisguy";
}
```

The event fires before the update operation climaxes. The *InputParameters* collection lists the parameters being passed to the update method. The collection is read-only, meaning that you can't add or delete elements. However, you can modify objects being transported, as the preceding code snippet demonstrates.

This technique is useful when, for whatever reasons, the *ObjectDataSource* control doesn't load all the data its method needs to perform the update. A similar approach can be taken for deletions and insertions as well.

The *SiteMapDataSource* Class

Site maps are a common feature of cutting-edge Web sites. A site map is the graph that represents all the pages and directories found in a Web site. Site map information is used to show users the logical coordinates of the page they are visiting, allow users to access site locations dynamically, and render all the navigation information in a graphical fashion (as shown in Figure 9-11).

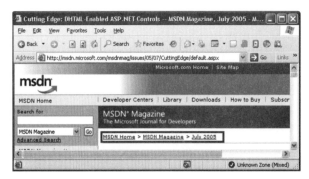

Figure 9-11   The graphical layout that the *MSDN Magazine* Web site uses to represent the location of a page in the site hierarchy.

ASP.NET 2.0 contains a rich navigation infrastructure that allows developers to specify the site structure. I cover site navigation in detail in *Programming Microsoft ASP.NET 2.0 Applications: Advanced Topics*. For now, it suffices to say that the site map is a hierarchical piece of information that can be used as input for a hierarchical data source control such as *SiteMapDataSource*. The output of *SiteMapDataSource* can bound to hierarchical data-bound controls such as *Menu*.

Displaying Site Map Information

The site map information can appear in many ways, the simplest of which is an XML file named *web.sitemap* located in the root of the application. To give you the essence of site maps and site map data sources, let's briefly review a few usage scenarios. Suppose you're writing a Web site and your client asks for a sequence of hyperlinks that indicate the location of the page in the site map. In ASP.NET 1.x, you have to create your own infrastructure to hold site map information and render the page location. (Typically, you would use a configuration file and a user control.) ASP.NET 2.0 provides richer support for site maps. You start by creating a configuration file named *web.sitemap* in the root of the Web application. The file describes the relationship between pages on the site. Your next step will depend on the expected output.

If the common representation shown in Figure 9-11 (a sequence of hyperlinks with a separator) is what you need, add a *SiteMapPath* control to the page. This control retrieves the site map and produces the necessary HTML markup. In this simple case, there is no need to resort to a site map data source control. If you need to build a more complex hierarchical layout—for example, a tree-based representation—you need the *SiteMapDataSource* control.

The *SiteMapDataSource* control pumps site map information to a hierarchical data-bound control (for example, the new *TreeView* control) so that it can display the site's structure. Here's a quick example:

```
<%@ Page Language="C#" %>
<html>
<body>
    <form runat="server">
        <asp:SiteMapDataSource runat="server" ID="MySiteMapSource" />
        <asp:TreeView runat="server" DataSourceId="MySiteMapSource" />
    </form>
</body>
</html>
```

Figure 9-12 shows the final output as it appears to the end user.

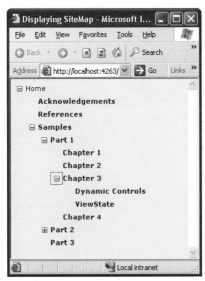

Figure 9-12   The site map information rendered through a *TreeView* control.

The site map information might look like the following:

```
<siteMap>
    <siteMapNode title="Home" url="default.aspx" >
        <siteMapNode title="Acknowledgements" url="ack.aspx"/>
        <siteMapNode title="References" url="ref.aspx" />
        <siteMapNode title="Samples">
            <siteMapNode title="Part 1">
                <siteMapNode title="Chapter 1" />
                <siteMapNode title="Chapter 2" />
                <siteMapNode title="Chapter 3">
                    <siteMapNode title="Dynamic Controls" url="…/dynctls.aspx" />
                    <siteMapNode title="ViewState" url="…/viewstate.aspx" />
                </siteMapNode>
                <siteMapNode title="Chapter 4" />
            </siteMapNode>
            <siteMapNode title="Part 2">
                <siteMapNode title="Chapter 9">
                    <siteMapNode title="Site map" url="…/sitemapinfo.aspx" />
                </siteMapNode>
            </siteMapNode>
            <siteMapNode title="Part 3" url="samples.aspx?partid=3" />
        </siteMapNode>
    </siteMapNode>
</siteMap>
```

Note that the *url* attribute is optional. If not defined, the node is intended to be an inert container and won't be made clickable.

> **Note**   As mentioned, ASP.NET 2.0 introduces a new type of data-bound control that was completely unsupported in previous versions—the hierarchical data-bound control. A new base class is defined to provide a minimum set of capabilities: *HierarchicalDataBoundControl*. The *TreeView* and *Menu* controls fall into this category.

Programming Interface of *SiteMapDataSource*

Table 9-15 details the properties available in the *SiteMapDataSource* class.

Table 9-15   Properties of *SiteMapDataSource*

Property	Description
Provider	Indicates the site map provider object associated with the data source control.
ShowStartingNode	True by default, indicates whether the starting node is retrieved and displayed.
SiteMapProvider	Gets and sets the name of the site map provider associated with the instance of the control.
StartFromCurrent-Node	False by default, indicates whether the node tree is retrieved relative to the current page.
StartingNodeOffset	Gets and sets a positive or negative offset from the starting node that determines the root hierarchy exposed by the control. Set to 0 by default.
StartingNodeUrl	Indicates the URL in the site map in which the node tree is rooted.

By default, the starting node is the root node of the hierarchy, but you can change the starting node through a pair of mutually exclusive properties—*StartFromCurrentNode* and *Starting-NodeUrl*. If you explicitly indicate the URL of the page that should appear as the root of the displayed hierarchy, make sure the *StartFromCurrentNode* property is *false*. Likewise, if you set *StartFromCurrentNode* to *true*, ensure the *StartingNodeUrl* property evaluates to the empty string.

Properly used, the *StartingNodeOffset* property lets you restrict the nodes of the site map that are actually displayed. The default value of 0 indicates that the root hierarchy exposed by the *SiteMapDataSource* control is the same as the starting node. A value greater than 0 goes as many levels down in the hierarchy proceeding from the root to the requested node and uses the node found as the root. Look at the sample site map we considered earlier. If you request *sitemapinfo.aspx* with an offset of 1, the displayed hierarchy will be rooted in the *Samples* node—that is, one level down the real root. If you set it to 2, the effective root will be the *Part 2* node. A negative offset, on the other hand, ensures that the specified number of child levels will be displayed if possible.

The *SiteMapDataSource* class features a couple of properties that relate to the site map provider: *SiteMapProvider* and *Provider*. The former specifies the name of the site map provider to use; the latter returns a reference to the object.

The *XmlDataSource* Class

The *XmlDataSource* control is a special type of data source control that supports both tabular and hierarchical views of data. The tabular view of XML data is just a list of nodes at a given level of hierarchy, whereas the hierarchical view shows the complete hierarchy. An XML node is an instance of the *XmlNode* class; the complete hierarchy is an instance of the *XmlDocument* class. The XML data source supports only read-only scenarios.

> **Important**   The *XmlDataSource* control is unique in that it is the only built-in data source control to implement both *IDataSource* and *IHierarchicalDataSource* interfaces. For both interfaces, though, the control doesn't go further than implementing the *Select* method. Hence, the *XmlDataSource* control is not suitable for Web applications using read/write XML data stores, as it doesn't support methods such as *Delete*, *Insert*, and *Update*.

Programming Interface of *XmlDataSource*

Table 9-16 details the properties of the *XmlDataSource* control.

Table 9-16   Properties of *XmlDataSource*

Property	Description
CacheDuration	Indicates in seconds how long the data should be maintained in the cache.
CacheExpirationPolicy	Indicates whether the cache duration is absolute or sliding. If absolute, data is invalidated after the specified number of seconds. If sliding, data is invalidated if not used for the specified duration.

Table 9-16   Properties of *XmlDataSource*

Property	Description
CacheKeyDependency	Indicates the name of a user-defined cache key that is linked to all cache entries created by the data source control. By expiring the key, you can clear the control's cache.
Data	Contains a block of XML text for the data source control to bind.
DataFile	Indicates the path to the file that contains data to display.
EnableCaching	Enables or disables caching support.
Transform	Contains a block of XSLT text that will be used to transform the XML data bound to the control.
TransformArgumentList	A list of input parameters for the XSLT transformation to apply to the source XML.
TransformFile	Indicates the path to the *.xsl* file that defines an XSLT transformation to be performed on the source XML data.
XPath	Indicates an XPath query to be applied to the XML data.

The *XmlDataSource* control can accept XML input data as a relative or absolute filename assigned to the *DataFile* property or as a string containing the XML content assigned to the *Data* property. If both properties are set, *DataFile* takes precedence. Note that the *Data* property can also be set declaratively through the *<Data>* tag. Furthermore, the contents assigned to *Data*—a potentially large chunk of text—are stored in the view state regardless of the caching settings you might have. If you bind the control to static text, the risk is that you move the XML data back and forth with the page view state while keeping it also stored in the cache for faster access. If you use *Data* and enable caching, consider disabling the view state for the control. (It should be noted, though, that disabling the view state on a control usually affects more than one property.)

If caching is enabled and you change the value of the *DataFile* or *Data* property, the cache is discarded. The *DataSourceChanged* event notifies pages of the event.

Displaying XML Data

The *XmlDataSource* control is commonly bound to a hierarchical control, such as the *TreeView* or *Menu*. (These are the only two built-in hierarchical controls we have in ASP.NET 2.0, but others can be created by developers and third-party vendors.)

To understand how the XML data source works, consider a file that is a kind of XML representation of a *DataSet*—the Employees table of Northwind:

```
<MyDataSet>
    <NorthwindEmployees>
        <Employee>
            <employeeid>1</employeeid>
            <lastname>Davolio</lastname>
            <firstname>Nancy</firstname>
```

```
            <title>Sales Representative</title>
        </Employee>
        ...
    <NorthwindEmployees>
<MyDataSet>
```

Next you bind this file to an instance of the *XmlDataSource* control and the data source to a tree view:

```
<asp:XmlDataSource runat="server" ID="XmlSource"
    DataFile="employees.xml" />
<asp:TreeView runat="server" DataSourceId="XmlSource">
</asp:TreeView>
```

The result (which is not as useful as it could be) is shown in Figure 9-13.

Figure 9-13   The layout (rather than contents) of the bound XML file displayed using a *TreeView* control.

To display data in a way that is really helpful to users, you need to configure node bindings in the tree view:

```
<asp:TreeView runat="server" DataSourceId="XmlSource">
    <DataBindings>
        <asp:TreeNodeBinding Depth="3" DataMember="employeeid"
            TextField="#innertext" />
        <asp:TreeNodeBinding Depth="3" DataMember="lastname"
            TextField="#innertext" />
        <asp:TreeNodeBinding Depth="3" DataMember="firstname"
            TextField="#innertext" />
        <asp:TreeNodeBinding Depth="3" DataMember="title"
            TextField="#innertext" />
    </DataBindings>
</asp:TreeView>
```

The *<DataBindings>* section of the *TreeView* control lets you control the layout and the contents of the tree nodes. The *<TreeNodeBinding>* node indicates the 0-based depth (attribute *Depth*) of the specified XML node (attribute *DataMember*), as well as which attributes determine the text displayed for the node in the tree view and value associated with the node. The *TextField* attribute can be set to the name of the attribute to bind or *#innertext* if you want to display the body of the node. Figure 9-14 provides a preview.

There's a lot more to know about the *TreeView* configuration. I delve into that in *Programming Microsoft ASP.NET 2.0 Applications: Advanced Topics.*

Figure 9-14   XML data bound to a *TreeView* control.

The contents returned by the *XmlDataSource* control can be filtered using XPath expressions:

```
<asp:xmldatasource runat="server" ID="XmlSource"
    DataFile="employees.xml"
    XPath="MyDataSet/NorthwindEmployees/Employee" />
```

The preceding expression displays only the *<Employee>* nodes, with no unique root node in the tree view. XPath expressions are case-sensitive.

> **Note**   The *XmlDataSource* control automatically caches data as the *EnableCaching* property is set to *true* by default. Note also that by default the cache duration is set to 0, which means an infinite stay for data. In other words, the data source will cache data until the XML file that it depends on is changed.

Transforming XML Data

The *XmlDataSource* class can also transform its data using Extensible Stylesheet Language Transformations (XSLT). You set the transform file by using the *TransformFile* property or by assigning the XSLT content to the string property named *Transform*. Using the *TransformArgumentList* property, you can also pass arguments to the style sheet to be used during the XSL transformation. An XSL transformation is often used when the structure of an XML document does not match the structure needed to process the XML data. Note that once the data is transformed, the *XmlDataSource* becomes read-only and the data cannot be modified or saved back to the original source document.

Conclusion

ASP.NET data binding has three faces—classic source-based binding as in ASP.NET 1.x, data source controls, and data-binding expressions. Data-binding expressions serve a different purpose from the other two binding techniques. Expressions are used declaratively and within templated controls. They represent calculated values bindable to any property. In ASP.NET 2.0, support for expressions has been empowered to go beyond the boundaries of classic data binding. ASP.NET 2.0 supports custom expressions that are evaluated when the page loads, not when the data-binding process is triggered.

The data-binding model of ASP.NET 1.x is maintained intact with enumerable collections of data bound to controls through the *DataSource* property and a few related others. In addition, a new family of controls makes its debut—data source controls. By virtue of being implemented as a control, a data source component can be declaratively persisted into a Web page without any further effort in code. In addition, data source controls can benefit from other parts of the page infrastructure, such as the view state and ASP.NET cache. Data source controls accept parameters, prepare and execute a command, and return results (if any). Commands include the typical data operations—select, insert, update, delete, and total count.

The most interesting consequence of data source controls is the tight integration with some new data-bound controls. These smarter data-bound controls (*GridView*, *DetailsView*) contain logic to automatically bind at appropriate times on behalf of the page developer, and they interact with the underlying data source intelligently, requiring you to write much less code. Existing data-bound controls have been extended to support data source controls, but only for select operations.

Data source controls make declarative, codeless programming easier and likely to happen in reality. Data source controls, though, are just tools and not necessarily the right tool for the job you need to do.

In the next chapter, we continue our examination of data binding from another perspective—data-bound controls.

Just the Facts

- In ASP.NET 2.0, all data-bound controls support two binding mechanisms: the classic binding available in ASP.NET 1.x done through enumerable data source objects, and data source controls.

- Data source controls are regular server controls with no user interface that intelligently cooperate with the control they're bound to in an effort to anticipate the user's next request.

- Data source controls simplify programming in a quite a few scenarios by reducing the code you need to write.

- ASP.NET 1.x data-bound controls have been modified to support data source controls; they have not been redesigned to take full advantage of data source controls. For this reason, new controls have been added, such as *GridView* and *DetailsView*.

- A new type of expression ($-expression) partners data-binding expressions to provide for declarative expressions that can be used primarily in the design-time configuration of data source controls.

- $-expressions differ from #-expressions because they are evaluated at parse time and their output becomes part of the page source.

- *ObjectDataSource* is the most interesting of the data source controls because it can bridge your presentation layer to the DAL, even remotely. The *ObjectDataSource* control takes advantage of existing tiers and overall promotes a domain-based design over a purely tiered design.

- *XmlDataSource* is both a hierarchical and tabular data source, but only supports read-only scenarios.

Chapter 10

Creating Bindable Grids of Data

Data-bound controls play a key role in the development of ASP.NET applications. Data-driven controls allow you to associate the whole interface, or individual properties, with one or more columns read out of a .NET-compliant data source. We already mentioned data-bound controls in Chapter 9 and reviewed their basics. In this chapter, we'll delve into the details of a couple of extremely versatile data-bound controls that are a fixed presence in any real-world ASP.NET application—the *DataGrid* control in ASP.NET 1.x and the *GridView* control in ASP.NET 2.0.

Both controls render a multicolumn, templated grid and provide a largely customizable user interface with read/write options. In spite of the rather advanced programming interface and the extremely rich set of attributes, the *DataGrid* and *GridView* controls simply generate an HTML table with interspersed hyperlinks to provide interactive functionalities such as sorting, paging, selection, and in-place editing.

Although they are customizable at will, grid controls feature a relatively rigid and inflexible graphical model. The data bound to a *DataGrid* or *GridView* is always rendered like a table, therefore, in terms of rows and columns. As we'll see later in the chapter, though, the contents of the cells in a column can be customizable to some extent using system-provided as well as user-defined templates.

The *DataGrid* is the principal control of most data-driven ASP.NET 1.x applications. Like all ASP.NET 1.x controls, the *DataGrid* is fully supported in ASP.NET 2.0 but is partnered with a newer control that is meant to replace it in the long run. The new grid control, *GridView*, is complemented by other view controls, such as *DetailsView* and *FormView*. (We'll cover *Details-View* and *FormView* in the next chapter.) The *GridView* is a major upgrade of the ASP.NET 1.x *DataGrid* control. It provides the same basic set of capabilities, plus a long list of extensions and improvements.

In this chapter, we'll first take a look at the *DataGrid* capabilities and try to identify and discuss its major shortcomings and limitations. Then we'll consider the *GridView* control and its modified programming interface. For brand-new ASP.NET 2.0 applications, choosing the *GridView* over the *DataGrid* is a no-brainer. For ASP.NET 1.x applications that are being maintained, a move to the *GridView* doesn't present any significant difficulties and such a move positions you well for future enhancements.

The *DataGrid* Control

The *DataGrid* is a column-based control that supports various types of data-bound columns, including text, templated, and command columns. You associate the control with a data source using either the *DataSource* property or, in ASP.NET 2.0, the *DataSourceID* property. The simplest way of displaying a table of data using the ASP.NET grid is as follows:

```
<asp:DataGrid runat="server" id="grid" />
```

Once the control has been placed into the page, you bind it to the data source and have it display the resulting markup.

The *DataGrid* Object Model

The *DataGrid* control provides a grid-like view of the contents of a data source. Each column represents a data source field, and each row represents a record. The *DataGrid* control supports several style and visual properties; in a more realistic scenario, the markup required to embed the control in a page is significantly larger and complex enough to include all those attributes. In ASP.NET 2.0, themes can wrap control-specific visual settings and apply them seamlessly while leaving the markup as slim as possible.

Properties of the *DataGrid* Control

Table 10-1 lists the properties of the control, except those that the control inherits from *Control* and *WebControl*.

Table 10-1   Properties of the *DataGrid* Control

Property	Description
AllowCustomPaging	Gets or sets whether custom paging is enabled. *AllowPaging* must be set to *true* for this setting to work.
AllowPaging	Gets or sets whether paging is enabled.
AllowSorting	Gets or sets whether sorting is enabled.
AlternatingItemStyle	Gets the style properties for alternating rows.
AutoGenerateColumns	Gets or sets whether columns are automatically created and displayed for each field in the data source. *True* by default.
BackImageUrl	Gets or sets the URL of the image to display as the background of the control.

Table 10-1   Properties of the *DataGrid* Control

Property	Description
Caption	The text to render in the control's caption. *Not available in ASP.NET 1.x.*
CaptionAlign	Alignment of the caption. *Not available in ASP.NET 1.x.*
CellPadding	Gets or sets the space (in pixels) remaining between the cell's border and the embedded text.
CellSpacing	Gets or sets the space (in pixels) remaining, both horizontally and vertically, between two consecutive cells.
Columns	Gets a collection of *DataGridColumn* objects.
CurrentPageIndex	Gets or sets the index of the currently displayed page.
DataKeyField	Gets or sets the key field in the bound data source.
DataKeys	Gets a collection that stores the key values of all records displayed as a row in the grid. The column used as the key is defined by the *DataKeyField* property.
DataMember	Indicates the specific table in a multimember data source to bind to the grid. The property works in conjunction with *DataSource*. If *DataSource* is a *DataSet* object, it contains the name of the particular table to bind.
DataSource	Gets or sets the data source object that contains the values to populate the control.
DataSourceID	Indicates the data source object to populate the control. *Not available in ASP.NET 1.x.*
EditItemIndex	Gets or sets the index of the grid's item to edit.
EditItemStyle	Gets the style properties for the item being edited.
FooterStyle	Gets the style properties for the footer section of the grid.
GridLines	Gets or sets whether all cells must have the border drawn.
HeaderStyle	Gets the style properties for the heading section of the grid.
HorizontalAlign	Gets or sets the horizontal alignment of the text in the grid.
Items	Gets the collection of the currently displayed items.
ItemStyle	Gets the style properties for the items in the grid.
PageCount	Gets the number of pages required to display all bound items.
PagerStyle	Gets the style properties for the paging section of the grid.
PageSize	Gets or sets the number of items to display on a single page.
SelectedIndex	Gets or sets the index of the currently selected item.
SelectedItem	Gets a *DataGridItem* object representing the selected item.
SelectedItemStyle	Gets the style properties for the currently selected item.
ShowFooter	Indicates whether the footer is displayed. *False* by default.
ShowHeader	Indicates the header is displayed. *True* by default.
UseAccessibleHeader	Indicates whether the control's header is rendered in an accessible format—that is, using *<th>* tags instead of *<td>*. *Not available in ASP.NET 1.x.*
VirtualItemCount	Gets or sets the virtual number of items in the *DataGrid* control when custom paging is used.

The characteristic traits of the *DataGrid* control are the *Columns* and *Items* collections, the style and data-binding properties. All columns in the grid are represented by an object with its own set of properties and methods. Several types of columns are available to implement the most common tasks. In general, not all rows in the bound data source are included in the HTML code for the client. The *Items* collection returns a collection of *DataGridItem* objects, one per each displayed row. The *DataGridItem* class is a specialized version of the *TableRow* class.

> **Note**   In ASP.NET 2.0, a bunch of new properties make their debut to improve the usability of the control especially for users with accessibility problems. *Caption*, *CaptionAlign*, and *UseAccessibleHeader* let you tweak the markup that the control generates to make it easier to users of Assistive Technology devices.

Constituent Elements of a *DataGrid*

The output of a *DataGrid* control is made of several constituent elements grouped in the *List-ItemType* enumeration. Each element plays a clear role and has a precise location in the user interface of the control, as Figure 10-1 shows.

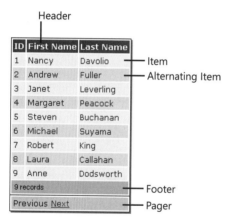

Figure 10-1   The layout of a *DataGrid* control.

The *DataGrid* user interface comprises the logical elements listed in Table 10-2. Each element has its own style property—that is, the set of graphical settings that are automatically applied by the control.

Table 10-2   Graphical Elements That Form a Data Grid

Item Type	Description
AlternatingItem	Represents a data-bound row placed in an odd position. Useful if you want to use different styles for alternating rows. *AlternatingItemStyle* is the property that lets you control the look and feel of the element.
EditItem	Represents the item currently displayed in edit mode. *EditItemStyle* lets you control the look and feel of the element.

Table 10-2 Graphical Elements That Form a Data Grid

Item Type	Description
Footer	Represents the grid's footer. The element can't be bound to a data source and is styled using the settings in the *FooterStyle* property.
Header	Represents the grid's header. The element can't be bound to a data source and is styled using the settings in the *HeaderStyle* property.
Item	Represents a data-bound row placed in an even position. Styled through the *ItemStyle* property.
Pager	Represents the pager element you use to scroll between pages. The element can't be bound to a data source and is styled using the settings in the *PagerStyle* property. The pager can be placed at the top or bottom of the grid's table and even in both places.
SelectedItem	Represents the item, or alternating item, currently selected. The property that defines its look and feel is *SelectedItemStyle*.

Each time one of the constituent elements is about to be created, the grid fires an *ItemCreated* event for you to perform some application-specific tasks. We'll return to grid events in a moment.

Data Source Rows and Displayed Rows

By design, the *DataGrid* control displays the data stored in a data source object—be it an enumerable data object or, in ASP.NET 2.0, a data source control. Each row in the bound data source is potentially a row in the grid. However, this one-to-one mapping doesn't always correspond to reality. Each displayed grid row finds a place in the *Items* collection. Each element in the *Items* collection is an instance of the *DataGridItem* class—a slightly richer table row object—and supplies a *DataItem* property set to the object that corresponds to the row in the bound data source. Note that only bindable items are contained in the *Items* collection. The header, footer, and pager are not included in the collection.

The index properties of the *DataGrid* refer to the rows displayed rather than to the underlying data source. When the item with an index of 1 is selected, the second displayed item is selected, but this piece of information says nothing about the position of the corresponding source record. The data source index for the item object is stored in the *DataSetIndex* property on the *DataGridItem* class. *DataSetIndex* returns the absolute position in the overall data source of the record represented by the current item. Although functional, this method isn't especially handy in some common scenarios, such as when you want to select a row and retrieve a bunch of associated records. In such a case, you need to know the value of the key field in the underlying data source row.

The *DataKeys* collection and the *DataKeyField* property provide an effective shortcut designed specifically to work in similar situations. When you configure a *DataGrid*, you can store the name of a key field in the *DataKeyField* property. During the data-binding phase, the control extracts from the data source the values for the specified key field that correspond to the rows being displayed. As a result, the index of the selected row in the *Items* collection can be used with *DataKeys* to get the key value for the underlying data source row. Let's consider the following declaration, which refers to a grid that displays information about the employees of a company:

```
<asp:DataGrid runat="server" id="grid" DataKeyField="employeeid" ... >
```

To get the ID of the selected employee—to be used to implement, say, a drill-down view—you simply use the following code:

```
// empID is the key of the currently selected item
int empID = grid.DataKeys[grid.SelectedIndex];
```

The *DataKeys* collection is automatically filled by the control based on the value of the *DataKeyField* property and the bound data source.

Events of the *DataGrid* Control

The *DataGrid* control has no specific methods worth mentioning. Table 10-3 lists the events that the control fires during its life cycle.

Table 10-3   Events of the *DataGrid* Control

Event	Description
CancelCommand	The user clicked to cancel any updates made on the current item being edited.
DeleteCommand	The user clicked to start a delete operation on the current item.
EditCommand	The user clicked to put the current item in edit mode.
ItemCommand	The user clicked any command button within the grid control.
ItemCreated	This event occurs after a new grid item is created.
ItemDataBound	This event occurs after a grid item is bound to data.
PageIndexChanged	The user clicked to see a new page of data.
SelectedIndexChanged	The user clicked to select a different item.
SortCommand	The user clicked to start a sort operation on a column.
UpdateCommand	The user clicked to save any updates made on the current item being edited.

The *CancelCommand* and *UpdateCommand* events are fired under special circumstances—that is, when an item is being edited. (We'll cover the *DataGrid* in-place editing feature later in the chapter.) The *CancelCommand* event signals that the user clicked the Cancel button to cancel all pending changes. The *UpdateCommand* event denotes the user's intention to persist all the changes. The other command events—*EditCommand*, *DeleteCommand*, and *SortCommand*—indicate that the user required a particular action by clicking on command buttons within the user interface of the grid.

In addition to the events just listed, the *DataGrid* control fires all the standard events of Web controls, including *Load*, *Init*, *PreRender*, and *DataBinding*. In particular, you might want to write a handler for *PreRender* if you need to modify the HTML code generated for the grid. The *DataBinding* event, on the other hand, is the entry point in the grid's binding process. The event is fired as the first step before the whole binding process begins, regardless of the type of object bound—be it an enumerable object or a data source control.

> **Note**   These command events mark a key difference between the *DataGrid* and the newer *GridView* control. While the *DataGrid* is limited to firing an event to let the page know the user's intention, the *GridView* proactively handles the event by executing the configured command through the bound data source control. The *DataGrid* supports data source controls too, but the support is limited to showing read-only data.

Binding Data to the Grid

A *DataGrid* control is formed by data-bindable columns. By default, the control includes all the data source columns in the view. You can change this behavior by setting the *AutoGenerate-Columns* property to *false*. In this case, only the columns explicitly listed in the *Columns* collection are displayed. The *DataGrid* control supports a variety of column types, which mostly differ from one another in how each represents the data. You are required to indicate the type of the column if you add it to the *Columns* collection; otherwise, if automatic generation is used, all columns are of the simplest type—the *BoundColumn* column type. Table 10-4 details the various types of columns supported.

Table 10-4   Types of Columns

Column Type	Description
BoundColumn	The contents of the column are bound to a field in a data source. Each cell displays as plain text.
ButtonColumn	Displays a button for each item in the column. The text of the button can be data-bound and buttons have a common command name.
EditCommandColumn	Particular type of button column associated with a command named *Edit*. When in edit mode, the whole row is drawn using text boxes rather than literals.
HyperLinkColumn	Displays the contents of each item in the column as a hyperlink. The text of the hyperlink can be bound to a column in the data source or it can be static text. The target URL can be data-bound, too. Clicking a hyperlink column causes the browser to jump to the specified URL.
TemplateColumn	This type displays each cell of the column following a specified ASP.NET template. It also allows you to provide custom behaviors.

Note that the *AutoGenerateColumns* property and the *Columns* collection are not mutually exclusive. If both properties are set to *true* and the collection is not empty, the grid will show the user-defined columns followed by all the ones that auto-generation would produce.

You normally bind columns using the *<columns>* tag in the body of the *<asp:datagrid>* server control, as the following code demonstrates:

```
<asp:datagrid runat="server" id="grid" ... >
   ...
  <columns>
    <asp:BoundColumn runat="server" DataField="employeeid"
        HeaderText="ID" />
    <asp:BoundColumn runat="server" DataField="firstname"
        HeaderText="First Name" />
    <asp:BoundColumn runat="server" DataField="lastname"
        HeaderText="Last Name" />
  </columns>
</asp:datagrid>
```

Alternately, you can create a new column of the desired class, fill its member properly, and then add the class instance to the *Columns* collection. Here is some code to add a *Bound-Column* object to a grid:

```
BoundColumn bc = new BoundColumn();
bc.DataField = "firstname";
bc.HeaderText = "First Name";
grid.Columns.Add(bc);
```

The order of the columns in the collection determines the order in which the columns are displayed in the *DataGrid* control.

> **Note**   The *Columns* collection doesn't persist its contents to the view state, and it is empty whenever the page posts back. To preserve any dynamically added column, you need to re-add it on each and every postback.

Data-Bound Columns

All grid column types inherit from the *DataGridColumn* class and have a few common properties such as the header text, footer and item style, and visibility flag. Table 10-5 details the properties shared by all types of columns.

Table 10-5   Common Properties for All Column Types

Property	Description
FooterStyle	Gets the style properties for the footer of the column
FooterText	Gets or sets the static text displayed in the footer of the column
HeaderImageUrl	Gets or sets the URL of an image to display in the header

Table 10-5   Common Properties for All Column Types

Property	Description
HeaderStyle	Gets the style properties for the header of the column
HeaderText	Gets or sets the static text displayed in the header of the column
ItemStyle	Gets the style properties for the item cells of the column
SortExpression	Gets or sets the expression to sort the data in the column
Visible	Gets or sets whether the column is visible

The *BoundColumn* class represents a column type that is bound to a data field. The key properties to set up a grid column are *DataField*, which represents the name of the column to bind, and *DataFormatString*, which allows you to format the displayed text to some extent. The *ReadOnly* property has an effect only if an edit command column is added to the grid. In this case, the cells in the column are switched to edit mode according to the value of the property.

The following code snippet adds two columns and specifies the header text and the source column for each. In addition, the second column is given a format string to make it look like a currency value with right alignment.

```
<asp:boundcolumn runat="server" datafield="quantityperunit"
    headertext="Packaging" />
<asp:boundcolumn runat="server" datafield="unitprice"
    headertext="Price" DataFormatString="{0:c}">
    <itemstyle width="80px" horizontalalign="right" />
</asp:boundcolumn>
```

Graphical settings for a column must be specified using a child style element.

HyperLink Columns

The *HyperLinkColumn* class is a column type that contains a hyperlink for each cell. The programmer can control the text of the hyperlink and the URL to navigate. Both fields can be bound to a column in the data source. The *DataTextField* takes the name of the field to use for the text of the hyperlink. *DataNavigateUrlField*, on the other hand, accepts the field that contains the URL. Another property, named *DataNavigateUrlFormatString*, defines the format of the final URL to use. By combining the two properties, you can redirect users to the same page, passing row-specific information on the query string, as shown in the following code:

```
<asp:hyperlinkcolumn runat="server" datatextfield="productname"
    headertext="Product"
    datanavigateurlfield="productid"
    datanavigateurlformatstring="productinfo.aspx?id={0}"
    target="ProductView">
    <itemstyle width="200px" />
</asp:hyperlinkcolumn>
```

The hyperlinks will point to the same page–*productinfo.aspx*–each with the product ID associated with the corresponding row of the bound data. The column class is responsible for building the real URL correctly.

> **Note**   By using the *DataNavigateUrlField* and *DataNavigateUrlFormatString* properties together, you can make the URL of the hyperlink parametric. However, by default you are limited to just one parameter—the value of the field bound through the *DataNavigateUrlField* property. To use a hyperlink bound to any number of arguments, you should resort to templated columns or use a *GridView*.

Button Columns

The *ButtonColumn* class represents a command column and contains a user-defined button for each cell in the column. Functionally similar to hyperlink columns, button columns are different because they generate a postback event on the same URL. Although the caption of each button can be bound to a data-source column, more often than not a button column has static text displayed through all the cells.

The key idea behind the button column is that you execute a particular action after the user clicks on a row. All buttons in the column are associated with some script code that posts the page back and executes the *ItemCommand* server-side procedure. Within that procedure, you use the command name (the *CommandName* property) to distinguish between multiple button columns, and you use the *ItemIndex* property of the *DataGridItem* class to know the particular row that was clicked. A reference to a *DataGridItem* object is passed through the *ItemCommand* event.

The *select* column is a special type of button column. It is a normal button column with the command name of *select*. When you click on such a column, the *DataGrid* automatically redraws the selected row using a different class of settings–those determined by the *SelectedItemStyle* property. There is no need for you to write an *ItemCommand* handler; the described behavior is built in:

```
<asp:ButtonColumn runat="server" text="Select" CommandName="Select" />
```

The style of the selected row–at most one at a time–is set using the *SelectedItemStyle* property. It can be as easy as the following code:

```
<selecteditemstyle backcolor="cyan" />
```

The change of the selected item is signaled with the *SelectedIndexChanged* event. However, before this event is fired, the application can handle the related *ItemCommand* event. When *SelectedIndexChanged* reaches the application, the *SelectedIndex* property indicates the new selected index.

Templated Columns

Templated columns allow you to create combinations of HTML text and server controls to design a custom layout for any cells in the column. The controls within a templated column can be bound to any combination of fields in the data source. In particular, you can group more fields in a single expression and even embellish it with HTML attributes such as bold-face or italic style. Templates are column-specific and cannot be applied to auto-generated columns. If you want more columns to share the same template, you can duplicate the code only in the ASP.NET page for each column.

A templated column is recognized by the *<TemplateColumn>* tag and rendered by the *Template-Column* class. The body of the tag can contain up to four different templates: *ItemTemplate*, *EditItemTemplate*, *HeaderTemplate*, and *FooterTemplate*. Just as with any other column type, a templated column can have header text and a sort expression. Templated columns, though, do not have an explicit data source field to bind. To bind a templated column to one or more data fields, you use a data-binding expression. (See Chapter 9.) In particular, you use the *Eval* method to evaluate data-bound expressions at run time and return the value properly cast. For example, the following code snippet shows a templated column that mimics the behavior of a *BoundColumn* object associated with the lastname column:

```
<asp:templatecolumn runat="server" headertext="Last Name">
    <itemtemplate>
        <asp:label runat="server" Text='<%#
            DataBinder.Eval(Container.DataItem, "lastname") %>' />
    </itemtemplate>
</asp:templatecolumn>
```

By using *DataBinder.Eval* (or simply *Eval* in ASP.NET 2.0), you can access any number of fields in the currently bound data source. In addition, you can combine them in any order to obtain any sort of expression, which is otherwise impossible using a simpler bound or button column.

Working with the *DataGrid*

The *DataGrid* control is not simply a tool to display static data; it also provides advanced functionalities to page, sort, and edit bound data. The interaction that is established between a *DataGrid* and the host page is limited to exchanging notifications in the form of postback events. The *DataGrid* lets the page know that something happened and leaves the page free to react as appropriate. This pattern is common to most supported operations, with the notable exception of item selection. As mentioned, in fact, if you add a Select button column to the grid and define a proper style for selected items, clicking on a Select button makes the page post back and forces the *DataGrid* to change the appearance of the corresponding row. Other operations for which the *DataGrid* simply fires an event to the page are paging, sorting, and in-place editing.

As you can see, these are relatively common operations that plenty of pages need to accomplish. If you choose to use a *DataGrid* control, be ready to write much more boilerplate code than you would with the newer *GridView* control.

Paging Through the Data Source

In real-world scenarios, the size of a data source easily exceeds the real estate of the page. Data paging is the contrivance that many applications adopt to both gain in scalability and present a more helpful page to the user. Especially on the Web, displaying only a few rows at a time is a more effective approach than downloading hundreds of records that stay hidden most of the time. The *DataGrid* control provides some built-in facilities to let the programmer easily switch to a new page according to the user's clicking.

The control needs to know how many items should be displayed per page, what type of functionality is required for the pager, and the data source to page through. In return for this, the control tracks the current page index, extracts the rows that fit into the particular page, and refreshes the user interface. Whenever the page index changes, an event is fired to the application—the *PageIndexChanged* event.

Note, however, that the host page is still responsible for ensuring that all the rows that fit into the new page are bound to the control. This holds true even if the *DataGrid* is bound to a data source control or a classic enumerable object. With a *DataGrid*, a handler for the *PageIndexChanged* event is always required. What you do in the handler might be different, though, depending on the actual data source. Here's the code you need to use if the *DataGrid* is bound to a data source control:

```
protected void grid_PageIndexChanged(object sender,
        DataGridPageChangedEventArgs e)
{
    grid.CurrentPageIndex = e.NewPageIndex;

    // Must be repeated to force a refresh
    grid.DataSourceID = "SqlDataSource1";
}
```

Note that you still need to reassign *DataSourceID* to trigger an internal data source changed event and cause the control to load its new dataset. If the grid is bound to an enumerable object, you simply assign a new bunch of rows to the *DataSource* property.

Overall, paging is a tough feature and a potential scalability killer. If you leave grid controls in charge of handling paging more or less automatically, caching data is a must. A data source control makes it as easy as turning on the *EnableCaching* property, as you saw in Chapter 9. Caching a lot of data, though, might pose a serious problem, especially if you have to do that for each user.

DataGrid controls also support custom paging, an alternative and cost-effective approach to paging that binds to the control only the records that fit in the current page:

```
protected void grid_PageIndexChanged(object sender,
        DataGridPageChangedEventArgs e)
{
    grid.CurrentPageIndex = e.NewPageIndex;
    grid.DataSource = GetRecordsInPage(grid.CurrentPageIndex);
}

protected object GetRecordsInPage(int pageIndex)
{
   // Retrieve and return data that fit in the given page
}
```

As we'll see later, the *GridView* doesn't explicitly support custom paging. On the other hand, the *GridView* doesn't prevent server paging from working if it is supported by the underlying data source control or the (data access layer) DAL.

Sorting Columns of Data

The *AllowSorting* property enables sorting on all or some of the *DataGrid*'s displayed columns. Just as for paging, clicking to sort data by a column doesn't really produce any visible effect unless you add a handler for the *SortCommand* event. Here's a simple handler you can use if the *DataGrid* is bound to a data source control:

```
protected void grid_SortCommand(object sender,
        DataGridSortCommandEventArgs e)
{
    SqlDataSource1.SelectCommand += " ORDER BY " + e.SortExpression;
    grid.DataSourceID = "SqlDataSource1";
}
```

Sorting is a potentially slow operation to accomplish and can have significant repercussions on scalability. For this reason, it is important to understand how it really works in the context of grids. In ASP.NET 1.x, you can employ in the *SortCommand* event handler only your own logic to sort. You can sort in memory using the *Sort* method of the *DataView* object (which is a very slow process, indeed); you can rely on the database sort capabilities (which is typically the fastest approach to sort data, but note that communication latency and network bandwidth may serve to slow things down from the user's perspective); sometimes, you can also maintain presorted caches of data. Whatever you choose, you need to know what you're doing.

In ASP.NET 2.0, data source controls tend to hide some details. If the data source control is configured to retrieve data via a *DataSet* (the default setting), sorting happens in memory via the *Sort* method. This approach is not really efficient, and it should be avoided unless you have only a few records to sort. If the data source control works via data readers and stored procedures, sorting can take place on the server and data will be returned in the correct order. In the end, sorting is a delicate operation no matter which controls you use. Only careful benchmarks and an application-specific combination of tools and options can deliver the perfect result. To get this, you need to understand how controls work internally.

Editing Existing Rows

A *DataGrid* control displays mostly read-only data. If editing is needed, you select the row to update and post a request for editing. The new page contains an edit form with input fields and links to persist or reject the changes. This pattern is probably the most effective one for editing data over the Web, and it's certainly the pattern that provides the highest level of flexibility. With *DataGrid* controls, though, a simpler model of data editing is possible. The new model is known as in-place editing and mimics the behavior of a Microsoft Office Excel worksheet. When you trigger the event that begins the editing phase, the visible part of the grid is redrawn and—like cells in Excel—the row selected for editing is rendered in a different way, using text-box controls instead of literals and labels. At the same time, the *DataGrid* control completes its own user interface with a couple of button links to allow you to commit or roll back changes.

In-place editing does not require much work to be completely set up, but at the same time it is not appropriate for all types of applications, and it is not functional in all operating contexts. All in all, if you have to edit the content of single and relatively small tables that have no special validation or business logic to apply, in-place editing is extremely handy and powerful.

The key object for in-place editing is the *EditCommandColumn* class. The column adds a link button to all rows of the grid. When the link is clicked, the page posts back and the cells of the row are drawn in edit mode. How a column behaves in edit mode depends on the column type. For example, button and hyperlink columns are completely ignored in edit mode. Bound and templated columns, on the other hand, change their rendering when the row is being edited. In particular, bound columns are rendered using text boxes in place of literals, whereas templated columns display the contents of the *<EditItemTemplate>* section, if any.

As with paging and sorting, code is required to have the *DataGrid* complete an in-place editing operation, too. You typically need to write three event handlers—*EditCommand*, to put the grid in edit mode; *CancelCommand*, to put the grid back in read-only mode; and *UpdateCommand*, to persist changes and refresh the grid. Handlers for *EditCommand* and *CancelCommand* are relatively simple and standard. Writing a handler for *UpdateCommand* might not be that easy, though.

Basically, the *UpdateCommand* handler must accomplish two key operations—retrieving input data and persisting changes. Both operations are hard-coded in the *GridView*, performed in collaboration with the underlying data source control, and mostly configured at design time by the page author.

> **Important** Admittedly, this section about *DataGrid* controls didn't get into the nitty-gritty details of how the control works and deliberately avoided describing how to implement paging, sorting, and editing properly in real-world scenarios. The reason for this approach lies in the structural difference that exists between *DataGrid* and *GridView* controls. To a large extent, the two controls provide the same set of abstract features—grid-like display, paging, sorting, editing, and templates. How each control implements individual features and binds to data is radically different. In one word, the *philosophy* behind each control is different. Now, the *GridView* control is newer, richer, and smarter, and it would probably have been the only grid control in ASP.NET 2.0 if it weren't for compatibility issues.
>
> If you have an existing ASP.NET application to maintain, and you don't feel like leaping to *GridView*, you already know all the details and techniques omitted here. If you're building a new application and want to take advantage of grids, you don't need to know about *Data-Grid* controls and are better off focusing entirely on *GridView* controls. The purpose of this section is to help people in the middle make a decision about which control to use while explaining why Microsoft decided to go with a new control that is designed to complement the changes in the data-binding model we explored in Chapter 9. The *GridView* control is also complemented by other view controls—specifically, *FormView* and *DetailsView*—that we'll cover in the next chapter.

The *GridView* Control

The *GridView* is the successor to the ASP.NET 1.x *DataGrid* control. It provides the same base set of capabilities, plus a long list of extensions and improvements. As mentioned, the *Data-Grid*—which is still fully supported in ASP.NET 2.0—is an extremely powerful and versatile control. However, it has one big drawback: it requires you to write a lot of custom code, even to handle relatively simple and common operations such as paging, sorting, editing, or deleting data. The *GridView* control was designed to work around this limitation and make two-way data binding happen with as little code as possible. The control is tightly coupled to the family of new data source controls, and it can handle direct data source updates as long as the underlying data source object supports these capabilities.

This virtually codeless two-way data binding is by far the most notable feature of the new *GridView* control, but other enhancements are numerous. The control is an improvement over the *DataGrid* control because it has the ability to define multiple primary key fields, new column types, and style and templating options. The *GridView* also has an extended eventing model that allows you to handle or cancel events.

The *GridView* Object Model

The *GridView* control provides a tabular grid-like view of the contents of a data source. Each column represents a data source field, and each row represents a record. The class is declared as follows:

```
public class GridView : CompositeDataBoundControl,
                        ICallbackContainer,
                        ICallbackEventHandler
```

The base class ensures data-binding and naming-container support. The *ICallbackContainer* and *ICallbackEventHandler* interfaces provide more effective paging and sorting than is now supported. It does this through client-side, out-of-band calls that use the new script callback technology. (I'll talk more about this later.) Let's begin our tour of the *GridView* control by looking at the control's programming interface.

Properties of the *GridView* Control

The *GridView* supports a large set of properties that fall into the following broad categories: behavior, visual settings, style, state, and templates. Table 10-6 details the properties that affect the behavior of the *GridView*.

Table 10-6   Behavior Properties of the *GridView* Control

Property	Description
AllowPaging	Indicates whether the control supports paging.
AllowSorting	Indicates whether the control supports sorting.
AutoGenerateColumns	Indicates whether columns are automatically created for each field in the data source. The default is *true*.
AutoGenerateDeleteButton	Indicates whether the control includes a button column to let users delete the record that is mapped to the clicked row.
AutoGenerateEditButton	Indicates whether the control includes a button column to let users edit the record that is mapped to the clicked row.
AutoGenerateSelectButton	Indicates whether the control includes a button column to let users select the record that is mapped to the clicked row.
DataMember	Indicates the specific table in a multimember data source to bind to the grid. The property works in conjunction with *DataSource*. If *DataSource* is a *DataSet* object, it contains the name of the particular table to bind.
DataSource	Gets or sets the data source object that contains the values to populate the control.
DataSourceID	Indicates the bound data source control.
EnableSortingAndPagingCallbacks	Indicates whether sorting and paging are accomplished using script callback functions. Disabled by default.
RowHeaderColumn	Name of the column to use as the column header. This property is designed for improving accessibility.

Table 10-6   Behavior Properties of the *GridView* Control

Property	Description
SortDirection	Gets the direction of the column current sort.
SortExpression	Gets the current sort expression.
UseAccessibleHeader	Specifies whether to render <th> tags for the column headers instead of default <td> tags.

The *SortDirection* and *SortExpression* properties specify the direction and the sort expression on the column that currently determines the order of the rows. Both properties are set by the control's built-in sorting mechanism when users click a column's header. The whole sorting engine is enabled and disabled through the *AllowSorting* property. The *EnableSortingAnd-PagingCallbacks* property toggles on and off the control's capability of using script callbacks to page and sort without doing roundtrips to the server and changing the entire page.

Each row displayed within a *GridView* control corresponds to a special type of grid item. The list of predefined types of items is nearly identical to that of the *DataGrid* and includes items such as the header, rows and alternating rows, footer, and pager. These items are static in the sense that they remain in place for the lifetime of the control in the application. Other types of items are active for a short period of time—the time needed to accomplish a certain operation. Dynamic items are the edit row, the selected row, and the *EmptyData* item. *EmptyData* identifies the body of the grid when the grid is bound to an empty data source.

> **Note**   The *GridView* control provides a few properties specifically designed for accessibility. They are *UseAccessibleHeader*, *Caption*, *CaptionAlign*, and *RowHeaderColumn*. When you set *RowHeaderColumn*, all the column cells will be rendered with the default header style (bold-face type). However, *ShowHeader*, *HeaderStyle*, and other header-related properties don't affect the column indicated by *RowHeaderColumn*.

Table 10-7 details the style properties available on the *GridView* control.

Table 10-7   Style Properties of the *GridView* Control

Style	Description
AlternatingRowStyle	Defines the style properties for every other row in the table
EditRowStyle	Defines the style properties for the row being edited
FooterStyle	Defines the style properties for the grid's footer
HeaderStyle	Defines the style properties for the grid's header
EmptyDataRowStyle	Defines the style properties for the empty row, which is rendered when the *GridView* is bound to empty data sources
PagerStyle	Defines the style properties for the grid's pager
RowStyle	Defines the style properties for the rows in the table
SelectedRowStyle	Defines the style properties for the currently selected row

Table 10-8 lists most of the properties that affect the appearance of the control, and Table 10-9 details the templating properties.

Table 10-8   Appearance Properties of the *GridView* Control

Property	Description
BackImageUrl	Indicates the URL to an image to display in the background
Caption	The text to render in the control's caption
CaptionAlign	Alignment of the caption text
CellPadding	Indicates the amount of space (in pixels) between the contents of a cell and the border
CellSpacing	Indicates the amount of space (in pixels) between cells
GridLines	Indicates the gridline style for the control
HorizontalAlign	Indicates the horizontal alignment of the control on the page
EmptyDataText	Indicates the text to render in the control when it is bound to an empty data source
PagerSettings	References an object that lets you set the properties of the pager buttons
ShowFooter	Indicates whether the footer row is displayed
ShowHeader	Indicates whether the header row is displayed

The *PagerSettings* object groups together all the visual properties you can set on the pager. Many of these properties should sound familiar to *DataGrid* programmers. The *PagerSettings* class also adds some new properties to accommodate new predefined buttons (first and last pages), and it uses images instead of text in the links. (You need to figure out a trick to do the same with a *DataGrid*.)

Table 10-9   Templating Properties of the *GridView* Control

Template	Description
EmptyDataTemplate	Indicates the template content to be rendered when the control is bound to an empty source. This property takes precedence over *EmptyDataText* if both are set. If neither is set, the grid isn't rendered if bound to an empty data source.
PagerTemplate	Indicates the template content to be rendered for the pager. This property overrides any settings you might have made through the *PagerSettings* property.

The final block of properties—the state properties—is shown in Table 10-10. State properties return information about the internal state of the control.

Table 10-10   State Properties

Property	Description
BottomPagerRow	Returns a *GridViewRow* object that represents the bottom pager of the grid.
Columns	Gets a collection of objects that represent the columns in the grid. The collection is always empty if columns are auto-generated.

Table 10-10   State Properties

Property	Description
DataKeyNames	Gets an array that contains the names of the primary key fields for the currently displayed items.
DataKeys	Gets a collection of *DataKey* objects that represent the values of the primary key fields set in *DataKeyNames* for the currently displayed records.
EditIndex	Gets and sets the 0-based index that identifies the row currently rendered in edit mode.
FooterRow	Returns a *GridViewRow* object that represents the footer.
HeaderRow	Returns a *GridViewRow* object that represents the header.
PageCount	Gets the number of pages required to display the records of the data source.
PageIndex	Gets and sets the 0-based index that identifies the currently displayed page of data.
PageSize	Indicates the number of records to display on a page.
Rows	Gets a collection of *GridViewRow* objects that represent the data rows currently displayed in the control.
SelectedDataKey	Returns the *DataKey* object for the currently selected record.
SelectedIndex	Gets and sets the 0-based index that identifies the row currently selected.
SelectedRow	Returns a *GridViewRow* object that represents the currently selected row.
SelectedValue	Returns the explicit value of the key as stored in the *DataKey* object. Similar to *SelectedDataKey*.
TopPagerRow	Returns a *GridViewRow* object that represents the top pager of the grid.

The *GridView* is designed to leverage the new data source object model, and it works best when bound to a data source control via the *DataSourceID* property. The *GridView* also supports the classic *DataSource* property, but if you bind data in that way, some of the features (such as built-in updates and paging) become unavailable.

Events of the *GridView* Control

The *GridView* control doesn't have methods other than *DataBind*. As mentioned, though, in many situations you don't need to call methods on the *GridView* control. The data-binding process is started implicitly when you bind the *GridView* to a data source control.

In ASP.NET 2.0, many controls, and the *Page* class itself, feature pairs of events of the type doing/done. Key operations in the control life cycle are wrapped by a pair of events—one firing before the operation takes place, and one firing immediately after the operation is completed. The *GridView* class is no exception. The list of events is shown in Table 10-11.

Table 10-11 Events Fired by the *GridView* Control

Event	Description
PageIndexChanging, *PageIndexChanged*	Both events occur when one of the pager buttons is clicked. They fire before and after the grid control handles the paging operation, respectively.
RowCancelingEdit	Occurs when the Cancel button of a row in edit mode is clicked, but before the row exits edit mode.
RowCommand	Occurs when a button is clicked.
RowCreated	Occurs when a row is created.
RowDataBound	Occurs when a data row is bound to data.
RowDeleting, RowDeleted	Both events occur when a row's Delete button is clicked. They fire before and after the grid control deletes the row, respectively.
RowEditing	Occurs when a row's Edit button is clicked but before the control enters edit mode.
RowUpdating, *RowUpdated*	Both events occur when a row's Update button is clicked. They fire before and after the grid control updates the row, respectively.
SelectedIndexChanging, *SelectedIndexChanged*	Both events occur when a row's Select button is clicked. The two events occur before and after the grid control handles the select operation, respectively.
Sorting, Sorted	Both events occur when the hyperlink to sort a column is clicked. They fire before and after the grid control handles the sort operation, respectively.

RowCreated and *RowDataBound* events are the same as the *DataGrid*'s *ItemCreated* and *ItemDataBound* events, with new names. They behave exactly as they do in ASP.NET 1.x. The same is true of the *RowCommand* event, which is the same as the *DataGrid*'s *ItemCommand* event.

The availability of events that announce a certain operation significantly enhances your programming power. By hooking the *RowUpdating* event, you can cross-check what is being updated and validate the new values. Likewise, you might want to handle the *RowUpdating* event to HTML-encode the values supplied by the client before they are persisted to the underlying data store. This simple trick helps you to fend off script injections.

Simple Data Binding

The following code demonstrates the simplest way to bind data to a *GridView* control. The data source object keeps the page virtually code-free.

```
<asp:ObjectDataSource ID="MySource" runat="server"
    TypeName="ProAspNet20.DAL.Customers"
    SelectMethod="LoadAll">
</asp:ObjectDataSource>
<asp:GridView runat="server" id="grid" DataSourceID="MySource"  />
```

Setting the *DataSourceID* property triggers the binding process, which runs the data source query and populates the user interface of the grid. You need not write any binding code. (Note that you still have to write the *LoadAll* method and the DAL.)

By default, the *GridView* control auto-generates enough columns to contain all the data coming through the data source. In other cases, you might want to control and style each column individually. For this to happen, the binding process should be refined a little bit.

Binding Data to a *GridView* Control

If no data source property is set, the *GridView* control doesn't render anything. If an empty data source object is bound and an *EmptyDataTemplate* template is specified, the results shown to the user have a more friendly look:

```
<asp:gridview runat="server" datasourceid="MySource">
   <emptydatatemplate>
      <asp:label runat="server">
         There's no data to show in this view.
      </asp:label>
   </emptydatatemplate>
</asp:gridview>
```

The *EmptyDataTemplate* property is ignored if the bound data source is not empty. Figure 10-2 shows the output generated by the empty template.

Figure 10-2   The *GridView* control in action on an empty data source.

When you use a declared set of columns, the *AutoGenerateColumns* property of the grid is typically set to *false*. However, this is not a strict requirement—a grid can have declared and auto-generated columns. In this case, declared columns appear first. Note also that auto-generated columns are not added to the *Columns* collection. As a result, when column auto-generation is used, the *Columns* collection is typically empty.

Configuring Columns

The *Columns* property is a collection of *DataControlField* objects. The *DataControlField* object is akin to the *DataGrid*'s *DataGridColumn* object, but it has a more general name because these field objects can be reused in other data-bound controls that do not necessarily render columns. (For example, in the *DetailsView* control, the same class is used to render a row.)

You can define your columns either declaratively or programmatically. In the latter case, you just instantiate any needed data field objects and add them to the *Columns* collection. The following code adds a data-bound column to the grid:

```
BoundField field = new BoundField();
field.DataField = "companyname";
field.HeaderText = "Company Name";
grid.ColumnFields.Add(field);
```

Columns of data are displayed in the order that the column fields appear in the collection. To statically declare your columns in the *.aspx* source file, you use the *<Columns>* tag, as shown here:

```
<columns>
    <asp:boundfield datafield="customerid" headertext="ID" />
    <asp:boundfield datafield="companyname" headertext="Company Name" />
</columns>
```

Table 10-12 lists the column field classes that can be used in a *GridView* control. All the classes inherit *DataControlField*.

Table 10-12   Supported Column Types in *GridView* Controls

Type	Description
BoundField	Default column type. Displays the value of a field as plain text.
ButtonField	Displays the value of a field as a command button. You can choose the link button or the push button style.
CheckBoxField	Displays the value of a field as a check box. It is commonly used to render Boolean values.
CommandField	Enhanced version of *ButtonField*, represents a special command such as *Select*, *Delete*, *Insert*, or *Update*. It's rarely useful with *GridView* controls; the field is tailor-made for *DetailsView* controls. (*GridView* and *DetailsView* share the set of classes derived from *DataControlField*.)
HyperLinkField	Displays the value of a field as a hyperlink. When the hyperlink is clicked, the browser navigates to the specified URL.
ImageField	Displays the value of a field as the *Src* property of an *<img>* HTML tag. The content of the bound field should be the URL to the physical image.
TemplateField	Displays user-defined content for each item in the column. You use this column type when you want to create a custom column field. The template can contain any number of data fields combined with literals, images, and other controls.

Table 10-13 lists the main properties shared by all column types.

Table 10-13   **Common Properties of** *GridView* **Columns**

Property	Description
AccessibleHeaderText	The text that represents abbreviated text read by screen readers of Assistive Technology devices.
FooterStyle	Gets the style object for the column's footer.
FooterText	Gets and sets the text for the column's footer.
HeaderImageUrl	Gets and sets the URL of the image to place in the column's header.
HeaderStyle	Gets the style object for the column's header.
HeaderText	Gets and sets the text for the column's header.
InsertVisible	Indicates whether the field is visible when its parent data-bound control is in insert mode. This property does not apply to *GridView* controls.
ItemStyle	Gets the style object for the various columns' cells.
ShowHeader	Indicates whether the column's header is rendered.
SortExpression	Gets and sets the expression used to sort the grid contents when the column's header is clicked. Typically, this string property is set to the name of the bound data field.

The properties listed in Table 10-13 represent a subset of the properties that each column type actually provides. In particular, each type of column defines a tailor-made set of properties to define and configure the bound field. Refer to the MSDN documentation for details on the programming interface of *GridView*'s column types.

Bound Fields

The *BoundField* class represents a field that is displayed as plain text in a data-bound control such as *GridView* or *DetailsView*. To specify the field to display, you set the *DataField* property to the field's name. You can apply a custom formatting string to the displayed value by setting the *DataFormatString* property. The *NullDisplayText* property lets you specify alternative text to display should the value be *null*. Finally, by setting the *ConvertEmptyStringToNull* property to *true*, you force the class to consider empty strings as null values.

A *BoundField* can be programmatically hidden from view through the *Visible* property while the *ReadOnly* property prevents the displayed value from being modified in edit mode. To display a caption in the header or footer sections, set the *HeaderText* and *FooterText* properties, respectively. You can also choose to display an image in the header instead of text. In this case, you set the *HeaderImageUrl* property.

Button Fields

A button field is useful to put a clickable element in a grid's column. You typically use a button field to trigger an action against the current row. A button field represents any action that you want to handle through a server-side event. When the button is clicked, the page posts back and fires a *RowCommand* event. Figure 10-3 shows a sample.

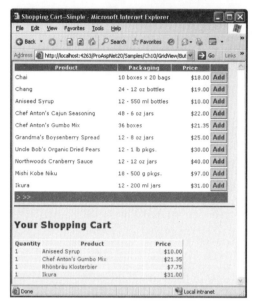

Figure 10-3   Button fields in a *GridView* control.

The following listing shows the markup code behind the grid in the figure:

```
<asp:GridView ID="GridView1" runat="server" DataSourceID="SqlDataSource1"
    AutoGenerateColumns="false" AllowPaging="true"
    OnRowCommand="GridView1_RowCommand">
    <HeaderStyle backcolor="gray" font-bold="true" height="200%" />
    <PagerStyle backcolor="gray" font-bold="true" height="200%" />
    <PagerSettings Mode="NextPreviousFirstLast" />
    <Columns>
       <asp:BoundField datafield="productname"
           headertext="Product" />
       <asp:BoundField datafield="quantityperunit"
           headertext="Packaging" />
       <asp:BoundField datafield="unitprice"
           headertext="Price" DataFormatString="{0:c}">
         <itemstyle width="80px" horizontalalign="right" />
       </asp:BoundField>
       <asp:ButtonField buttontype="Button" text="Add" CommandName="Add" />
    </Columns>
</asp:GridView>
```

Product information is displayed using a few *BoundField* objects. The sample button column allows you to add the product to the shopping cart. When users click the button, the *RowCommand* server event is fired. In case multiple button columns are available, the *CommandName* attribute lets you figure out which button was clicked. The value you assign to *CommandName* is any unique string that the code-behind class can understand. Here's an example:

```
void GridView1_RowCommand(object sender, GridViewCommandEventArgs e)
{
    if (e.CommandName.Equals("Add"))
```

```
    {
        // Get the index of the clicked row
        int index = Convert.ToInt32(e.CommandArgument);

        // Create a new shopping item and add it to the cart
        AddToShoppingCart(index);
    }
}
```

In the sample, the button column shows a fixed text for all data items. You get this by setting the *Text* property on the *ButtonField* class. If you want to bind the button text to a particular field on the current data item, you set the *DataTextField* property to the name of that field.

You can choose different styles for the button—push, link, or image. To render the button as an image, do as follows:

```
<asp:buttonfield buttontype="Image" CommandName="Add"
    ImageUrl="/proaspnet20/images/cart.gif"  />
```

To add a ToolTip to the button (or the image), you need to handle the *RowCreated* event. (I'll discuss this in more detail later in the chapter.)

Hyperlink Fields

Hyperlink columns point the user to a different URL, optionally displayed in an inner frame. Both the text and URL of the link can be obtained from the bound source. In particular, the URL can be set in either of two ways: through a direct binding to a data source field or by using a hard-coded URL with a customized query string. You choose the direct binding if the URL is stored in one of the data source fields. In this case, you set the *DataNavigateUrlFields* property to the name of the column. In some situations, though, the URL to access is application-specific and not stored in the data source. In this case, you can set the *DataNavigateUrl-FormatString* property with a hard-coded URL and with an array of parameters in the query string, as follows:

```
<asp:HyperLinkField DataTextField="productname"
    HeaderText="Product"
    DataNavigateUrlFields="productid"
    DataNavigateUrlFormatString="productinfo.aspx?id={0}"
    Target="ProductView" />
```

When the user clicks, the browser fills the specified frame window with the contents of the *productinfo.aspx?id=xxx* URL, where *xxx* comes from the *productid* field. The URL can include multiple parameters. To include more data-bound values, just set the *DataNavigateUrlFields* property to a comma-separated list of field names. This behavior extends that of the *Data-Grid*'s hyperlink column in that it supports multiple parameters.

The text of the hyperlink can be formatted too. The *DataTextFormatString* property can contain any valid markup and uses the {0} placeholder to reserve space for the data-bound value. (See Figure 10-4.)

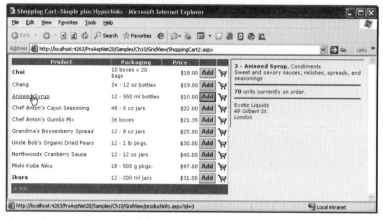

Figure 10-4   Hyperlink fields in a *GridView* control.

Tip   When choosing a target for the hyperlinked pages, you can also use any of the following standard targets: *_self*, *_parent*, *_new*. Both Microsoft Internet Explorer and Firefox support *_search*, which uses a companion Web panel docked at the left edge of the browser's real estate. (See Figure 10-5.)

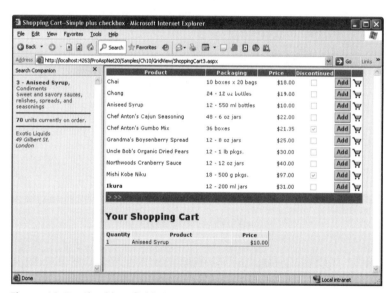

Figure 10-5   Checkbox fields in a *GridView* control.

CheckBox Fields

The column types we hitherto considered are nothing new for seasoned ASP.NET 1.x developers. Although renamed, their overall behavior remains very similar to that of analogous column types for *DataGrids*. The *CheckBoxField* type, on the other hand, is a new entry in

ASP.NET 2.0 and is limited to *GridView* and other view controls. The simplest way in which you can get a checkbox column in ASP.NET 1.x (or in general for *DataGrids*) is through templates.

The *CheckBoxField* column is a relatively simple bound column that displays a check box. You can bind it only to a data field that contains Boolean values. A valid Boolean value is a value taken from a column of type *Bit* in a SQL Server table (and analogous types in other databases) or a property of type *bool* if the control is bound to a custom collection. Any other form of binding will result in a parsing exception. In particular, you get an exception if you bind a *CheckBoxField* column to an integer property, thus implicitly assuming that 0 is false and non-zero values are true.

Image Fields

The *ImageField* column type represents a field that is displayed as an image in a data-bound control. The cell contains an *<img>* element, so the underlying field must reference a valid URL. You can compose the URL at will, though. For example, you can use the *DataImage-UrlField* to perform a direct binding where the content of the field fills the *Src* attribute of the *<img>* tag. Alternately, you can make the column cells point to an external page (or HTTP handler) that retrieves the bytes of the image from any source and passes them down to the browser. The following code illustrates this approach:

```
<Columns>
  <asp:ImageField DataImageUrlField="employeeid"
    DataImageUrlFormatString="showemployeepicture.aspx?id={0}"
    DataAlternateTextField="lastname">
    <ControlStyle width="120px" />
  </asp:ImageField>
  <asp:TemplateField headertext="Employee">
    <ItemStyle Width="220px" />
    <ItemTemplate>
        <b><%# Eval("titleofcourtesy") + " " +
               Eval("lastname") + ", " +
               Eval("firstname") %></b> <br />
               <%# Eval("title")%>
               <hr />
               <i><%# Eval("notes")%></i>
    </ItemTemplate>
  </asp:templatefield>
</Columns>
```

Cells in the *ImageField* column are filled with the output of the next URL:

```
ShowEmployeePicture.aspx?id=xxx
```

Needless to say, *xxx* is the value in the *employeeid* field associated with *DataImageUrlField*. Interestingly enough, the alternate text can also be data bound. You use the *DataAlternateText-Field* property. Figure 10-6 gives a sneak preview of the feature. The page in Figure 10-6 employs a template column to render the employee's information. I'll return to the subject of template columns in a moment.

Figure 10-6 Image fields in a *GridView* control.

The following code demonstrates the world's simplest page to retrieve and serve an image out of a database table:

```
void Page_Load(object sender, EventArgs e)
{
    int id = Convert.ToInt32(Request.QueryString["id"]);
    string connString = "...";
    string cmdText = "SELECT photo FROM employees WHERE employeeid=@empID";

    using (SqlConnection conn = new SqlConnection(connString))
    {
        SqlCommand cmd = new SqlCommand(cmdText, conn);
        cmd.Parameters.AddWithValue("@empID", id);
        byte[] img = null;
        conn.Open();

        try
        {
            img = (byte[])cmd.ExecuteScalar();
            if (img != null)
            {
                Response.ContentType = "image/png";
                Response.OutputStream.Write(img, EMP_IMG_OFFSET, img.Length);
            }
        }
        catch
        {
```

```
        Response.WriteFile("/proaspnet20/images/noimage.gif");
    }
    conn.Close();
}
```

The preceding code serves a standard image if the value of the field specified is *null*. You can obtain the same result by setting the *NullImageUrl* property if you're using direct binding—that is, not passing through an external page or handler.

> **Note**   The EMP_IMG_OFFSET constant in the code snippet should normally be just 0. However, given the particular structure of the photo column of the Northwind's *Employees* database, it has to be 78. But, again, this is required only with that table.

Templated Fields

Figure 10-6 shows a customized column where the values of several fields are combined. This is exactly what you can get by using templates. A *TemplateField* column gives each row in the grid a personalized user interface that is completely defined by the page developer. You can define templates for various rendering stages, including the default view, in-place editing, the header, and the footer. The supported templates are listed in Table 10-14.

Table 10-14   Supported Templates

Template	Description
AlternatingItemTemplate	Defines the contents and appearance of alternating rows. If not specified, the *ItemTemplate* is used.
EditItemTemplate	Defines the contents and appearance of the row currently being edited. This template should contain input fields and possibly validators.
FooterTemplate	Defines the contents and appearance of the row's footer.
HeaderTemplate	Defines the contents and appearance of the row's header.
ItemTemplate	Defines the default contents and appearance of the rows.

A templated view can contain anything that makes sense to the application you're building—server controls, literals, and data-bound expressions. Data-bound expressions allow you to insert values contained in the current data row. You can use as many fields as needed in a template. Notice, though, that not all templates support data-bound expressions. The header and footer templates are not data-bound, and any attempt to use expressions will result in an exception.

The following code shows how to define the item template for a product column. The column displays on two lines and includes the name of the product and some information about the packaging. You use data-bound expressions (which are discussed in Chapter 9) to refer to data fields.

```
<asp:templatefield headertext="Product">
    <itemtemplate>
```

```
        <b><%# Eval("productname")%></b> <br />
        available in <%# Eval("quantityperunit")%>
    </itemtemplate>
</asp:templatefield>
```

Figure 10-7 demonstrates template fields in action.

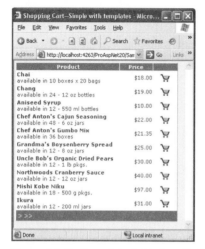

Figure 10-7 Template fields in a *GridView* control.

Note The *TemplateField* class also features an *InsertTemplate* property. However, this type of template is never used by the *GridView* control. The *InsertTemplate* is used by the *FormView* control instead. As mentioned earlier, in ASP.NET 2.0 view controls share some field classes, such as *TemplateField*. As a result, *TemplateField* (and a few more classes) provide a superset of properties that serves the needs of multiple view controls. We'll cover the *FormView* control in the next chapter.

Paging Data

The *GridView* is designed to take advantage of specific capabilities of the underlying data source control. In this way, the grid control can handle common operations on data such as sorting, paging, updating, and deleting. In general, not all data source components support all possible and feasible data operations. Data source components expose Boolean properties (such as the *CanSort* property) to signal whether they can perform a given operation.

Important If a *GridView* control is bound to its data source through the *DataSource* property—that is, it doesn't leverage data source controls—its overall behavior as far as paging and other operations are concerned (for example, sorting and editing) is nearly identical to that of the *DataGrid* control. In this case, the *GridView* fires events and expects the binding code in the page to provide instructions and fresh data. In the remainder of this chapter, unless explicitly mentioned, we refer to a *GridView* bound to a data source control.

To some extent, the *GridView* makes transparent for the page developer the implementation of commonly required features such as sorting and paging. In most cases, you need only a fraction of the code you need with the *DataGrid*; in some cases, no code at all is required. This said, don't forget what one old and wise proverb says—not all that glitters is gold. Put another way, be aware that the less code you write, the more you rely on the existing infrastructure to get things done. In doing so, you let the system make important decisions on your behalf. Paging and sorting are key operations in Web applications. You can still accept what the *GridView* does by default, but if you get to know exactly what happens under the hood, you have a better chance of diagnosing and fixing in a timely manner any performance problems that show up in the lifetime of the application.

Codeless Data Paging

The ability to scroll a potentially large set of data is an important but challenging feature for modern, distributed applications. An effective paging mechanism allows customers to interact with a database without holding resources. To enable paging on a *GridView* control, all you do is set the *AllowPaging* property to *true*. When the *AllowPaging* property is set to *true*, the grid displays a pager bar and prepares to detect a user's pager button clicks.

When a user clicks to see a new page, the page posts back, but the *GridView* traps the event and handles it internally. This marks a major difference between *GridView* and the *DataGrid* and programming model you might know from ASP.NET 1.x. With the *GridView*, there's no need to write a handler for the *PageIndexChanged* event. The event is still exposed (and partnered with *PageIndexChanging*), but you should handle it only to perform extra actions. The *GridView* knows how to retrieve and display the requested new page. Let's take a look at the following control declaration:

```
<asp:GridView ID="GridView1" runat="server"
    DataSourceID="SqlDataSource1" AllowPaging="true" />
```

Any data *SqlDataSource1* binds to the grid is immediately pageable. As in Figure 10-8, the control displays a pager with a few predefined links (first, previous, next, and last) and automatically selects the correct subset of rows that fit in the selected page.

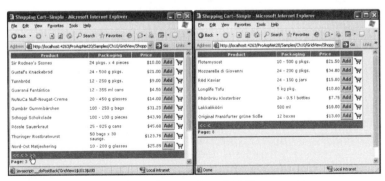

Figure 10-8   Moving through pages in a *GridView* control.

The default user interface you get with the *GridView* doesn't include the page number. Adding a page number label is as easy as writing a handler for the *PageIndexChanged* event:

```
protected void GridView1_PageIndexChanged(object sender, EventArgs e)
{
    ShowPageIndex();
}
private void ShowPageIndex()
{
    CurrentPage.Text = (GridView1.PageIndex + 1).ToString();
}
```

Once again, note that the *PageIndexChanged* handler is not involved with data binding or page selection as it is with *DataGrids*. If you don't need any post-paging operation, you can blissfully omit it altogether.

What's the cost of this apparently free (and magical) paging mechanism?

The *GridView* control doesn't really know how to get a new page. It simply asks the bound data source control to return the rows that fit in the specified page. Paging is ultimately up to the data source control. When a grid is bound to a *SqlDataSource* control, paging requires that the whole data source be bound to the control. When a grid is bound to an *ObjectDataSource* control, paging depends on the capabilities of the business object you're connecting to.

Let's tackle *SqlDataSource* first. It is mandatory that you set *DataSourceMode* to *DataSet* (the default setting). This means that the whole dataset is retrieved and only the few records that fit in the current page size are displayed. In an extreme scenario, you might end up downloading 1,000 records for each postback to show only 10. Things go much better if you enable caching on *SqlDataSource* by setting *EnableCaching* to *true*. In this case, the whole data set is downloaded only once and stored in the ASP.NET cache for the specified duration. As long as the data stays cached, any page is displayed almost for free. However, a potentially large chunk of data is stored in memory. This option is therefore recommended only for relatively small sets of records shared by all users.

> **Tip**   If you want to page records at the database level, the best that you can do is code the desired behavior in a stored procedure and bind the stored procedure to the *SelectCommand* property of the *SqlDataSource* control. In this case, turn caching off.

Moving the Burden of Paging to the DAL

As we discussed in Chapter 9, the *ObjectDataSource* control supplies a rather generic interface for paging that heavily relies on the capabilities of the underlying business and data access layers (DALs).

The key point is that you should have a paging-enabled business object. You configure the *ObjectDataSource* control based on the characteristics of your business object method. Once you have identified the select method, you overload it with a version that takes two extra parameters—the page size and start index for the page. In the end, the select method must be able to retrieve pages of records. In the declaration of the *ObjectDataSource* control, you set the *StartRowIndexParameterName* and *MaximumRowsParameterName* properties to the name of the method parameter that denotes the start index and page size, respectively.

One more step is needed to enable the *GridView* to page the data source provided by the *ObjectDataSource* control. You also need to set the *EnablePaging* property of *ObjectDataSource* to *true*:

```
<asp:ObjectDataSource ID="ObjectDataSource1" runat="server"
    EnablePaging="true"
    TypeName="ProAspNet20.DAL.Customers"
    StartRowIndexParameterName="firstRow"
    MaximumRowsParameterName="totalRows"
    SelectMethod="LoadByCountry">
    <SelectParameters>
        <asp:ControlParameter Name="country" ControlID="Countries"
            PropertyName="SelectedValue" />
    </SelectParameters>
</asp:ObjectDataSource>

<asp:GridView ID="GridView1" runat="server" AutoGenerateColumns="false"
    DataSourceID="ObjectDataSource1" AllowPaging="true"
    OnPageIndexChanged="GridView1_PageIndexChanged">
    <PagerSettings Mode="NextPreviousFirstLast" />
    <Columns>
        <asp:BoundField DataField="id" HeaderText="ID" />
        <asp:BoundField DataField="companyname" HeaderText="Company" />
        <asp:BoundField DataField="contactname" HeaderText="Contact" />
    </Columns>
</asp:GridView>
<b>Page: </b><asp:Label runat="server" ID="CurrentPage" />
```

In the preceding code, you explicitly specify only the parameters whose contents are important for the method to work. The two paging-related parameters are left to the *GridView* to set. The page size parameter is automatically bound to the *PageSize* property of the *GridView*; the first index to retrieve is determined by multiplying page size by page index. Here are the prototypes of the *LoadByCountry* method:

```
public static CustomerCollection LoadByCountry(string country) {
    LoadByCountry(country, -1, 0);
}
public static CustomerCollection LoadByCountry(string country,
        int totalRows, int firstRow) {
    // Retrieve the specified subset of records
}
```

The mechanics of *ObjectDataSource* doesn't say much about the effectiveness of the paging algorithm. How the business object actually retrieves the records in the requested page is an implementation- and application-specific detail. In the sample code, *LoadByCountry* runs the original query and retrieves a data reader to the whole data set. Next, it discards all the records that don't fit in the specified range. This implementation is a good compromise between simplicity and effectiveness. It is not the best solution possible, but it's easy to implement and demonstrate. The memory consumption is limited to one record at a time, but the database returns the whole data set.

Paging Algorithms

The *GridView* doesn't support the *AllowCustomPaging* property you find on *DataGrids*. However, customizing the paging algorithm is definitely possible. At its core, a custom paging algorithm provides a way to extract pages of records that minimizes caching of records. Ideally, you would ask the database to page the results of a particular query. Very few databases, though, support this feature. Several alternative approaches exist, with pros and cons.

A possible strategy entails creating temporary tables to select only the subset of records you really need. You build a stored procedure and pass it parameters to indicate the page size and index. Alternately, you can use nested SELECT commands and the TOP statement to retrieve all the records up to the last record in the requested page, reverse the order, and discard unneeded records. Again, the TOP clause is not common to all databases. Another possible approach based on dynamically built SQL code is discussed in the following blog post: *http://weblogs.sqlteam.com/jeffs/archive/2004/03/22/1085.aspx*.

If you can collaborate with the database administrator (DBA), you can require that an ad hoc column be added to index the queries. In this case, the DAL must guarantee that the values in the column form a regular succession of values and can be computable. The simplest way of accomplishing this is by giving the column progressive numbers.

Configuring the Pager

When the *AllowPaging* property is set to *true*, the grid displays a pager bar. You can control the characteristics of the pager to a large extent, through the *<PagerSettings>* and *<PagerStyle>* tags or their equivalent properties. The pager of the *GridView* control also supports first and last page buttons and lets you assign an image to each button. (This is also possible for *DataGrids*, but it requires a lot of code.) The pager can work in either of two modes—displaying explicit page numbers, or providing a relative navigation system. In the former case, the pager contains numeric links, one representing a page index. In the latter case, buttons are present to navigate to the next or previous page and even to the first or last page. The *Mode* property rules the user interface of the pager. Available modes are listed in the Table 10-15.

Table 10-15   Modes of a Grid Pager

Mode	Description
NextPrevious	Displays next and previous buttons to access the next and previous pages of the grid
NextPreviousFirstLast	Displays next and previous buttons plus first and last buttons to directly access first and last pages of the grid
Numeric	Displays numeric link buttons corresponding to the pages of the grid
NumericFirstLast	Displays numeric link buttons corresponding to the pages of the grid plus first and last buttons to directly access first and last pages of the grid

Ad hoc pairs of properties—*xxxPageText* and *xxxPageImageUrl*—let you set the labels for these buttons as desired. The *xxx* stands for any of the following: *First*, *Last*, *Next*, or *Previous*. Figure 10-9 shows a sample page in action.

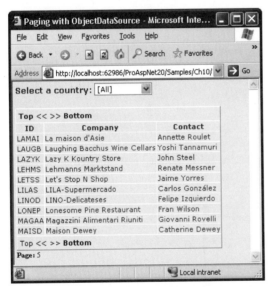

Figure 10-9   A pageable *GridView* with two pagers.

Depending on the size of the grid, the first and last rows in a grid might not necessarily fit in the screen real estate. To make it easier for users to page regardless of the scrollbar position, you can enable top and bottom pagers for a grid. You do this by setting the *Position* attribute on the *<PagerSettings>* element:

```
<PagerSettings Position="TopAndBottom" />
```

Other options are to display the pager only at the top or only at the bottom of the grid.

The pager of the *GridView* control can be entirely replaced with a new one, in case of need. (See Figure 10-10.) You do this by adding the *<PagerTemplate>* element to the control's declaration. Here's an example:

```
<PagerTemplate>
    <asp:Button ID="BtnFirst" runat="server" commandname="First"
        Text="First" />
    <asp:Button ID="BtnPrev" runat="server" commandname="Prev"
        Text="<<" />
    <asp:Button ID="BtnNext" runat="server" commandname="Next"
        Text=">>" />
    <asp:Button ID="BtnLast" runat="server" commandname="Last"
        Text="Last" />
</PagerTemplate>
```

To handle clickings on the buttons, you write a *RowCommand* event handler and set the page index explicitly:

```
void GridView1_RowCommand(object sender, GridViewCommandEventArgs e)
{
    if (e.CommandName == "Last")
        GridView1.PageIndex = GridView1.PageCount - 1;
    if (e.CommandName == "First")
        GridView1.PageIndex = 0;
    if (e.CommandName == "Next")
        GridView1.PageIndex ++;
    if (e.CommandName == "Prev")
        GridView1.PageIndex --;
}
```

Admittedly, this code is quite simple and should be fleshed out a little bit, at least to make it capable of disabling buttons when the first or last index is reached.

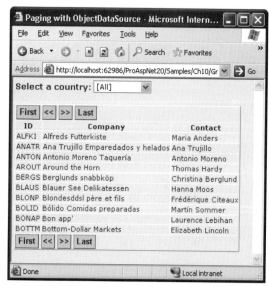

Figure 10-10   A pageable *GridView* with a custom pager.

Sorting Data

Sorting is a delicate, nonlinear operation that normally is quite expensive if performed on the client. Generally speaking, in fact, the best place to sort records is in the database environment because of the super-optimized code you end up running most of the time. Be aware of this as we examine the sorting infrastructure of the *GridView* control and data source controls. The *GridView* doesn't implement a sorting algorithm; instead, it relies on the data source control (or the page, if bound to an enumerable object) to provide sorted data.

Codeless Data Sorting

To enable the *GridView*'s sorting capabilities, you set the *AllowSorting* property to *true*. When sorting is enabled, the *GridView* gains the ability to render the header text of columns as links. You can associate each column with a sorting expression by using the *SortExpression* property. A sorting expression is any comma-separated sequence of column names. Each column name can be enriched with an order qualifier such as DESC or ASC. DESC indicates a descending order, while ASC denotes the ascending order. The ASC qualifier is the default; if omitted, the column is sorted ascendingly. The following code sets up the GridView column for sorting on the *productname* data source column:

```
<asp:GridView runat="server" id="MyGridView" DataSourceID="MySource"
    AllowSorting="true" AutoGenerateColumns="false">
    <Columns>
        <asp:BoundField datafield="productname" headertext="Product"
            sortexpression="productname" />
        <asp:BoundField datafield="quantityperunit"
            headertext="Packaging" />
    </Columns>
</asp:GridView>
```

Just as for paging, with a *GridView* no manually written code is required to make sorting work. Properly configured, the *GridView*'s sorting infrastructure works without further intervention and in a bidirectional way—that is, if you click on a column sorted descendingly, it is sorted ascendingly and vice versa. You need to add some custom code only if you want to implement more advanced capabilities such as showing a glyph in the header to indicate the direction. (I'll say more about that in a moment.)

Just as for paging, the main snag with sorting is how the underlying data source control implements it. Let's see what happens when the grid is bound to a *SqlDataSource* object. Other than setting *AllowSorting* to *true* and adding the sort expression to the sortable columns, no other action is required. (See Figure 10-11.)

When the user clicks to sort, the grid asks the *SqlDataSource* control to return sorted data. As mentioned, the *SqlDataSource* control returns a *DataSet* by default. If this is the case, the control retrieves the data, builds a *DataView* out of it, and calls the *DataView*'s *Sort* method. This approach works fine, but it's not exactly the fastest way you have to sort. You might still find it to be a good fit for your application, but be aware that sorting is performed using the Web server's memory. Combined with caching, both paging and sorting in memory are a feasible solution for shared and relatively small sets of records.

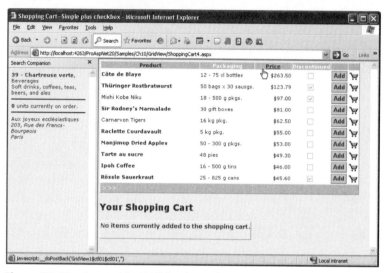

Figure 10-11 A sortable *GridView* bound to a *SqlDataSource* control.

Is there any chance to get pre-sorted data from the database server? The first step is to set the *DataSourceMode* property of the *SqlDataSource* control to *DataReader*. If you leave it set to *DataSet*, sorting will occur in memory. The second step requires you to write a stored procedure to retrieve data. To get data sorted, you also set the *SortParameterName* property of the data source control to the name of the stored procedure parameter that indicates the sort expression. Obviously, you need the stored procedure to build its command text dynamically to incorporate the proper *ORDER BY* clause. Here's how to modify the *CustOrderHist*, Northwind's stored procedure, to make its results sortable at will:

```
CREATE PROCEDURE CustOrderHistSorted
     @CustomerID nchar(5), @SortedBy varchar(20)='total'  AS
SET QUOTED_IDENTIFIER OFF
IF @SortedBy = ''
BEGIN
   SET @SortedBy = 'total'
END

EXEC (
   'SELECT ProductName, Total=SUM(Quantity)  ' +
   'FROM Products P, [Order Details] OD, Orders O, Customers C ' +
   'WHERE C.CustomerID = "' + @CustomerID + '" ' +
   'AND C.CustomerID = O.CustomerID AND O.OrderID = OD.OrderID ' +
   'AND OD.ProductID = P.ProductID GROUP BY ProductName ' +
   'ORDER BY ' + @SortedBy)
GO
```

At this point, the grid is ready to show sorted columns of data and the burden of sorting has moved to the database management system (DBMS):

```
<asp:SqlDataSource ID="SqlDataSource1" runat="server"
    DataSourceMode="DataReader"
    ConnectionString='<%$ ConnectionStrings:LocalNWind %>'
    SortParameterName="SortedBy"
    SelectCommand="CustOrderHistSorted"
    SelectCommandType="StoredProcedure">
  <SelectParameters>
    <asp:ControlParameter ControlID="CustList"
        Name="CustomerID" PropertyName="SelectedValue" />
  </SelectParameters>
</asp:SqlDataSource>
```

It is essential to know that sorting data on the database, as shown here, is incompatible with caching. You need to set *EnableCaching* to *false*; otherwise, an exception is thrown. As a result, you go back to the database every time the user clicks to sort.

If you use the *DataSet* mode and enable caching, you initially get data from the database, sorted as expected, but successive sorting operations are resolved in memory. Finally, if you use the *DataSet* mode and disable caching, you still go down to the database for sorting each time. Note that this option is mentioned only for completeness: the effect is the same as using *DataReader*, but a data reader is a more efficient approach when caching is not required.

In general, the availability of the *SortParameterName* property opens up a world of possibility for sorting the contents of other data-bound controls (for example, *Repeater* and custom controls) that mostly consume data and don't require paging or caching.

Moving the Burden of Sorting to the DAL

What if you use an *ObjectDataSource* control instead? In this case, the burden of sorting should be moved to the DAL or business layer and exposed to the data source control by the programming interface of the bound business object. Let's modify the *LoadByCountry* method we considered earlier for paging and add to it a new parameter to indicate the sort expression:

```
public static CustomerCollection LoadByCountry(
    string country, int totalRows, int firstRow, string sortExpression)
{
    CustomerCollection coll = new CustomerCollection();
    using (SqlConnection conn = new SqlConnection(ConnectionString))
    {
        SqlCommand cmd;
        cmd = new SqlCommand(cmdLoadByCountry, conn);
        cmd.Parameters.AddWithValue("@country", country);
        if (!String.IsNullOrEmpty(sortExpression))
            cmd.CommandText += " ORDER BY " + sortExpression;
        conn.Open();
        SqlDataReader reader = cmd.ExecuteReader();
        HelperMethods.FillCustomerList(coll, reader, totalRows, firstRow);
```

```
        reader.Close();
        conn.Close();
    }
    return coll;
}
```

The *cmdLoadByCountry* constant represents the SQL command or stored procedure we use to retrieve data. As you can see, this implementation of the method simply adds an optional *ORDER BY* clause to the existing command. This might not be the best approach ever devised, but it certainly fits the bill of having the burden of sorting moved down to the DAL and from there to the database. At this point, you set the *SortParameterName* on the *ObjectDataSource* control to the method's parameter that determines the sorting—in this case, *sortExpression*:

```
<asp:ObjectDataSource ID="ObjectDataSource1" runat="server"
    EnablePaging="true"
    TypeName="ProAspNet20.DAL.Customers"
    SortParameterName="sortExpression"
    StartRowIndexParameterName="firstRow"
    MaximumRowsParameterName="totalRows"
    SelectMethod="LoadByCountry">
    <SelectParameters>
        ...
    </SelectParameters>
</asp:ObjectDataSource>
```

The advantage of this approach is that you take full control of the sorting machinery, and you can decide how, where, and when to implement it. You might have to write some code in your DAL for sorting, but consider that you only write highly focused code. In fact, no infrastructural code is required, as the machinery is set up for you by ASP.NET.

> **Note**   One more item worth mentioning about sorting on a *GridView* control is that you can cancel the sorting operation if need be. To do this, you write a handler for the *Sorting* event, get the event argument data (of type *GridViewSortEventArgs*), and set its *Cancel* property to *true*.

Give Users Feedback

The *GridView* control doesn't automatically add any visual element to the output that indicates the direction of the sorting. This is one of the few cases in which some coding is needed to complete sorting:

```
<script runat="server">
void GridView1_RowCreated (object sender, GridViewRowEventArgs e) {
    if (e.Row.RowType == DataControlRowType.Header)
        AddGlyph(MyGridView, e.Row);
}

void AddGlyph(GridView grid, GridViewRow item) {
    Label glyph = new Label();
    glyph.EnableTheming = false;
    glyph.Font.Name = "webdings";
```

```
    glyph.Font.Size = FontUnit.Small;
    glyph.Text = (grid.SortDirection==SortDirection.Ascending ?"5" :"6");

    // Find the column you sorted by
    for(int i=0; i<grid.Columns.Count; i++) {
        string colExpr = grid.Columns[i].SortExpression;
        if (colExpr != "" && colExpr == grid.SortExpression)
            item.Cells[i].Controls.Add (glyph);
    }
}
</script>
```

The idea is that you write a handler for the *RowCreated* event and look for the moment when the header is created. Next you create a new *Label* control that represents the glyph you want to add. Where should the *Label* control be added?

The newly created *Label* control has font and text adequately set to generate a glyph (typically ▲ and ▼) that indicates the direction of the sorting. (The glyphs correspond to 5 and 6 in the Microsoft Webdings font.) You must add it alongside the header text of the clicked column. The index of the column can be stored to the view state during the *Sorting* event. Alternately, it can simply be retrieved, comparing the current sort expression—the grid's *SortExpression* property—to the column's sort expression. Once you know the index of the column, you retrieve the corresponding table cells and add the *Label*:

```
item.Cells[i].Controls.Add (glyph);
```

The results are shown in Figure 10-12. If your page is based on a theme, the font of the *Label* control—essential for rendering the glyph correctly—might be overridden. To avoid that, you should disable theming support for the label control. The *EnableTheming* property does just that.

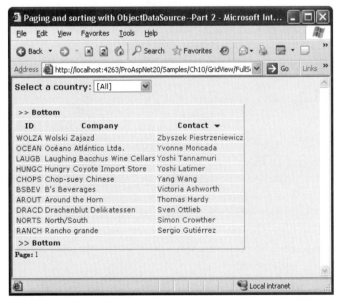

Figure 10-12   Enhancing the sorting capabilities of the *GridView* control.

Using Callbacks for Paging and Sorting

Both sorting and paging operations require a postback with subsequent full refresh of the page. In most cases, this is a heavy operation, as the page usually contains lots of graphics. To provide the user with a better experience, wouldn't it be nice if the grid could go down to the Web server, grab the new set of records, and update only a portion of the interface? Thanks to ASP.NET script callbacks (which I cover in greater detail in my other recent book, *Programming Microsoft ASP.NET 2.0 Applications: Advanced Topics* [Microsoft Press, 2005]), the *GridView* control is capable of offering this feature. All that you have to do is turn on the Boolean property *EnableSortingAndPagingCallbacks*.

As mentioned, the feature relies on the services of the ASP.NET script callback engine, which is designed to work also with non–Internet Explorer browsers, including Firefox, Netscape 6.x and newer, Safari 1.2, and the latest Opera browser.

SqlDataSource vs. *ObjectDataSource*

A few considerations will help clarify when to use *SqlDataSource* and *ObjectDataSource* controls. First, remember that these data source controls are not the only two choices for developers who want to do sane data binding. By far, though, they are the most popular and commonly used. It is also essential to bear in mind that data binding in ASP.NET 2.0 is in no way limited to using data source controls. This said, *SqlDataSource* and *ObjectDataSource* are just tools in the ASP.NET toolbox and should be used if they're right for the job.

As I see things, *SqlDataSource* is optimized for a disconnected approach to data binding. It works at its best if you retrieve data through a *DataSet*. Only in this case are paging, sorting, and caching capabilities enabled. Of these three functionalities, only sorting is somehow replicable in data reader mode. If using *DataSets* is fine for your application, using *SqlDataSource* is an excellent choice. It gives you ready-made solutions with mostly declarative code that is simple to write, but it's not necessarily effective in a real-world application. Put another way, using *SqlDataSource* in an application might be good for certain features, but it's hardly sufficient to power the whole DAL.

Should you instead realize that you need more control over paging and sorting operations (such as custom paging or server-side sorting), switching to *ObjectDataSource* appears to me a sounder idea. In this case, you start by designing and implementing a fully fledged DAL and, optionally, a business layer, too. In this layer, you craft any capabilities you need to be supported from the grid—paging, sorting, or even data caching. Note that caching is not supported if you use custom collections instead of ADO.NET container classes, but implementing a personal caching layer is not a hard challenge.

> With *ObjectDataSource*, you make yourself responsible for the implementation of such key features more or less like with *DataGrid*s in ASP.NET 1.x. What's the deal? You don't simply inject sparse code in some code-behind class; you inject logic in the application's DAL. You're still writing code, but the quality of the code you get to write is quite different!
>
> In addition, the *ObjectDataSource* control fully supports custom entity classes and custom collections. The support for generics in the .NET Framework 2.0 makes writing custom collections a snap, and it significantly reduces the cost of writing a fully custom DAL built on made-to-measure and domain-specific objects.

Editing Data

A major strength of the *GridView* control—which makes up for a major shortcoming of the *DataGrid*—is the ability to handle updates to the data source. The *DataGrid* control provides only an infrastructure for data editing. It provides the necessary user interface elements and fires appropriate events when the user modifies the value of a certain data field, but it does not submit those changes back to the data source. Developers are left with the disappointing realization that they have to write a huge amount of boilerplate code to really persist changes.

With the *GridView* control, when the bound data source supports updates, the control can automatically perform this operation, thus providing a truly out-of-the-box solution. The data source control signals its capability to update through the *CanUpdate* Boolean property.

Much like the *DataGrid*, the *GridView* can render a column of command buttons for each row in the grid. These special command columns contain buttons to edit or delete the current record. With the *DataGrid*, you must explicitly create an edit command column using a special column type—the *EditCommandColumn* class. The *GridView* simplifies things quite a bit for update and delete operations.

In-Place Editing and Updates

In-place editing refers to the grid's ability to support changes to the currently displayed records. You enable in-place editing on a grid view by turning on the *AutoGenerateEditButton* Boolean property:

```
<asp:gridview runat="server" id="GridView1" datasourceid="MySource"
    autogeneratecolumns="false" autogenerateeditbutton="true">
...
</asp:gridview>
```

When the *AutoGenerateEditButton* property is set to *true*, the *GridView* displays an additional column, like that shown in Figure 10-13. By clicking the Edit button, you put the selected row in edit mode and can enter new data at will.

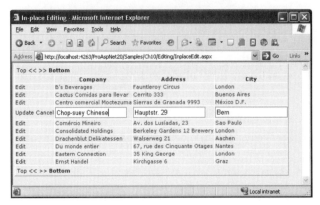

Figure 10-13   A *GridView* control that supports in-place editing.

To stop editing and lose any changes, users simply click the Cancel button. *GridView* can handle this click without any external support; the row returns to its original read-only state; and the *EditIndex* property takes back its −1 default value—meaning no row is currently being edited. But what if users click the update link? *GridView* first fires the *RowUpdating* event and then internally checks the *CanUpdate* property on the data source control. If *CanUpdate* returns false, an exception is thrown. *CanUpdate* returns false if the data source control has no update command defined.

Suppose your grid is bound to a *SqlDataSource* object. To persist changes when the user updates, you have to design your code as follows:

```
<asp:sqldatasource runat="server" ID="EmployeesSource"
     ConnectionString="<%$ ConnectionStrings:LocalNWind %>"
     SelectCommand="SELECT employeeid, firstname, lastname FROM employees"
     UpdateCommand="UPDATE employees SET
             firstname=@firstname, lastname=@lastname
             WHERE employeeid=@original_employeeid">
</asp:sqldatasource>
<asp:gridview runat="server" id="GridView1" datasourceid="EmployeesSource"
        AutoGenerateColumns="false"
        DataKeyNames="employeeid" AutoGenerateEditButton="true">
        <columns>
            <asp:boundfield datafield="firstname" headertext="First" />
            <asp:boundfield datafield="lastname" headertext="Last" />
        </columns>
</asp:gridview>
```

The *UpdateCommand* attribute is set to the SQL command to use to perform updates. When you write the command, you declare as many parameters as needed. However, if you stick with a particular naming convention, parameter values are automatically resolved. Parameters that represent fields to update (such as *firstname*) must match the name of *DataField* property of a grid column. The parameter used in the WHERE clause to identify the working record must match the *DataKeyNames* property—the key for the displayed records. The *original_XXX* format string is required for identity parameters. You can change this scheme through the *OldValuesParameterFormatString* property on the data source control.

The successful completion of an update command is signaled throughout the grid via the *RowUpdated* event.

> **Note** The *GridView* collects values from the input fields and populates a dictionary of name/value pairs that indicate the new values for each field of the row. The *GridView* also exposes a *RowUpdating* event that allows the programmer to validate the values being passed to the data source object. In addition, the *GridView* automatically calls *Page.IsValid* before starting the update operation on the associated data source. If *Page.IsValid* returns false, the operation is canceled. This is especially useful if you're using a custom template with validators.

If the grid is bound to an *ObjectDataSource* control, things go a bit differently. The bound business object must have an update method. This method will receive as many arguments as it needs to work. You can decide to pass parameters individually or grouped in a unique data structure. This second option is preferable if you have a well-done DAL. Here's an example:

```
<asp:ObjectDataSource ID="CustomersSource" runat="server"
    TypeName="ProAspNet20.DAL.Customers"
    SelectMethod="LoadAll"
    UpdateMethod="Save"
    DataObjectTypeName="ProAspNet20.DAL.Customer">
</asp:ObjectDataSource>
<asp:GridView ID="GridView1" runat="server" DataSourceID="CustomersSource"
    DataKeyNames="id" AutoGenerateColumns="false">
    AutoGenerateEditButton="true"
    <Columns>
        <asp:BoundField DataField="companyname" HeaderText="Company" />
        <asp:BoundField DataField="street" HeaderText="Address" />
        <asp:BoundField DataField="city" HeaderText="City" />
    </Columns>
</asp:GridView>
```

The *Save* method can have the following prototype and implementation:

```
public static void Save(Customer cust)
{
    using (SqlConnection conn = new SqlConnection(ConnectionString))
    {
        SqlCommand cmd = new SqlCommand(cmdSave, conn);
        cmd.Parameters.AddWithValue("@id", cust.ID);
        cmd.Parameters.AddWithValue("@companyname", cust.CompanyName);
        cmd.Parameters.AddWithValue("@city", cust.City);
        cmd.Parameters.AddWithValue("@address", cust.Street);
        ...

        conn.Open();
        cmd.ExecuteNonQuery();
        conn.Close();
        return;
    }
}
```

The physical SQL command (or stored procedure) to run is nothing more than a classic UPDATE statement with a list of SET clauses. The *DataObjectTypeName* attribute indicates the name of a class that the *ObjectDataSource* uses for a parameter in a data operation.

> **Note** If you set the *DataObjectTypeName* property, all data methods can either be parameterless or accept an object of the specified type. This happens regardless of whether you declarative fill the parameters collection for the method. The *DataObjectTypeName* property takes precedence over parameter collections.

Deleting Displayed Records

From the *GridView*'s standpoint, deleting records is not much different from updating. In both cases, the *GridView* takes advantage of a data source ability to perform data operations. You enable record deletion by specifying a value of *true* for the *AutoGenerateDeleteButton* property. The *GridView* renders a column of buttons that, if clicked, invokes the delete command for the row on the bound data source control. The data source method is passed a dictionary of key field name/value pairs that are used to uniquely identify the row to delete:

```
<asp:sqldatasource runat="server" ID="EmployeesSource"
    ConnectionString="<%$ ConnectionStrings:LocalNWind %>"
    SelectCommand="SELECT employeeid, firstname, lastname FROM employees"
    UpdateCommand="UPDATE employees SET
            firstname=@firstname, lastname=@lastname
        WHERE employeeid=@original_employeeid"
    DeleteCommand="DELETE employees WHERE
            employeeid=@original_employeeid" />
```

The *GridView* doesn't provide any feedback about the operation that will take place. Before proceeding, it calls *Page.IsValid*, which is useful if you have a custom template with validators to check. In addition, the *RowDeleting* event gives you another chance to programmatically control the legitimacy of the operation.

The delete operation fails if the record can't be deleted because of database-specific constraints. For example, the record can't be deleted if child records refer to it through a relationship. In this case, an exception is thrown.

To delete a record through an *ObjectDataSource* control, you give your business object a couple of methods, as follows:

```
public static void Delete(Customer cust)
{
    Delete(cust.ID);
}
public static void Delete(string id)
{
    using (SqlConnection conn = new SqlConnection(ConnectionString))
    {
        SqlCommand cmd = new SqlCommand(cmdDelete, conn);
```

```
        cmd.Parameters.AddWithValue("@id", id);
        conn.Open();
        cmd.ExecuteNonQuery();
        conn.Close();
        return;
    }
}
```

Overloading the delete method is not mandatory, but it can be useful and certainly make your DAL more flexible and easier to use.

Inserting New Records

In its current form, the *GridView* control doesn't support inserting data against a data source object. This omission is a result of the *GridView* implementation and not the capabilities and characteristics of the underlying data source. In fact, all data source controls support an insert command property. As you'll see in the next chapter, the insertion of new records is a scenario fully supported by the *DetailsView* and *FormView* control.

In ASP.NET 1.x, a common practice to make *DataGrid* controls support record insertions entails that you modify the footer or the pager to make room for empty text boxes and buttons. The *GridView* supports the same model and makes it slightly simpler through the *Pager-Template* property as far as the pager is concerned. Modifying the contents of the footer is possible through the *RowCreated* event (which I'll say more about in a moment). Note, though, that if the grid is bound to an empty data, the footer bar is hidden. What if you want your users to be able to add a new record to an empty grid? Resort to the *EmptyDataTemplate*, as follows:

```
<emptydatatemplate>
    <asp:label ID="Label1" runat="server">
      There's no data to show in this view.
      <asp:Button runat="server" ID="btnAddNew" CommandName="AddNew"
          Text="Add New Record" />
    </asp:label>
</emptydatatemplate>
```

To trap the user's clicking on the button, you write a handler for the *RowCommand* event:

```
void Gridview1_RowCommand(object sender, GridViewCommandEventArgs e)
{
    if (e.CommandName == "AddNew")
    { ... }
}
```

Advanced Capabilities

To complete the overview of the *GridView* control, we just need to take a look at a couple of common programming scenarios—drill-down and row customization. A grid presents a list of items to the user; in many cases, the user needs to select one of those items and start an operation on it. As discussed earlier, button columns exist to facilitate this task. We'll delve deeper into this topic in a moment. Row customization is another common feature, which gives you a chance to modify the standard rendering of the grid. You can edit the row layout, add or remove cells, or modify visual attributes on a per-row basis so that certain rows show up distinct from others (for example, rows representing negative values).

Executing an Operation on a Given Row

Let's return to a problem that we briefly mentioned earlier in the chapter while discussing button columns. Imagine you're building an e-commerce application; one of your pages shows a grid of products with buttons for users to add products to their shopping cart. You add a button column and write a handler for the *RowCommand* event:

```
void GridView1_RowCommand(object sender, GridViewCommandEventArgs e)
{
    if (e.CommandName.Equals("Add"))
    {
        // Get the index of the clicked row
        int index = Convert.ToInt32(e.CommandArgument);

        // Create a new shopping item and add it to the cart
        AddToShoppingCart(index);
    }
}
```

This is where we left off earlier. Let's go one step ahead now and expand the code of *AddTo-ShoppingCart*. What's the purpose of this method? Typically, it retrieves some information regarding the clicked product and stores that in the data structure that represents the shopping cart. In the sample code, the shopping cart is a custom collection named *ShoppingCart*:

```
public class ShoppingCart : List<ShoppingItem>
{
    public ShoppingCart()
    {
    }
}
```

ShoppingItem is a custom class that describes a bought product. It contains a few properties—product ID, product name, price per unit, and quantity bought. The shopping cart is stored in the session state and exposed through a page-wide property named *MyShoppingCart*:

```
protected ShoppingCart MyShoppingCart
{
    get
    {
        object o = Session["ShoppingCart"];
        if (o == null) {
            InitShoppingCart();
            return (ShoppingCart) Session["ShoppingCart"];
        }
        return (ShoppingCart) o;
    }
}
```

```
private void InitShoppingCart()
{
    ShoppingCart cart = new ShoppingCart();
    Session["ShoppingCart"] = cart;
}
```

At its core, the goal of *AddToShoppingCart* is merely that of creating a *ShoppingItem* object filled with the information of the clicked product. How would you retrieve that information?

As you can see, the *GridView* stores the index of the clicked row in the *CommandArgument* property of the *GridViewCommandEventArgs* structure. This information is necessary but not sufficient for our purposes. We need to translate that index into the key of the product behind the grid's row. Better yet, we need to translate the grid row index into a data set index to retrieve the data item object rendered in the clicked grid's row.

The *DataKeyNames* property of the *GridView* indicates the names of the data fields to persist in the view state to be retrieved later during postback events such as *RowCommand*. Implemented as a string array, *DataKeyNames* is the *GridView*'s counterpart of the *DataKeyField* of *DataGrid* controls. It carries the value of the primary key for a displayed row in a *DataGrid* and a slew of properties for a *GridView*:

```
<asp:GridView ID="GridView1" runat="server"
        DataSourceID="SqlDataSource1"
        DataKeyNames="productid,productname,unitprice" ... />
```

How many fields should you list in *DataKeyNames*? Consider that every field you list there takes up some view-state space. On the other hand, if you limit yourself to storing only the primary key field, you need to run a query to retrieve all the data you need. Which approach is better depends on what you really need to do. In our sample scenario, we need to make a copy of a product that is already cached in the Web server's memory. There's no need to run a query to retrieve data we already know. To fill a *ShoppingItem* object, you need the product ID, name, and unit price:

```
private void AddToShoppingCart(int rowIndex)
{
    DataKey data = GridView1.DataKeys[rowIndex];
    ShoppingItem item = new ShoppingItem();
    item.NumberOfItems = 1;
    item.ProductID = (int) data.Values["productid"];
    item.ProductName = data.Values["productname"].ToString();
    item.UnitPrice = (decimal) data.Values["unitprice"];
    MyShoppingCart.Add(item);

    ShoppingCartGrid.DataSource = MyShoppingCart;
    ShoppingCartGrid.DataBind();
}
```

The values of the fields listed in *DataKeyNames* are packed in the *DataKeys* array—an old acquaintance for *DataGrid* developers. *DataKeys* is an array of *DataKey* objects. *DataKey*, in turn, is a sort of ordered dictionary. You access the values of the persisted fields through the *Values* collection, as shown in the preceding code.

For user-interface purposes, the contents of the shopping cart are bound to a second *GridView* control so that users can see what's in their basket at any time. The binding takes place through the classic *DataSource* object. Look back to Figure 10-3 for a view of this feature.

> **Caution** Each grid row gets bound to a data item—a row from the data source—only when the control is rendered out. A postback event such as *RowCommand* fires before this stage is reached. As a result, the *DataItem* property of the clicked *GridViewRow* object—where the data we need is expected to be—is inevitably null if accessed from within the *RowCommand* handler. That's why you need *DataKeyNames* and the related *DataKeys* properties.

Selecting a Given Row

A more general mechanism to select clicked rows can be implemented through a special command button—the select button. As with delete and edit buttons, you bring it on by setting the *AutoGenerateSelectButton* Boolean property. To fully take advantage of the selection feature, it is recommended that you also add a style for selected rows:

```
<asp:GridView ID="GridView1" runat="server" ... >
    <SelectedRowStyle BackColor="cyan" />
    ...
</asp:GridView>
```

When users click a select-enabled button, the page receives a more specific *SelectedIndexChanged* event. Some properties such as *SelectedIndex*, *SelectedRow*, and *SelectedDataKey* are updated too. For completeness, note that when a row is selected the page first receives a *RowCommand* event, and later it is reached by the *SelectedIndexChanged* event. When *RowCommand* fires, though, none of the select properties is updated yet.

The following code shows how to rewrite the previous example to add the product being selected to the cart:

```
protected void GridView1_SelectedIndexChanged(object sender, EventArgs e)
{
    AddToShoppingCart();
}
private void AddToShoppingCart()
{
    DataKey data = GridView1.SelectedDataKey;
    ShoppingItem item = new ShoppingItem();
    item.NumberOfItems = 1;
    item.ProductID = (int) data.Values["productid"];
    item.ProductName = data.Values["productname"].ToString();
    item.UnitPrice = (decimal) data.Values["unitprice"];
    MyShoppingCart.Add(item);

    ShoppingCartGrid.DataSource = MyShoppingCart;
    ShoppingCartGrid.DataBind();
}
```

As you can see, there's no need to pass the row index, as the corresponding *DataKey* object is served by the *SelectedDataKey* property. (See Figure 10-14.)

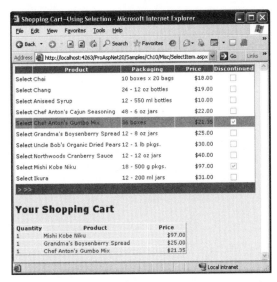

Figure 10-14 Adding the selected item to the shopping cart.

Row Customization

Want a quick example of why it's often important to render grid rows in a customized way? Take a look at Figure 10-14. The user just added to the cart a product that has been discontinued. Wouldn't it be nice if you could disable any rows matching certain criteria or, more simply, customize the row layout according to runtime conditions? Let's see how to do it.

There are two *GridView* events that are essential for the task—*RowCreated* and *RowDataBound*. The former is fired when any grid row is being created—whether it's a header, footer, item, alternating item, pager, and so on. The latter fires when the newly created row is bound to its data item—that is, the corresponding record in the bound data source. The *RowDataBound* event is not fired for all rows in the grid, but only for those which represent bound items. No event fires for the header, footer, and pager.

As a first example, let's see how to disable the Select link for rows where the *Discontinued* field returns true. In this case, you need a handler to *RowDataBound* because the required customization depends on the values on the bound data row. As mentioned, this information is not available yet when *RowCreated* fires:

```
void GridView1_RowDataBound(object sender, GridViewRowEventArgs e)
{
    if (e.Row.RowType == DataControlRowType.DataRow)
    {
        object dataItem = e.Row.DataItem;
```

```
        bool discontinued = (bool) DataBinder.Eval(dataItem, "discontinued");
        e.Row.Enabled = !discontinued;
    }
}
```

In general, you start by checking the type of the row. To be precise, this test is not strictly necessary for a *RowDataBound* event, which fires only for data rows. The data item—that is, the corresponding record—is retrieved through the *DataItem* property of the *GridViewRow* object. Next, you retrieve the field of interest and apply your logic. You might not know in advance the type of the data object bound to the row. The *DataBinder.Eval* method is a generic accessor that works through reflection and regardless of the underlying object. If you want to disable the whole row (and contained controls), you can turn off the *Enabled* property of the grid row object. To access a particular control, you need to find your way in the grid's object model. Here's how to access (and disable) the Select link alone:

```
((WebControl)e.Row.Cells[0].Controls[0]).Enabled = !discontinued;
```

This code works because in the sample grid the Select link is always the first control in the first cell of each data row. Figure 10-15 shows the previous product list with discontinued products disabled.

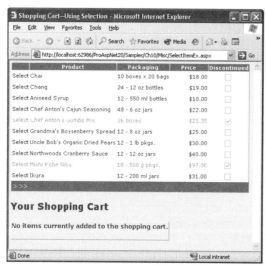

Figure 10-15   The rows corresponding to discontinued products are now disabled.

Once you gain access to the grid row object model, you can do virtually whatever you want.

Conclusion

In this chapter, we examined the grid controls available in ASP.NET—*DataGrid* and the newer *GridView*. Grids are a type of component that all Web applications need to employ in one shape or another. All Web applications, in fact, at a certain point of their life cycles are called to display data. More often than not, this data is in tabular format.

As long as the data to be displayed can be articulated in rows and columns, a grid is ideal for displaying it. Such controls provides facilities to select and edit single rows, page through a bound data source, and sort views. In addition, you can customize all the cells in a column by using any data-bound template made of any combination of HTML and ASP.NET text. To top it off, a fair number of events signal to user applications the key events in the control's life cycle.

The in-place editing feature is a piece of cake to use, as it is powerful and easy to configure. Even though this type of editing–designed to resemble Excel worksheets–is not appropriate for all applications and pages, as long as you can functionally afford the feature, in-place editing can save you a lot of coding and increase productivity by at least one order of magnitude.

Why are there two grid controls in ASP.NET 2.0? Let's state the answer clearly–the *DataGrid* control is supported mostly for backward compatibility. If you're writing a new ASP.NET 2.0 application, choosing to use the *GridView* is a no-brainer. The *GridView* has a newer and more effective design and totally embraces the data-binding model of ASP.NET 2.0. The key shortcoming of ASP.NET 1.x data binding is that it requires too much code for common, relatively boilerplate operations. This has been addressed with the introduction of data source controls. But data source controls require richer data-bound controls that are capable of working with the new model. This explains why ASP.NET 2.0 offers a brand-new control–the *GridView*– rather than just enhancing the existing *DataGrid*.

In the next chapter, we'll cover a pair of controls named *DetailsView* and *FormView*–the perfect complements to the *GridView*. These two controls fill another hole in the ASP.NET 1.x data toolbox, as they offer a smart interface for displaying individual records.

Just the Facts

- ASP.NET comes with two grid controls—*DataGrid* and *GridView*. The *DataGrid* works as it did in ASP.NET 1.x, whereas the *GridView* has a newer and more effective design and totally embraces the new data-binding model of ASP.NET 2.0.

- The *GridView* supports more column types, including checkbox and image columns.

- The *GridView* provides paging, sorting, and editing capabilities, and it relies on the bound data source control for effective implementation. If bound to an enumerable data source object (ASP.NET 1.x-style binding), it behaves like a *DataGrid* control.

- If bound to a *SqlDataSource* control, the *GridView* heavily relies on the *DataSet* capabilities for paging and sorting data in memory.

- If bound to an *ObjectDataSource* control, the *GridView* requires a fully fledged DAL that contains any custom logic for paging, sorting, and sometimes caching.

- Compared to the *DataGrid* control, the *GridView* provides an extended eventing model: pre/post pairs of events, possibility of canceling ongoing operations, and more events.

- To retrieve information about a clicked row, you use the *CommandArgument* property of the event data structure to get the index and you use the newest version of the *DataKeys* collection to access selected fields on the data item. With *DataGrid*, you can select only the primary key field and you need to run a query to access row data in drill-down scenarios.

About the Author

Dino Esposito is the Microsoft ASP.NET and ADO.NET expert at Solid Quality Learning, a premier training and consulting firm.

Dino writes the "Cutting Edge" column for *MSDN Magazine* and regularly contributes Microsoft .NET Framework articles to the Microsoft ASP.NET and Visual Studio Developer Centers and other magazines, including *asp.netPRO Magazine*, *CoDe Magazine*, and the *Dr. Dobb's ASP.NET-2-The-Max* newsletter. His books include *Programming Microsoft ASP.NET* (Microsoft Press, 2003), *Building Web Solutions with ASP.NET and ADO.NET* (Microsoft Press, 2002), and *Applied XML Programming for Microsoft .NET* (Microsoft Press, 2002). Up-to-date information about Dino's upcoming articles and books can be found in his blog at *http://weblogs.asp.net/despos*.

As a member of the International .NET Association (INETA) team of speakers, Dino is a frequent speaker at local community events, particularly in Europe and the United States.

Before becoming a full-time author, consultant, and trainer, Dino worked for several top consulting companies. Based in Rome, Italy, he pioneered DNA systems in Europe, and in 1994 designed one of the first serious Web applications—an image data bank. These days, you can find Dino at leading conferences such as DevConnections, DevWeek, WinDev, and Microsoft TechEd.

Additional Resources for Visual Basic Developers

Published and Forthcoming Titles from Microsoft Press

Microsoft® Visual Basic® 2005 Express Edition: Build a Program Now!
Patrice Pelland • ISBN 0-7356-2213-2

Featuring a full working edition of the software, this fun and highly visual guide walks you through a complete programming project—a desktop weather-reporting application—from start to finish. You'll get an introduction to the Microsoft Visual Studio® development environment and learn how to put the lightweight, easy-to-use tools in Visual Basic Express to work right away—creating, compiling, testing, and delivering your first ready-to-use program. You'll get expert tips, coaching, and visual examples each step of the way, along with pointers to additional learning resources.

Microsoft Visual Basic 2005 *Step by Step*
Michael Halvorson • ISBN 0-7356-2131-4

With enhancements across its visual designers, code editor, language, and debugger that help accelerate the development and deployment of robust, elegant applications across the Web, a business group, or an enterprise, Visual Basic 2005 focuses on enabling developers to rapidly build applications. Now you can teach yourself the essentials of working with Visual Studio 2005 and the new features of the Visual

Basic language—one step at a time. Each chapter puts you to work, showing you how, when, and why to use specific features of Visual Basic and guiding as you create actual components and working applications for Microsoft Windows®. You'll also explore data management and Web-based development topics.

Programming Microsoft Visual Basic 2005 *Core Reference*
Francesco Balena • ISBN 0-7356-2183-7

Get the expert insights, indispensable reference, and practical instruction needed to exploit the core language features and capabilities in Visual Basic 2005. Well-known Visual Basic programming author Francesco Balena expertly guides you through the fundamentals, including modules, keywords, and inheritance, and builds your mastery of more advanced topics such as delegates, assemblies, and My Namespace. Combining

in-depth reference with extensive, hands-on code examples and best-practices advice, this *Core Reference* delivers the key resources that you need to develop professional-level programming skills for smart clients and the Web.

Programming Microsoft Visual Basic 2005 *Framework Reference*
Francesco Balena • ISBN 0-7356-2175-6

Complementing *Programming Microsoft Visual Basic 2005 Core Reference*, this book covers a wide range of additional topics and information critical to Visual Basic developers, including Windows Forms, working with Microsoft ADO.NET 2.0 and ASP.NET 2.0, Web services, security, remoting, and much more. Packed with sample code and real-world examples, this book will help developers move from understanding to mastery.

Programming Microsoft Windows Forms
Charles Petzold • ISBN 0-7356-2153-5

Programming Microsoft Web Forms
Douglas J. Reilly • ISBN 0-7356-2179-9

Debugging, Tuning, and Testing Microsoft .NET 2.0 Applications
John Robbins • ISBN 0-7356-2202-7

Microsoft ASP.NET 2.0 *Step by Step*
George Shepherd • ISBN 0-7356-2201-9

Microsoft ADO.NET 2.0 *Step by Step*
Rebecca Riordan • ISBN 0-7356-2164-0

Programming Microsoft ASP.NET 2.0 *Core Reference*
Dino Esposito • ISBN 0-7356-2176-4

For more information about Microsoft Press® books and other learning products, visit: **www.microsoft.com/books** *and* **www.microsoft.com/learning**

Additional Resources for C# Developers

Published and Forthcoming Titles from Microsoft Press

Microsoft® Visual C#® 2005 Express Edition: Build a Program Now!
Patrice Pelland • ISBN 0-7356-2229-9

In this lively, eye-opening, and hands-on book, all you need is a computer and the desire to learn how to program with Visual C# 2005 Express Edition. Featuring a full working edition of the software, this fun and highly visual guide walks you through a complete programming project—a desktop weather-reporting application—from start to finish. You'll get an unintimidating introduction to the Microsoft Visual Studio® development environment and learn how to put the lightweight, easy-to-use tools in Visual C# Express to work right away—creating, compiling, testing, and delivering your first, ready-to-use program. You'll get expert tips, coaching, and visual examples at each step of the way, along with pointers to additional learning resources.

Microsoft Visual C# 2005 *Step by Step*
John Sharp • ISBN 0-7356-2129-2

Visual C#, a feature of Visual Studio 2005, is a modern programming language designed to deliver a productive environment for creating business frameworks and reusable object-oriented components. Now you can teach yourself essential techniques with Visual C#—and start building components and Microsoft Windows®–based applications—one step at a time. With *Step by Step*, you work at your own pace through hands-on, learn-by-doing exercises. Whether you're a beginning programmer or new to this particular language, you'll learn how, when, and why to use specific features of Visual C# 2005. Each chapter puts you to work, building your knowledge of core capabilities and guiding you as you create your first C#-based applications for Windows, data management, and the Web.

Programming Microsoft Visual C# 2005 Framework Reference
Francesco Balena • ISBN 0-7356-2182-9

Complementing *Programming Microsoft Visual C# 2005 Core Reference*, this book covers a wide range of additional topics and information critical to Visual C# developers, including Windows Forms, working with Microsoft ADO.NET 2.0 and Microsoft ASP.NET 2.0, Web services, security, remoting, and much more. Packed with sample code and real-world examples, this book will help developers move from understanding to mastery.

Programming Microsoft Visual C# 2005 *Core Reference*
Donis Marshall • ISBN 0-7356-2181-0

Get the in-depth reference and pragmatic, real-world insights you need to exploit the enhanced language features and core capabilities in Visual C# 2005. Programming expert Donis Marshall deftly builds your proficiency with classes, structs, and other fundamentals, and advances your expertise with more advanced topics such as debugging, threading, and memory management. Combining incisive reference with hands-on coding examples and best practices, this *Core Reference* focuses on mastering the C# skills you need to build innovative solutions for smart clients and the Web.

CLR via C#, Second Edition
Jeffrey Richter • ISBN 0-7356-2163-2

In this new edition of Jeffrey Richter's popular book, you get focused, pragmatic guidance on how to exploit the common language runtime (CLR) functionality in Microsoft .NET Framework 2.0 for applications of all types—from Web Forms, Windows Forms, and Web services to solutions for Microsoft SQL Server™, Microsoft code names "Avalon" and "Indigo," consoles, Microsoft Windows NT® Service, and more. Targeted to advanced developers and software designers, this book takes you under the covers of .NET for an in-depth understanding of its structure, functions, and operational components, demonstrating the most practical ways to apply this knowledge to your own development efforts. You'll master fundamental design tenets for .NET and get hands-on insights for creating high-performance applications more easily and efficiently. The book features extensive code examples in Visual C# 2005.

Programming Microsoft Windows Forms
Charles Petzold • ISBN 0-7356-2153-5

CLR via C++
Jeffrey Richter with Stanley B. Lippman
ISBN 0-7356-2248-5

Programming Microsoft Web Forms
Douglas J. Reilly • ISBN 0-7356-2179-9

Debugging, Tuning, and Testing Microsoft .NET 2.0 Applications
John Robbins • ISBN 0-7356-2202-7

For more information about Microsoft Press® books and other learning products,
visit: **www.microsoft.com/books** *and* **www.microsoft.com/learning**

Additional Resources for Web Developers

Published and Forthcoming Titles from Microsoft Press

Microsoft® Visual Web Developer™ 2005 Express Edition: Build a Web Site Now!
Jim Buyens • ISBN 0-7356-2212-4

With this lively, eye-opening, and hands-on book, all you need is a computer and the desire to learn how to create Web pages now using Visual Web Developer Express Edition! Featuring a full working edition of the software, this fun and highly visual guide walks you through a complete Web page project from set-up to launch. You'll get an introduction to the Microsoft Visual Studio® environment and learn how to put the light-weight, easy-to-use tools in Visual Web Developer Express to work right away—building your first, dynamic Web pages with Microsoft ASP.NET 2.0. You'll get expert tips, coaching, and visual examples at each step of the way, along with pointers to additional learning resources.

Microsoft ASP.NET 2.0 Programming
Step by Step
George Shepherd • ISBN 0-7356-2201-9

With dramatic improvements in performance, productivity, and security features, Visual Studio 2005 and ASP.NET 2.0 deliver a simplified, high-performance, and powerful Web development experience. ASP.NET 2.0 features a new set of controls and infrastructure that simplify Web-based data access and include functionality that facilitates code reuse, visual consistency, and aesthetic appeal. Now you can teach yourself the essentials of working with ASP.NET 2.0 in the Visual Studio environment—one step at a time. With *Step by Step*, you work at your own pace through hands-on, learn-by-doing exercises. Whether you're a beginning programmer or new to this version of the technology, you'll understand the core capabilities and fundamental techniques for ASP.NET 2.0. Each chapter puts you to work, showing you how, when, and why to use specific features of the ASP.NET 2.0 rapid application development environment and guiding you as you create actual components and working applications for the Web, including advanced features such as personalization.

Programming Microsoft ASP.NET 2.0
Core Reference
Dino Esposito • ISBN 0-7356-2176-4

Delve into the core topics for ASP.NET 2.0 programming, mastering the essential skills and capabilities needed to build high-performance Web applications successfully. Well-known ASP.NET author Dino Esposito deftly builds your expertise with Web forms, Visual Studio, core controls, master pages, data access, data binding, state management, security services, and other must-know topics—combining definitive reference with practical, hands-on programming instruction. Packed with expert guidance and pragmatic examples, this *Core Reference* delivers the key resources that you need to develop professional-level Web programming skills.

Programming Microsoft ASP.NET 2.0
Applications: *Advanced Topics*
Dino Esposito • ISBN 0-7356-2177-2

Master advanced topics in ASP.NET 2.0 programming—gaining the essential insights and in-depth understanding that you need to build sophisticated, highly functional Web applications successfully. Topics include Web forms, Visual Studio 2005, core controls, master pages, data access, data binding, state management, and security considerations. Developers often discover that the more they use ASP.NET, the more they need to know. With expert guidance from ASP.NET authority Dino Esposito, you get the in-depth, comprehensive information that leads to full mastery of the technology.

Programming Microsoft Windows® Forms
Charles Petzold • ISBN 0-7356-2153-5

Programming Microsoft Web Forms
Douglas J. Reilly • ISBN 0-7356-2179-9

CLR via C++
Jeffrey Richter with Stanley B. Lippman
ISBN 0-7356-2248-5

Debugging, Tuning, and Testing Microsoft .NET 2.0 Applications
John Robbins • ISBN 0-7356-2202-7

CLR via C#, Second Edition
Jeffrey Richter • ISBN 0-7356-2163-2

For more information about Microsoft Press® books and other learning products, visit: **www.microsoft.com/books** *and* **www.microsoft.com/learning**

Additional Resources for Database Developers

Published and Forthcoming Titles from Microsoft Press

Microsoft® SQL Server™ 2005 Express Edition
Step by Step
Jackie Goldstein ● ISBN 0-7356-2184-5

Teach yourself how to get database projects up and running quickly with SQL Server Express Edition—one step at a time! SQL Server Express is a free, easy-to-use database product that is based on SQL Server 2005 technology. It's designed for building simple, dynamic applications, with all the rich functionality of the SQL Server database engine and using the same data access APIs such as Microsoft ADO.NET, SQL Native Client, and T-SQL. With *Step by Step*, you work at your own pace through hands-on, learn-by-doing exercises. Whether you're new to database programming or new to SQL Server, you'll learn how, when, and why to use specific features of this simple but powerful database development environment. Each chapter puts you to work, building your knowledge of core capabilities and guiding you as you create actual components and working applications. You'll also discover how SQL Server Express works seamlessly with the Microsoft Visual Studio® 2005 environment, simplifying the design, development, and deployment of your applications.

Programming Microsoft ADO.NET 2.0
Applications: *Advanced Topics*
Glenn Johnson ● ISBN 0-7356-2141-1

Get in-depth coverage and expert insights on advanced ADO.NET programming topics such as optimization, DataView, and large objects (BLOBs and CLOBs). Targeting experienced, professional software developers who design and develop enterprise applications, this book assumes that the reader knows and understands the basic functionality and concepts of ADO.NET 2.0 and that he or she is ready to move to mastering data-manipulation skills in Microsoft Windows. The book, complete with pragmatic and instructive code examples, is structured so that readers can jump in for reference on each topic as needed.

Microsoft ADO.NET 2.0
Step by Step
Rebecca Riordan ● ISBN 0-7356-2164-0

In Microsoft .NET Framework 2.0, data access is enhanced not only through the addition of new data access controls, services, and the ability to integrate more seamlessly with SQL Server 2005, but also through improvements to the ADO.NET class libraries themselves. Now you can teach yourself the essentials of working with ADO.NET 2.0 in the Visual Studio environment—one step at a time. With *Step by Step*, you work at your own pace through hands-on, learn-by-doing exercises. Whether you're a beginning programmer or new to this version of the technology, you'll understand the core capabilities and fundamental techniques for ADO.NET 2.0. Each chapter puts you to work, showing you how, when, and why to use specific features of the ADO.NET 2.0 rapid application development environment and guiding as you create actual components and working applications for Microsoft Windows®.

Programming Microsoft ADO.NET 2.0
Core Reference
David Sceppa ● ISBN 0-7356-2206-X

This *Core Reference* demonstrates how to use ADO.NET 2.0, a technology within Visual Studio 2005, to access, sort, and manipulate data in standalone, enterprise, and Web-enabled applications. Discover best practices for writing, testing, and debugging database application code using the new tools and wizards in Visual Studio 2005, and put them to work with extensive code samples, tutorials, and insider tips. The book describes the ADO.NET object model, its XML features for Web extensibility, integration with Microsoft SQL Server 2000 and SQL Server 2005, and other core topics.

Programming Microsoft Windows Forms
Charles Petzold ● ISBN 0-7356-2153-5

Programming Microsoft Web Forms
Douglas J. Reilly ● ISBN 0-7356-2179-9

Inside Microsoft SQL Server 2005: The Storage Engine (Volume 1)
Kalen Delaney ● ISBN 0-7356-2105-5

Debugging, Tuning, and Testing Microsoft .NET 2.0 Applications
John Robbins ● ISBN 0-7356-2202-7

Microsoft SQL Server 2005 Programming *Step by Step*
Fernando Guerrero ● ISBN 0-7356-2207-8

Programming Microsoft SQL Server 2005
Andrew J. Brust, Stephen Forte, and William H. Zack
ISBN 0-7356-1923-9

For more information about Microsoft Press® books and other learning products,
visit: **www.microsoft.com/books** *and* **www.microsoft.com/learning**

Additional Learning Tools for ASP.NET

Whether you are brand new to ASP.NET or upgrading to ASP.NET 2.0, Microsoft Learning has a wide range of tools to help increase skills and productivity—to design, develop and deploy powerful, dynamic Web applications.

Microsoft E-Learning

With Microsoft E-Learning you get rich, interactive training and virtual labs so you can learn by doing in a safe environment. These e-learning courses include pre- and post- assessments to track your progress as you learn, and can be downloaded to your desktop for offline use.

Get started today at *www.microsoftelearning.com/ visualstudio2005* and take the following course for **FREE**:

- **Course 2913: Creating Your First Microsoft® ASP.NET 2.0 Web Application**
  This three-hour online course covers the entities that form the foundation of Web applications written with ASP.NET 2.0. This course is a great starting point for anyone who has not worked with Visual Studio 2005 or ASP.NET 2.0 before.

Also, check out special deals on the following ASP.NET 2.0 E-Learning courses:

- Collection 3201: Developing Microsoft® ASP.NET 2.0 Web Applications
- Course 2914: Writing Master Pages and Content Pages in Microsoft® ASP.NET 2.0
- Course 2915: Working with ADO.NET 2.0 Within Microsoft® ASP.NET 2.0
- Course 2916: Working with Microsoft® ASP.NET 2.0 Wizards and Site Navigation
- Course 2917: Working with State Management in Microsoft® ASP.NET 2.0
- Course 2918: Working with Web Parts in Microsoft® ASP.NET 2.0
- Course 2919: Working with User Profiles and Themes in Microsoft® ASP.NET 2.0
- Course 2920: Improving Security in a Microsoft® ASP.NET 2.0 Web Application
- Course 2921: Working with Microsoft® ASP.NET 2.0 Configuration and Instrumentation

Instructor-led Courses

Microsoft Certified Partners for Learning Solutions offer a variety of courses and workshops designed to provide in-depth knowledge, hands-on experience, and the latest technical information on ASP.NET 2.0. Check for availability of the following courses in your area at: *www.microsoft.com/learning/training*

- **Course 3201: Developing Microsoft ASP.NET 2.0 Web Applications**
  This three-day course provides students with the knowledge and skills to create ASP.NET 2.0 applications. It will show the advancements from ASP.NET 1.x to ASP.NET 2.0 in creating applications. The course focuses on the new features and functionality of ASP.NET. The course includes sample code in both Microsoft Visual Basic .NET and Microsoft Visual C#.

- **Course 2543: Core Web Application Development with Visual Studio 2005**
  Three-day instructor-led workshop focused on user interfaces, Web site structure and functionality, and implementation details.

- **Course 2544: Advanced Web Application Development with Visual Studio 2005**
  Two-day instructor-led workshop focused on advanced user interfaces, Web site functionality, and implementation details using the advanced features of ASP.NET 2.0 and Visual Studio 2005.

Microsoft Certified Technology Specialist: .NET Framework 2.0 Web Applications

Developers holding the Microsoft Certified Technology Specialist: .NET Framework 2.0 Web Applications certification have demonstrated the breadth and depth of skills and knowledge of Web application technology and data access in Web applications. Get more information on this certification including exam requirements at *http://www.microsoft.com/learning/mcp/mcts/webapps/*

For more information about Microsoft Learning products for developers, visit *www.microsoft.com/learning*

Microsoft | Learning

Learn More. Go Further.